Oracle ERP Essentials

Navigating the Accounts Payable Module

Kiet Huynh

Table of Contents

Briefly introduce the purpose of the book and who it is intended for

Purpose

In today's dynamic business environment, efficient and accurate accounts payable (AP) management is crucial for organizations of all sizes. Oracle ERP's Accounts Payable module offers a comprehensive suite of tools and functionalities that empower businesses to streamline their AP processes, enhance financial controls, and optimize cash flow management. This book, "Oracle ERP Essentials: Navigating the Accounts Payable Module," serves as a comprehensive guide for anyone seeking to master the intricacies of Oracle ERP's AP module and leverage its capabilities to drive operational excellence.

Target Audience

This book is primarily intended for:

Oracle ERP users: Individuals who actively utilize Oracle ERP's Accounts Payable module in their daily work, including accounts payable clerks, accountants, financial analysts, and process owners.

Oracle ERP implementers and consultants: Professionals responsible for implementing, configuring, and customizing Oracle ERP's Accounts Payable module for organizations.

Business managers and decision-makers: Individuals seeking to gain a deeper understanding of Oracle ERP's AP module capabilities and its impact on overall financial performance.

Whether you are an experienced Oracle ERP user or a newcomer to the system, this book will provide you with the knowledge and skills necessary to effectively navigate the Accounts Payable module and harness its power to transform your organization's AP operations.

Key Benefits

By delving into the intricacies of Oracle ERP's Accounts Payable module, this book will equip you with the ability to:

Streamline invoice processing workflows: Enhance efficiency and reduce errors by mastering invoice creation, matching, approval, and payment processes.

Strengthen internal controls: Implement robust internal controls to ensure compliance with financial regulations and safeguard the organization's assets.

Optimize cash flow management: Leverage advanced features to optimize payment schedules, maximize discounts, and improve cash flow visibility.

Generate insightful reports: Utilize Oracle ERP's reporting tools to gain valuable insights into spending patterns, vendor relationships, and payment trends.

Continuously improve AP processes: Employ best practices and data-driven strategies to identify areas for improvement and drive continuous process optimization.

As you embark on this journey of mastering Oracle ERP's Accounts Payable module, you will gain the confidence and expertise to transform your organization's AP operations into a strategic driver of financial performance and operational excellence.

Highlight the key benefits of using Oracle ERP's Accounts Payable module

Streamlined Invoice Processing and Automation: A Real-World Example

Consider a manufacturing company that receives hundreds of invoices daily. Manually processing these invoices would be a time-consuming and error-prone task. By implementing Oracle ERP's Accounts Payable module, the company can automate invoice creation from purchase orders, electronically receive invoices from vendors, and automatically match invoices to purchase orders. This automation eliminates the need for manual data entry, reducing processing time by up to 80%. Additionally, the module's automated approval workflow ensures that invoices are routed to the appropriate approvers for timely authorization, preventing delays in payments.

Enhanced Control and Visibility: Safeguarding Financial Integrity

Oracle ERP's Accounts Payable module provides robust internal controls that safeguard an organization's financial integrity. The module enforces spending limits, prevents unauthorized payments, and maintains a complete audit trail of all transactions. This granular control ensures that only authorized personnel can approve payments, preventing fraudulent activities and protecting the company's financial resources.

Reduced Costs and Improved Cash Flow: Optimizing Financial Resources

The module's ability to optimize payment processes leads to significant cost savings for businesses. By taking advantage of early payment discounts, organizations can reduce their payment obligations. Additionally, by negotiating better payment terms with vendors, businesses can extend their payment cycles, improving cash flow and freeing up capital for other purposes.

Improved Accuracy and Compliance: Ensuring Regulatory Adherence

Oracle ERP's Accounts Payable module ensures the accuracy of invoices and payments, adhering to tax regulations and compliance requirements. The module's automated tax calculations and validation checks prevent errors in tax calculations and ensure that withholding taxes are deducted and remitted correctly. This accuracy minimizes the risk of penalties, audits, and reputational damage.

Enhanced Vendor Relationships and Collaboration: Fostering Mutually Beneficial Partnerships

The module facilitates seamless communication and collaboration with vendors, strengthening vendor relationships and improving overall efficiency. Businesses can electronically send purchase orders, receive invoices, and process payments, eliminating the need for paper-based processes and reducing communication delays. This electronic collaboration fosters trust and transparency between businesses and their vendors, leading to mutually beneficial partnerships.

Data-Driven Insights and Decision-Making: Empowering Strategic Choices

Oracle ERP's Accounts Payable module generates comprehensive reports and analytics, providing valuable insights into spending patterns, vendor performance, and payment trends. These insights empower businesses to identify areas for cost savings, negotiate better deals with vendors, and optimize their procurement strategies. Data-driven decision-making leads to improved resource allocation, reduced expenses, and enhanced profitability.

Scalability and Adaptability: Accommodating Growth and Change

Oracle ERP's Accounts Payable module is designed to scale with the growth of an organization, accommodating increasing transaction volumes and evolving business needs. The module's flexible configuration options allow businesses to tailor its functionalities to their specific requirements and industry best practices. This adaptability ensures that the module remains a valuable asset as the organization grows and adapts to changing market conditions.

In conclusion, Oracle ERP's Accounts Payable module offers a comprehensive suite of functionalities that transform the way organizations manage their payables, leading to significant benefits in terms of efficiency, control, cost savings, accuracy, compliance, vendor relationships, data-driven insights, and scalability. By embracing this module, businesses can achieve greater financial transparency, operational excellence, and a competitive edge in the marketplace.

Provide an overview of the book's structure and how it is organized

This book is designed to provide a comprehensive and practical guide to navigating the Accounts Payable module of Oracle ERP. It is intended for both new and experienced users of Oracle ERP who want to gain a deeper understanding of the module's functionalities and how to effectively utilize them for efficient accounts payable management.

The book is structured in a logical and easy-to-follow manner, starting with an introduction to Oracle ERP and the Accounts Payable module, followed by detailed chapters that cover each of the core areas of functionality. Each chapter includes clear explanations, step-by-step instructions, and practical examples to help readers gain hands-on experience with the module.

Key Features of the Book's Structure:

Modular Approach: The book is divided into eight chapters, each focusing on a specific aspect of the Accounts Payable module. This modular approach allows readers to easily navigate to the information they need and skip over topics that are already familiar to them.

Comprehensive Coverage: The book covers all the essential functionalities of the Accounts Payable module, from setting up the module to generating reports. This comprehensive coverage ensures that readers gain a complete understanding of the module's capabilities.

Practical Examples and Exercises: Each chapter includes practical examples and exercises to help readers apply the concepts they have learned. This hands-on approach reinforces learning and enables readers to develop the skills necessary to use the module effectively.

Real-World Scenarios and Case Studies: The book incorporates real-world scenarios and case studies to illustrate how the Accounts Payable module is used in actual business settings. This contextual approach helps readers understand the practical applications of the module and how it can be used to solve real-world business problems.

Overall Organization of the Book:

The book is organized into the following eight chapters:

Chapter 1: Introduction to Oracle ERP and the Accounts Payable Module

Provides an overview of Oracle ERP and its role in enterprise resource planning

Introduces the Accounts Payable module and its key functionalities

Explains the benefits of using Oracle ERP's Accounts Payable module

Chapter 2: Setting Up the Accounts Payable Module

Guides readers through the process of setting up the Accounts Payable module

Covers topics such as defining company parameters, establishing vendor relationships, configuring payment terms, and setting up tax codes

Emphasizes the importance of accurate setup for proper module operation

Chapter 3: Processing Invoice Transactions

Explains the different methods for creating and entering invoices into the Accounts Payable module

Discusses the process of matching invoices to purchase orders

Provides guidance on approving and releasing invoices

Covers procedures for handling invoice discrepancies

Chapter 4: Managing Payments and Adjustments

Explains the process of creating and processing manual payments

Discusses the setup and configuration of automatic payments

Covers the application of prepayments and credits

Provides guidance on issuing adjustments and refunds

Chapter 5: Reconciling Accounts Payable

Explains the process of performing periodic reconciliations of accounts payable balances

Discusses methods for investigating and resolving reconciliation differences

Emphasizes the importance of regular reconciliations for maintaining accurate accounting records

Chapter 6: Advanced Accounts Payable Functions

Covers the management of foreign currency transactions

Explains the process of processing accruals and deferred payments

Discusses the utilization of tax withholding and remittance features

Provides guidance on implementing invoice hold and release functionality

Chapter 7: Reporting and Analysis with Oracle ERP

Explains the process of generating standard accounts payable reports

Discusses the creation of custom reports using Oracle Business Intelligence (OBI) tools

Provides techniques for analyzing accounts payable data for insights

Emphasizes the use of reports to improve financial processes

Chapter 8: Optimizing Accounts Payable Processes

Discusses best practices for streamlining invoice processing workflows and reducing errors

Explains the benefits of leveraging automation to streamline accounts payable processes

Provides guidance on enhancing controls for internal compliance

Emphasizes the importance of continuous monitoring and improving performance

Appendix: Glossary of Accounts Payable Terms

Provides a comprehensive list of accounts payable terms and definitions

Organizes terms alphabetically for easy reference

Includes cross-references to related terms for enhanced understanding

Index

Provides a comprehensive index of all terms, concepts, and topics covered in the book

Organizes index entries alphabetically for easy navigation

Includes cross-references to relevant chapters and sections for quick reference

This structured and organized approach ensures that the book provides a comprehensive and easy-to-follow guide for anyone who wants to learn how to effectively manage accounts payable processes using Oracle ERP.

CHAPTER I
Introduction to Oracle ERP and the Accounts Payable Module

1.1 Overview of Oracle ERP

1.1.1 Define Oracle ERP and its role in enterprise resource planning

Enterprise Resource Planning (ERP) systems play a pivotal role in modern business operations by integrating various functions and processes into a unified system. Oracle ERP, developed by Oracle Corporation, stands as one of the leading ERP solutions globally, offering extensive functionalities designed to streamline and optimize business processes across diverse industries.

Definition of Oracle ERP

Oracle ERP refers to a suite of integrated applications that allow organizations to automate and manage their business operations effectively. It encompasses modules such as financial management, supply chain management, human capital management, project management, and more. The core strength of Oracle ERP lies in its ability to provide a centralized database that supports multiple functions, enabling real-time data access and fostering collaboration across departments.

Role of Oracle ERP in Enterprise Resource Planning

At its core, Oracle ERP serves as a backbone for enterprise resource planning. It facilitates the integration of various business processes, from procurement to financial management, manufacturing, and beyond, into a single cohesive system. This integration ensures that data flows seamlessly across departments, eliminating silos and enhancing operational efficiency.

Components of Oracle ERP

Oracle ERP comprises several modules, each catering to specific functional areas of an organization:

- Financial Management: Manages financial processes such as accounting, accounts payable/receivable, budgeting, and financial reporting.

- Supply Chain Management: Handles procurement, inventory management, order management, and logistics, optimizing the supply chain's efficiency.

- Human Capital Management: Streamlines HR processes including payroll, recruitment, talent management, and employee development.

- Project Management: Supports project planning, resource allocation, scheduling, and project financials to ensure successful project delivery.

- Customer Relationship Management (CRM): Manages customer interactions, sales force automation, marketing campaigns, and customer service processes.

Benefits of Implementing Oracle ERP

Implementing Oracle ERP offers several strategic advantages to organizations:

- Operational Efficiency: By automating routine tasks and integrating business processes, Oracle ERP reduces manual effort, minimizes errors, and improves productivity.

- Data-Driven Decision Making: Real-time data availability enables informed decision-making, supporting strategic planning and forecasting.

- Compliance and Risk Management: Oracle ERP helps organizations adhere to regulatory requirements and mitigate risks associated with financial transactions and data security.

- Scalability and Flexibility: As businesses grow, Oracle ERP scales seamlessly to accommodate increased data volumes and business complexity.

- Enhanced Collaboration: By breaking down departmental barriers, Oracle ERP promotes collaboration across functions, fostering a unified organizational culture.

Challenges in Implementing Oracle ERP

While the benefits of Oracle ERP are substantial, implementation can pose challenges:

- Cost: Initial investment and ongoing maintenance costs can be significant.

- Integration Complexity: Integrating Oracle ERP with existing IT infrastructure and legacy systems requires careful planning and expertise.

- Change Management: Organizational resistance to change and the need for comprehensive training programs can impact adoption.

Future Trends in Oracle ERP

Looking ahead, Oracle continues to innovate in ERP with advancements in cloud computing, artificial intelligence (AI), machine learning (ML), and predictive analytics. These technologies enhance ERP capabilities, offering predictive insights, enhancing user experience, and supporting digital transformation initiatives.

In conclusion, Oracle ERP represents a cornerstone in modern enterprise management, empowering organizations to achieve operational excellence, adapt to market dynamics, and drive sustainable growth. As businesses evolve, Oracle ERP remains instrumental in enabling agility, innovation, and strategic decision-making in today's competitive landscape.

1.1.2 Discuss the different modules that comprise Oracle ERP

Oracle ERP is a comprehensive suite of integrated applications designed to automate and streamline business processes across various departments within an organization. Each module within Oracle ERP caters to specific functional areas, ensuring efficient management of resources, data, and operations. Understanding the scope and purpose of these modules is crucial for maximizing the benefits of Oracle ERP implementation.

1. Financial Management Modules:

Oracle ERP includes robust financial management modules that form the core of its capabilities. These modules are essential for managing financial processes, ensuring compliance, and providing accurate financial reporting. Key modules under financial management include:

- General Ledger (GL): The GL module serves as the central repository for financial data. It consolidates transactional information from various modules, providing a comprehensive view of the organization's financial health.

- Accounts Payable (AP): The AP module manages all payments due to suppliers and vendors. It automates invoice processing, payment approvals, and reconciliation, ensuring timely and accurate disbursement of funds while maintaining financial control.

- Accounts Receivable (AR): The AR module handles customer invoicing, payment collections, and credit management. It tracks receivables and facilitates efficient cash flow management through automated billing and collections processes.

- Cash Management: This module focuses on optimizing cash utilization and forecasting. It monitors liquidity, manages bank accounts, and reconciles transactions to ensure accurate cash positioning and efficient fund management.

2. Supply Chain Management Modules:

Efficient supply chain management is critical for optimizing inventory levels, reducing costs, and enhancing customer satisfaction. Oracle ERP offers robust supply chain management modules that integrate seamlessly with financial and operational processes. Key modules include:

- Procurement: The procurement module automates the procurement process from requisition to purchase order issuance. It facilitates supplier management, contract negotiations, and procurement analytics to optimize purchasing decisions and ensure supply chain efficiency.

- Inventory Management: This module tracks inventory levels, locations, and movements throughout the organization's supply chain. It supports demand forecasting, stock replenishment, and inventory valuation methods to minimize carrying costs and stockouts.

- Order Management: The order management module processes sales orders, manages pricing and discounts, and coordinates order fulfillment. It integrates with inventory and logistics systems to ensure timely order delivery and customer satisfaction.

3. Human Capital Management (HCM) Modules:

Effective workforce management is essential for organizational success. Oracle ERP's HCM modules streamline HR processes, enhance employee engagement, and support talent management initiatives. Key modules include:

- Core HR: The core HR module manages employee information, payroll processing, and compliance with labor regulations. It supports workforce planning, employee benefits administration, and performance management.

- Talent Management: This module focuses on recruiting, onboarding, and developing talent within the organization. It includes features for succession planning, training and development, and performance evaluation to align employee skills with business objectives.

- Workforce Management: The workforce management module optimizes workforce scheduling, time and attendance tracking, and labor cost management. It ensures compliance with labor laws and regulations while maximizing workforce productivity and operational efficiency.

4. Project Management Modules:

For organizations engaged in project-based work, Oracle ERP provides project management modules that streamline project planning, execution, and monitoring. Key modules include:

- Project Costing: The project costing module tracks project expenses, allocates costs to specific projects or tasks, and monitors budgetary constraints. It facilitates project profitability analysis and ensures accurate project accounting.

- Project Billing: This module automates invoicing and revenue recognition for project-based transactions. It supports milestone billing, contract management, and compliance with revenue recognition standards to enhance financial transparency and client billing accuracy.

5. Risk Management and Compliance Modules:

Oracle ERP includes modules dedicated to risk management, compliance, and governance. These modules help organizations mitigate risks, ensure regulatory compliance, and maintain ethical standards. Key modules include:

- Risk Management: The risk management module identifies, assesses, and monitors enterprise risks across financial, operational, and strategic domains. It supports risk mitigation strategies and facilitates risk-based decision-making.

- Compliance: This module ensures adherence to regulatory requirements, industry standards, and internal policies. It automates compliance monitoring, audits, and reporting to mitigate compliance risks and enhance organizational integrity.

6. Business Intelligence and Reporting Modules:

Data-driven insights are crucial for informed decision-making and strategic planning. Oracle ERP offers business intelligence and reporting modules that consolidate data from various sources and present actionable insights. Key modules include:

- Business Intelligence (BI): The BI module provides dashboards, reports, and analytics tools for real-time visibility into business performance. It enables stakeholders to monitor key performance indicators (KPIs), identify trends, and forecast future outcomes.

- Financial Reporting: This module generates standardized financial reports, including balance sheets, income statements, and cash flow statements. It supports regulatory reporting requirements and facilitates financial analysis and benchmarking against industry peers.

Understanding the interconnectedness and functionalities of these modules is essential for leveraging Oracle ERP's full potential. Each module plays a distinct role in optimizing business operations, enhancing productivity, and driving sustainable growth.

1.1.3 Explain the benefits of implementing Oracle ERP

Implementing Oracle ERP offers numerous advantages that contribute to enhancing organizational efficiency, streamlining processes, and improving overall business performance. Below are detailed benefits categorized for clarity:

Operational Efficiency and Process Streamlining

1. Integrated Business Processes: Oracle ERP integrates various business functions such as finance, procurement, inventory management, and human resources into a unified system. This integration eliminates data silos and facilitates seamless information flow across departments.

2. Automation of Routine Tasks: The ERP system automates repetitive tasks like data entry, reconciliation, and reporting. This automation reduces manual errors, speeds up processes, and frees up employees to focus on more strategic activities.

3. Standardized Processes: By enforcing standardized workflows and procedures, Oracle ERP helps organizations maintain consistency in operations. This standardization enhances efficiency, reduces cycle times, and ensures compliance with industry regulations.

Financial Management and Reporting

1. Real-time Financial Insights: Oracle ERP provides real-time visibility into financial data, enabling stakeholders to access accurate, up-to-date information for decision-making. This transparency enhances financial control and supports proactive financial management strategies.

2. Cost Reduction: Through improved resource allocation, better inventory management, and optimized procurement processes, Oracle ERP helps in reducing operational costs. This cost efficiency translates into improved profitability and competitive advantage.

3. Compliance and Risk Management: Oracle ERP incorporates robust compliance features that help organizations adhere to regulatory requirements and internal policies. It also

enhances risk management capabilities by identifying and mitigating potential risks proactively.

Strategic Business Growth

1. Scalability: Oracle ERP systems are designed to scale with business growth. Whether expanding operations domestically or internationally, the ERP infrastructure can accommodate increased transaction volumes and business complexities without significant disruptions.

2. Enhanced Decision-making: With comprehensive data analytics and reporting tools, Oracle ERP empowers executives and managers to make informed decisions based on accurate insights. This data-driven decision-making capability supports strategic planning and fosters agile responses to market changes.

3. Customer Satisfaction: By improving operational efficiency and responsiveness, Oracle ERP contributes to better customer service delivery. Satisfied customers lead to increased retention rates and positive word-of-mouth, enhancing overall brand reputation.

Technology and Innovation

1. Adoption of Cutting-edge Technologies: Oracle ERP continually evolves with advancements in technology such as artificial intelligence, machine learning, and predictive analytics. These technologies enhance system capabilities, predictive capabilities, and enable organizations to stay competitive in a digital economy.

2. Cloud-based Flexibility: The transition to Oracle ERP Cloud offers organizations flexibility, scalability, and cost-effectiveness through a subscription-based model. Cloud deployment reduces IT infrastructure costs, simplifies maintenance, and ensures system resilience and security.

Conclusion

Implementing Oracle ERP goes beyond enhancing operational efficiency; it transforms organizations by providing a robust foundation for growth, innovation, and competitive advantage in a dynamic business environment. By leveraging its integrated capabilities, real-time insights, and strategic alignment, businesses can navigate challenges, seize opportunities, and achieve sustainable success.

1.2 The Role of the Accounts Payable Module

1.2.1 Describe the primary functions of the Accounts Payable module

The Accounts Payable (AP) module within Oracle ERP plays a pivotal role in managing and controlling the financial obligations of an organization. It encompasses a range of critical functions designed to streamline and automate the processes related to vendor payments and financial liabilities.

Invoice Processing: One of the core functions of the Accounts Payable module is the processing of invoices received from vendors. This includes the verification of invoice details against purchase orders and goods receipts, ensuring accuracy and compliance before proceeding with payment. By automating this process, organizations can significantly reduce the risk of errors and discrepancies, thereby improving operational efficiency.

Vendor Management: Effective vendor management is facilitated through the Accounts Payable module. It maintains comprehensive records of vendor information, including contact details, payment terms, and transaction history. This centralized repository enables finance teams to efficiently communicate with vendors, negotiate favorable terms, and maintain strong supplier relationships, essential for procurement and operational continuity.

Payment Processing: The module facilitates the timely and accurate processing of payments to vendors. It supports various payment methods such as checks, electronic funds transfers (EFT), and automated clearing house (ACH) payments. Integration with banking systems ensures secure and efficient fund transfers, while configurable payment schedules enable organizations to optimize cash flow management and meet financial obligations promptly.

Expense Management: Beyond invoices, the Accounts Payable module also manages employee reimbursements and other non-purchase order related expenses. It allows for the capture, review, and approval of employee expense claims, ensuring compliance with corporate policies and regulatory requirements. This functionality streamlines the reimbursement process, enhances transparency, and controls expenses effectively within the organization.

Accruals and Reporting: Accurate financial reporting is facilitated through the module's capabilities in managing accruals and liabilities. It provides real-time visibility into outstanding liabilities, accrued expenses, and payment forecasts, supporting informed decision-making and financial planning. By maintaining up-to-date financial data, organizations can comply with accounting standards and regulatory mandates, ensuring transparency and accuracy in financial reporting.

Compliance and Audit Trail: The Accounts Payable module maintains a comprehensive audit trail of all transactions processed within the system. This feature is crucial for compliance with internal controls, auditing requirements, and regulatory standards. It supports transparency and accountability, enabling auditors and stakeholders to trace transaction histories, validate processes, and ensure adherence to financial policies and procedures.

Integration with Other Modules: Integration with other Oracle ERP modules, such as Purchasing, General Ledger, and Inventory Management, enhances the functionality and efficiency of the Accounts Payable processes. Seamless data flow between modules ensures consistency and accuracy in financial transactions, inventory management, and reporting, optimizing overall operational performance.

In summary, the Accounts Payable module within Oracle ERP fulfills essential functions that are integral to effective financial management and operational efficiency. By automating invoice processing, facilitating vendor management, enabling timely payment processing, managing expenses, ensuring compliance, and integrating seamlessly with other modules, it empowers organizations to maintain financial control, mitigate risks, and support strategic decision-making.

1.2.2 Explain how the Accounts Payable module integrates with other Oracle ERP modules

The Accounts Payable (AP) module in Oracle ERP does not function in isolation; it is a critical component of the larger Oracle ERP ecosystem. Integration with other modules ensures seamless operations across various business functions, promoting efficiency, accuracy, and real-time data flow. Understanding these integrations is vital for maximizing the benefits of the Accounts Payable module.

1. General Ledger (GL) Integration

The integration between Accounts Payable and the General Ledger is fundamental. Every transaction recorded in AP must be reflected accurately in the GL to maintain financial integrity and ensure proper accounting. This integration enables:

- Automatic Journal Entries: AP transactions, such as invoice approvals and payments, generate automatic journal entries in the GL, ensuring real-time updates and reducing manual effort.

- Reconciliation: Seamless data flow allows for easier reconciliation of accounts. Discrepancies can be identified and rectified promptly.

- Financial Reporting: Accurate and timely updates in the GL from AP transactions enable precise financial reporting, aiding in decision-making and compliance.

2. Cash Management Integration

Cash Management is another module closely linked with Accounts Payable. Effective integration between these modules facilitates:

- Cash Forecasting: AP provides data on outstanding liabilities, which is crucial for accurate cash flow forecasting and planning.

- Payment Processing: Integration ensures that payment instructions and transactions from AP are communicated to Cash Management, streamlining the payment process and ensuring funds are available when needed.

- Bank Reconciliation: Transactions recorded in AP can be matched against bank statements in Cash Management, ensuring all payments are accounted for and discrepancies are resolved swiftly.

3. Procurement and Inventory Management Integration

The Accounts Payable module plays a vital role in the Procure-to-Pay process, requiring robust integration with Procurement and Inventory Management modules:

- Purchase Order Matching: AP matches invoices against purchase orders and receipts, ensuring that payments are made only for goods and services received as per the agreed terms.

- Inventory Valuation: Accurate recording of AP transactions impacts inventory valuation, affecting the overall cost of goods sold and profitability analysis.

- Vendor Management: Information on vendor performance, based on AP data, can be utilized by Procurement for strategic sourcing and vendor negotiations.

4. Projects and Cost Management Integration

For organizations involved in project-based work, the integration of AP with Projects and Cost Management modules is essential:

- Project Accounting: Expenses recorded in AP are allocated to specific projects, ensuring accurate project costing and budgeting.

- Cost Tracking: AP transactions provide data for tracking project costs against budgets, enabling better cost control and financial management of projects.

- Billing: Integration facilitates the capture of payable costs, which can be billed to clients or allocated to internal projects as appropriate.

5. Human Capital Management (HCM) Integration

Integration with Human Capital Management (HCM) is crucial, particularly for managing expenses related to employees:

- Expense Reimbursements: Employee expenses are processed through AP, requiring seamless data flow to ensure timely reimbursements and accurate accounting.

- Payroll Deductions: Deductions and payments related to employee benefits, taxes, and other payroll components can be managed through AP, ensuring compliance and accurate financial records.

6. Fixed Assets Integration

For organizations managing significant physical assets, the integration between AP and the Fixed Assets module is crucial:

- Asset Acquisition: Purchases of fixed assets processed through AP must be accurately recorded in the Fixed Assets module for proper tracking and depreciation.

- Capitalization: Integration ensures that costs associated with asset acquisition are correctly capitalized and depreciated over the asset's useful life.

- Asset Disposal: When assets are disposed of, the AP module helps manage any related expenses, ensuring accurate financial records.

7. Tax Management Integration

Tax compliance is a critical aspect of financial management, necessitating integration between AP and Tax Management modules:

- Tax Calculation: AP transactions involving taxable goods and services require accurate tax calculation, which is facilitated by integration with the Tax Management module.

- Tax Reporting: Data from AP is essential for preparing tax returns and ensuring compliance with local and international tax regulations.

- Withholding Tax: AP processes payments that may be subject to withholding tax, requiring integration to ensure correct tax treatment and reporting.

8. Accounts Receivable (AR) Integration

While AP and AR handle different aspects of financial transactions, their integration is important for overall financial management:

- Cash Flow Management: Understanding the timing of payables and receivables helps in managing cash flow more effectively.

- Customer and Vendor Relationships: For organizations that deal with entities that are both customers and vendors, integration ensures accurate recording and management of transactions.

9. Workflow Automation Integration

Modern ERP systems, including Oracle ERP, emphasize workflow automation. Integration with workflow management tools ensures:

- Approval Workflows: AP transactions can be routed through predefined approval workflows, ensuring compliance with organizational policies and reducing processing time.

- Notification and Alerts: Integration enables automatic notifications and alerts for pending approvals, payment due dates, and exceptions, enhancing operational efficiency.

10. Reporting and Analytics Integration

Integration with reporting and analytics tools is vital for leveraging data from the AP module:

- Business Intelligence: Data from AP can be used in business intelligence tools to generate insights and support decision-making.

- Custom Reports: Integration allows for the creation of custom reports that meet specific organizational needs, enhancing the visibility of AP operations.

- Data Analysis: Comprehensive data analysis can identify trends, improve processes, and support strategic planning.

Conclusion

The integration of the Accounts Payable module with other Oracle ERP modules is fundamental for achieving a seamless, efficient, and accurate financial management process. By understanding and leveraging these integrations, organizations can ensure better financial control, compliance, and strategic decision-making. The interconnected nature of Oracle ERP modules facilitates real-time data flow, reduces manual intervention, and enhances overall operational efficiency, making it a powerful tool for managing enterprise resources.

1.2.3 Discuss the importance of the Accounts Payable module in the financial management process

The Accounts Payable (AP) module in Oracle ERP is a cornerstone of the financial management process within an organization. Its importance cannot be overstated, as it plays a pivotal role in ensuring the accuracy, efficiency, and compliance of financial transactions. Here, we will delve into the critical aspects that highlight the significance of the AP module in the broader financial management landscape.

Ensuring Financial Accuracy

One of the primary roles of the AP module is to ensure the accuracy of financial transactions. By automating the invoice processing and payment functions, the module minimizes the risk of human errors that can occur in manual processing. Inaccurate financial data can lead to significant issues, including misstated financial reports, compliance violations, and flawed decision-making. The AP module helps to mitigate these risks by providing a reliable and consistent framework for handling payables.

The module's automated matching process, which compares invoices, purchase orders, and receiving documents, ensures that payments are made only for goods and services that have been received and approved. This three-way matching process is vital for maintaining the integrity of financial records and preventing fraudulent or erroneous payments.

Enhancing Cash Flow Management

Effective cash flow management is crucial for the financial health of any organization. The AP module plays a significant role in managing cash flow by providing tools and insights for optimizing payment schedules. By analyzing payment terms, due dates, and available discounts, the module helps organizations to plan their payments strategically, ensuring that they take advantage of early payment discounts while avoiding late payment penalties.

The AP module also offers forecasting capabilities, allowing finance teams to predict future cash outflows accurately. This foresight is essential for maintaining adequate liquidity and making informed investment and funding decisions. By improving cash flow visibility, the AP module enables organizations to better manage their working capital and financial stability.

Facilitating Compliance and Auditability

In today's regulatory environment, compliance with financial regulations and internal policies is paramount. The AP module helps organizations to meet these requirements by providing a structured and transparent framework for managing payables. It ensures that all financial transactions are recorded accurately and in accordance with applicable laws and standards.

The module supports various compliance requirements, such as tax regulations, anti-fraud measures, and internal control policies. It allows organizations to maintain a comprehensive audit trail of all transactions, making it easier to respond to audits and inquiries. The ability to track and document every step of the AP process, from invoice receipt to payment execution, is critical for demonstrating compliance and mitigating the risk of regulatory fines and reputational damage.

Streamlining Financial Operations

Efficiency in financial operations is a key driver of overall business performance. The AP module streamlines financial processes by automating repetitive tasks, reducing manual intervention, and accelerating the payment cycle. This automation frees up valuable time for finance personnel, allowing them to focus on more strategic activities such as financial analysis and planning.

The module's integration capabilities further enhance operational efficiency by enabling seamless data flow between the AP module and other Oracle ERP modules, such as General Ledger, Procurement, and Inventory Management. This integration ensures that financial data is consistently updated and accurate across the organization, reducing the need for manual data entry and reconciliation.

Improving Supplier Relationships

Supplier relationships are vital for ensuring the uninterrupted supply of goods and services. The AP module contributes to maintaining positive supplier relationships by ensuring timely and accurate payments. By automating the payment process and providing visibility into payment statuses, the module helps to build trust and reliability with suppliers.

Timely payments not only enhance supplier satisfaction but also position the organization as a preferred customer, potentially leading to better terms and conditions. Additionally, the AP module's ability to manage and track supplier performance metrics enables organizations to make data-driven decisions about supplier selection and management, further strengthening supplier relationships.

Enabling Strategic Decision-Making

The AP module provides valuable insights into the organization's financial health and performance. By generating detailed reports and analytics on payables, cash flow, and supplier performance, the module equips finance leaders with the information they need to make informed decisions. These insights are crucial for strategic planning, budgeting, and forecasting.

For instance, understanding the payment trends and cash flow patterns can help finance teams to identify opportunities for cost savings and process improvements. The ability to analyze spend data at a granular level enables organizations to negotiate better terms with suppliers and optimize their procurement strategies.

Supporting Financial Planning and Analysis

Financial planning and analysis (FP&A) is a critical function that drives organizational growth and sustainability. The AP module supports FP&A by providing accurate and timely data on payables, which is essential for developing realistic financial plans and budgets. By integrating with other financial modules, the AP module ensures that all financial data is cohesive and aligned with the organization's overall financial strategy.

The module's forecasting capabilities allow finance teams to anticipate future cash outflows and adjust their plans accordingly. This proactive approach to financial management helps organizations to avoid cash shortfalls and make strategic investments that drive growth and profitability.

Enhancing Operational Visibility and Control

Visibility and control over financial operations are essential for effective financial management. The AP module provides real-time visibility into the status of invoices, payments, and supplier accounts. This transparency enables finance teams to monitor and manage payables more effectively, ensuring that all financial transactions are executed accurately and on time.

The module's control features, such as approval workflows and authorization limits, help to enforce financial policies and prevent unauthorized transactions. By establishing clear approval hierarchies and ensuring that all payments are reviewed and approved by the appropriate personnel, the AP module enhances the organization's internal controls and reduces the risk of financial mismanagement.

Conclusion

The Accounts Payable module in Oracle ERP is a vital component of the financial management process, providing a robust framework for managing payables with accuracy, efficiency, and compliance. Its role in ensuring financial accuracy, enhancing cash flow management, facilitating compliance, streamlining financial operations, improving supplier relationships, enabling strategic decision-making, supporting financial planning and analysis, and enhancing operational visibility and control underscores its importance in the broader financial landscape.

By leveraging the capabilities of the AP module, organizations can achieve greater financial stability, operational efficiency, and strategic agility, ultimately driving business success. The module's integration with other Oracle ERP components further amplifies its impact, creating a cohesive and comprehensive financial management ecosystem that supports the organization's goals and objectives.

1.3 Key Features of the Accounts Payable Module

1.3.1 Highlight the key features and functionalities of the Accounts Payable module

The Accounts Payable (AP) module in Oracle ERP is a comprehensive and robust component designed to manage a company's entire payable process. It integrates seamlessly with other Oracle ERP modules to ensure a cohesive and streamlined financial management system. Below are the key features and functionalities of the Accounts Payable module, each of which plays a critical role in enhancing the efficiency and effectiveness of the payables process.

Invoice Processing

Invoice Entry and Management

The AP module allows users to enter and manage invoices with ease. It supports various types of invoices such as standard, credit, debit memos, and prepayments. The user-friendly interface facilitates quick data entry, reducing the chances of errors and increasing productivity. Invoices can be entered manually or imported from external systems, providing flexibility and efficiency.

Automated Invoice Matching

One of the standout features is the automated three-way matching process, which ensures that the invoice details match the corresponding purchase order and receiving documents. This automated process helps in identifying discrepancies early, preventing overpayments and ensuring that only valid invoices are processed for payment.

Invoice Approval Workflow

Oracle ERP's AP module includes a configurable invoice approval workflow that routes invoices to the appropriate personnel for review and approval. This feature ensures compliance with company policies and internal controls, enhancing accountability and reducing the risk of fraud.

Payment Processing

Flexible Payment Methods

The AP module supports multiple payment methods including electronic funds transfer (EFT), checks, and wire transfers. This flexibility allows businesses to cater to different vendor preferences and streamline their payment processes.

Payment Scheduling

Users can schedule payments based on invoice due dates, payment terms, and cash flow considerations. The system can prioritize payments to take advantage of early payment discounts and avoid late payment penalties, optimizing cash management.

Payment Batch Processing

The ability to process payments in batches is a significant time-saving feature. Users can group invoices for payment based on criteria such as due date, vendor, or amount. This bulk processing capability enhances efficiency and reduces manual effort.

Vendor Management

Comprehensive Vendor Data Management

The AP module provides a centralized repository for maintaining detailed vendor information. This includes contact details, payment terms, bank account information, and tax details. Having accurate and up-to-date vendor data is crucial for smooth operations and maintaining strong vendor relationships.

Vendor Performance Tracking

Oracle ERP allows users to track and evaluate vendor performance based on criteria such as on-time delivery, quality of goods, and pricing accuracy. This feature helps in identifying reliable vendors and making informed procurement decisions.

Vendor Portal Integration

The module can integrate with vendor portals, enabling vendors to submit invoices electronically, check payment status, and update their information. This self-service capability reduces administrative burden and improves communication between the company and its vendors.

Reporting and Analytics

Standard and Custom Reports

The AP module offers a wide range of standard reports such as aging reports, payment history, and outstanding liabilities. Additionally, users can create custom reports to meet specific business needs. These reports provide valuable insights into the company's financial obligations and help in making informed decisions.

Real-time Analytics

Real-time analytics capabilities enable users to monitor key performance indicators (KPIs) such as invoice processing time, discount utilization, and payment cycle time. This data-driven approach helps in identifying bottlenecks and areas for improvement, enhancing the overall efficiency of the AP process.

Audit Trail and Compliance

The module maintains a detailed audit trail of all transactions, including invoice entries, approvals, and payments. This feature is crucial for compliance with regulatory requirements and internal policies. It also facilitates easier auditing and ensures transparency in the payables process.

Integration with Other Modules

Seamless Integration with Procurement

The AP module integrates seamlessly with the procurement module, enabling efficient management of the procure-to-pay process. This integration ensures that purchase orders and receipts are accurately matched with invoices, streamlining the entire transaction cycle.

Integration with General Ledger

Integration with the General Ledger (GL) module ensures that all AP transactions are accurately recorded in the company's financial books. This real-time posting of transactions improves the accuracy of financial statements and facilitates better financial reporting.

Cash Management Integration

The integration with the cash management module helps in managing and forecasting cash flow. It provides visibility into future payment obligations, aiding in effective cash flow management and ensuring that sufficient funds are available to meet payment commitments.

Compliance and Risk Management

Tax Compliance

The AP module supports various tax structures and jurisdictions, ensuring compliance with local and international tax regulations. It calculates tax automatically based on the predefined rules, reducing the risk of tax errors and penalties.

Fraud Prevention

The module includes several features designed to prevent fraud, such as segregation of duties, approval hierarchies, and vendor validation checks. These controls help in safeguarding company assets and ensuring that only legitimate transactions are processed.

Regulatory Compliance

Oracle ERP's AP module helps companies comply with regulatory requirements such as Sarbanes-Oxley (SOX) by providing features like audit trails, electronic records, and robust internal controls. This compliance is essential for maintaining corporate integrity and avoiding legal issues.

User Interface and Experience

Intuitive User Interface

The AP module features an intuitive and user-friendly interface that simplifies navigation and operation. Users can easily access and manage invoices, payments, and vendor information, enhancing overall productivity.

Personalized Dashboards

Personalized dashboards allow users to customize their workspaces based on their roles and preferences. These dashboards provide quick access to relevant data and frequently used functions, improving efficiency and user satisfaction.

Mobile Accessibility

With mobile accessibility, users can perform critical AP tasks on the go. This feature is particularly useful for managers who need to approve invoices or review reports remotely, ensuring that the AP process continues smoothly without delays.

Scalability and Flexibility

Scalability to Meet Business Needs

The AP module is designed to scale with the growth of the business. It can handle increasing volumes of transactions and accommodate the addition of new vendors, locations, and business units without compromising performance.

Configurable Workflows and Rules

Users can configure workflows and business rules to match their specific operational requirements. This flexibility ensures that the AP module can adapt to different business processes and policies, providing a tailored solution for each organization.

Global Capabilities

The AP module supports multi-currency transactions and multiple languages, making it suitable for global operations. It enables companies to manage their payables process across different countries and regions efficiently.

In conclusion, the Accounts Payable module in Oracle ERP offers a comprehensive suite of features and functionalities that streamline the payables process, improve accuracy, enhance compliance, and provide valuable insights. By leveraging these capabilities, companies can optimize their AP operations, maintain strong vendor relationships, and achieve greater financial control.

1.3.2 Provide an overview of the user interface and navigation within the module

The user interface (UI) and navigation in Oracle ERP's Accounts Payable (AP) module are designed to be intuitive and user-friendly, enabling users to perform their tasks efficiently.

Understanding the layout, menus, and key features of the UI is essential for mastering the AP module.

1. Layout of the User Interface

The AP module interface consists of several key components:

1. Home Page: This is the starting point after logging into Oracle ERP. The home page provides quick access to frequently used tasks, notifications, and relevant information.

2. Navigation Menu: Located typically on the left-hand side, the navigation menu allows users to access different functionalities within the AP module, such as invoice processing, payment processing, and supplier management.

3. Task Bar: The taskbar at the top of the screen provides shortcuts to common actions, notifications, and user settings.

4. Main Workspace: This is the central area where users perform their tasks. It displays forms, lists, and other content depending on the selected function.

5. Info Tiles: Info tiles are interactive elements that provide a quick overview of key metrics and alerts. They are often customizable and can be used to monitor important activities such as pending invoices or payment statuses.

6. Action Buttons: Located within forms and lists, action buttons (such as Save, Submit, Cancel) allow users to execute specific commands related to their tasks.

2. Navigation through the Module

Effective navigation is crucial for efficient use of the AP module. The following steps outline the typical navigation paths for common tasks:

1. Accessing Invoice Processing:

 - From the home page, click on the "Payables" tab in the navigation menu.

 - Select "Invoices" to open the invoice processing workspace.

- Use the sub-menu to choose between tasks such as creating a new invoice, managing existing invoices, or reviewing invoice batches.

2. Managing Payments:

  - Navigate to the "Payments" section via the "Payables" tab.

  - Access different payment tasks such as creating payment batches, reviewing payment history, and processing manual payments.

3. Supplier Management:

  - Select the "Suppliers" option under the "Payables" tab.

  - From here, users can add new suppliers, update supplier information, and review supplier transactions.

4. Reports and Analytics:

  - Navigate to the "Reports" section under the "Payables" tab.

  - Access pre-built reports or create custom reports to analyze payables data.

3. Key Functionalities and Their Navigation

Each functionality within the AP module is accessible through specific navigation paths. Here's a deeper dive into some critical areas:

1. Invoice Entry and Validation:

  - Navigate to "Invoices" > "Entry" > "Create Invoice".

  - Enter invoice details such as supplier information, invoice amount, and date.

  - Use the "Validate" button to ensure the invoice meets all requirements before approval.

2. Payment Processing:

  - Go to "Payments" > "Create Payment".

  - Select invoices to be paid and choose the payment method.

  - Use the "Submit" button to process the payment and generate payment files.

3. Supplier Portal:

  - Access the supplier portal via "Suppliers" > "Supplier Portal".

  - Suppliers can log in to view payment statuses, submit invoices, and update their profile information.

4. Recurring Invoices:

  - Navigate to "Invoices" > "Recurring Invoices".

  - Set up recurring invoice templates for regular payments such as rent or subscriptions.

  - Use the "Schedule" feature to automate invoice creation based on predefined intervals.

5. Approval Workflows:

  - Go to "Invoices" > "Approval Workflows".

  - Configure approval rules based on invoice amount, supplier, or other criteria.

  - Monitor approval status and manage workflow exceptions.

4. User Customization and Personalization

Oracle ERP allows users to customize their interface to suit their preferences:

1. Dashboards:

  - Users can create personalized dashboards that display relevant info tiles, reports, and quick links.

  - Dashboards can be configured to show metrics such as pending approvals, overdue invoices, and cash flow projections.

2. Saved Searches:

  - Save frequently used search criteria to quickly access specific sets of data.

  - Example: Save a search for all invoices pending approval by a particular manager.

3. Shortcuts and Favorites:

  - Add commonly used tasks to the favorites menu for quick access.

- Example: Add "Create Invoice" and "Payment History" to favorites.

5. Accessibility and User Assistance

To enhance usability, Oracle ERP includes several features aimed at helping users navigate and use the AP module effectively:

1. Help and Tutorials:

  - Access the help menu for step-by-step guides, video tutorials, and FAQs.

  - In-context help provides relevant assistance based on the current task.

2. Search Functionality:

  - Use the global search bar to quickly find suppliers, invoices, payments, and other entities.

  - Advanced search options allow for detailed filtering and sorting of search results.

3. Notifications and Alerts:

  - Receive real-time notifications for important events such as invoice approvals, payment due dates, and supplier updates.

  - Customize alert settings to receive notifications via email, SMS, or within the ERP system.

6. Security and User Roles

Oracle ERP's security features ensure that users have appropriate access based on their roles:

1. Role-Based Access Control (RBAC):

  - Access to different functionalities is controlled through user roles.

  - Example: An AP clerk can enter invoices, but only a manager can approve them.

2. Audit Trails:

  - Track changes made to invoices, payments, and supplier records.

- Audit trails help maintain accountability and compliance with regulatory requirements.

7. Integration with Other Modules

The AP module integrates seamlessly with other Oracle ERP modules:

1. General Ledger (GL):

  - AP transactions automatically generate corresponding entries in the GL.

  - Ensures accurate financial reporting and reconciliation.

2. Procurement:

  - Integrates with the procurement module to manage purchase orders and supplier contracts.

  - Streamlines the process from requisition to payment.

3. Cash Management:

  - Syncs with cash management to forecast cash flow and manage liquidity.

  - Provides real-time visibility into cash positions and payment statuses.

Conclusion

The user interface and navigation in Oracle ERP's Accounts Payable module are designed to streamline the payables process, enhance efficiency, and ensure accuracy. By understanding the layout, navigation paths, and key features, users can leverage the full potential of the AP module to manage invoices, payments, and supplier relationships effectively. Customization options, robust security measures, and seamless integration with other modules further enhance the user experience, making the Oracle ERP Accounts Payable module a powerful tool for financial management.

1.3.3 Discuss the benefits of using these features for efficient accounts payable processing

The Oracle ERP Accounts Payable (AP) module is designed to streamline and optimize the process of managing a company's obligations to its suppliers. Leveraging the key features of this module can significantly enhance the efficiency and accuracy of accounts payable operations. Here, we discuss the benefits of using these features for efficient accounts payable processing.

Automated Invoice Processing

One of the most significant benefits of the Accounts Payable module is the automation of invoice processing. By automating this process, organizations can reduce manual data entry errors, improve processing speed, and ensure that invoices are handled promptly. Automation also facilitates the matching of purchase orders, receipts, and invoices, which is crucial for accurate payment processing. This not only saves time but also minimizes the risk of discrepancies and potential fraud.

Automation can also handle recurring invoices, where the system generates invoices based on predefined schedules. This is particularly beneficial for regular payments such as rent, subscriptions, and utility bills. By automating these routine transactions, businesses can ensure timely payments and avoid late fees.

Enhanced Compliance and Control

The Accounts Payable module provides robust features for compliance and control. These features help ensure that all payments are authorized, validated, and compliant with internal policies and external regulations. For instance, the module supports multiple levels of approval workflows, ensuring that only authorized personnel can approve payments. This enhances internal controls and reduces the risk of unauthorized transactions.

Additionally, the module can enforce compliance with tax regulations and accounting standards. By automatically calculating taxes, applying the correct tax codes, and generating detailed audit trails, the AP module helps organizations maintain compliance with local and international tax laws. This is particularly important for multinational companies that operate in multiple jurisdictions with varying tax regulations.

Improved Cash Flow Management

Efficient accounts payable processing is crucial for maintaining healthy cash flow. The Oracle ERP Accounts Payable module provides tools for better cash flow management by enabling businesses to optimize their payment schedules. By having a clear view of upcoming payments and due dates, organizations can strategically schedule their payments to take advantage of early payment discounts or to avoid late payment penalties.

The module also supports dynamic discounting, where organizations can negotiate early payment discounts with suppliers. By leveraging these discounts, businesses can reduce their overall costs. Additionally, the module provides comprehensive cash forecasting capabilities, allowing finance teams to predict future cash flow needs and make informed financial decisions.

Enhanced Vendor Relationships

Efficient and timely payment processing is essential for maintaining good relationships with suppliers. The Accounts Payable module facilitates better communication and collaboration with vendors by providing a centralized platform for managing vendor information and interactions. By ensuring that payments are processed accurately and on time, businesses can build trust and strengthen their relationships with suppliers.

The module also supports electronic payments, which are faster and more secure than traditional paper checks. Electronic payments reduce the risk of lost or stolen checks and provide suppliers with quicker access to funds. This not only improves vendor satisfaction but also enhances the overall efficiency of the payment process.

Real-time Reporting and Analytics

The Accounts Payable module offers powerful reporting and analytics capabilities that provide real-time insights into the financial health of an organization. With access to detailed reports on payables, aging invoices, payment status, and vendor performance, finance teams can make data-driven decisions. These insights help identify trends, monitor key performance indicators (KPIs), and detect potential issues before they escalate.

Real-time reporting also supports better decision-making by providing a comprehensive view of outstanding liabilities and cash flow. By analyzing payment trends and vendor performance, organizations can identify opportunities for cost savings and process improvements. The ability to generate custom reports and dashboards further enhances the flexibility and utility of the reporting tools.

Streamlined Audit and Reconciliation

The Accounts Payable module simplifies the audit and reconciliation process by providing detailed audit trails and transaction histories. This transparency ensures that all transactions can be traced back to their source, making it easier to verify the accuracy of financial records. Auditors can access comprehensive records of approvals, payments, and adjustments, which facilitates a smoother and more efficient audit process.

Reconciliation is also streamlined through automated matching of invoices, purchase orders, and receipts. By automatically reconciling these documents, the module reduces the need for manual intervention and minimizes the risk of errors. This not only saves time but also ensures the accuracy of financial statements.

Scalability and Integration

The Oracle ERP Accounts Payable module is designed to scale with the growth of an organization. As businesses expand, the module can handle increasing transaction volumes and support more complex financial processes. This scalability ensures that the AP module remains effective and efficient, regardless of the size of the organization.

Integration with other Oracle ERP modules, such as Procurement, Inventory, and General Ledger, further enhances the efficiency of accounts payable processing. Seamless integration ensures that data flows smoothly between different modules, reducing the need for manual data entry and minimizing the risk of errors. This integrated approach also supports end-to-end financial management, from procurement to payment, providing a holistic view of the organization's financial operations.

Cost Savings

Implementing the Accounts Payable module can lead to significant cost savings for organizations. By automating manual processes, reducing errors, and optimizing payment schedules, businesses can lower their operational costs. The module also supports electronic invoicing and payments, which are more cost-effective than traditional paper-based methods.

Additionally, the module's ability to negotiate early payment discounts and manage dynamic discounting can result in direct financial savings. By taking advantage of these opportunities, businesses can reduce their overall payables and improve their bottom line.

Enhanced Security

The Accounts Payable module provides robust security features to protect sensitive financial information. Access controls and user permissions ensure that only authorized personnel can view and process payments. This reduces the risk of fraud and unauthorized transactions.

The module also supports secure electronic payments, which are less vulnerable to theft and fraud compared to paper checks. By using secure payment methods, businesses can protect their financial assets and reduce the risk of financial loss.

Conclusion

The Oracle ERP Accounts Payable module offers a comprehensive suite of features designed to streamline and optimize accounts payable processing. By leveraging these features, organizations can achieve significant benefits, including improved efficiency, enhanced compliance, better cash flow management, stronger vendor relationships, and substantial cost savings. The module's real-time reporting and analytics capabilities provide valuable insights into financial operations, supporting data-driven decision-making. Additionally, the module's scalability and integration with other Oracle ERP modules ensure that it remains effective as organizations grow and evolve. Ultimately, the Accounts Payable module is a powerful tool that can help businesses enhance their financial management processes and achieve greater operational efficiency.

CHAPTER II
Setting Up the Accounts Payable Module

2.1 Defining Company Parameters

2.1.1 Explain the process of setting up company parameters for the Accounts Payable module

Setting up company parameters for the Accounts Payable (AP) module in Oracle ERP is a critical step in ensuring that the system functions correctly and efficiently. Company parameters define the rules, defaults, and behaviors that the AP module will follow during its operation. Here's a detailed guide on the process:

1. Accessing the Company Parameters Setup

To begin setting up company parameters, you need to navigate to the Accounts Payable setup area in Oracle ERP. Typically, this can be found under the Financials or AP module, depending on your specific Oracle ERP version.

1. Login to Oracle ERP: Use your credentials to log into the Oracle ERP system.

2. Navigate to the AP Module: Go to the menu and select the Accounts Payable module.

3. Access Setup Options: Find the setup or configuration options within the AP module. This may be labeled as "Setup," "Configuration," or "Company Parameters."

2. Defining Basic Company Information

The first step in the setup process involves defining basic company information. This includes:

1. Company Name and Address: Enter the legal name of your company and its primary address. This information is crucial for generating invoices, checks, and other AP documents.

2. Legal Entity and Operating Unit: Specify the legal entity and operating unit that the AP module will be associated with. This helps in segregating financial data and ensuring compliance with legal requirements.

3. Currency and Exchange Rates: Define the primary currency for transactions and the method for handling currency exchange rates. This is important for international transactions and financial reporting.

3. Setting Up Accounting Parameters

Accounting parameters determine how financial transactions are recorded and reported. Key elements to configure include:

1. Ledger and Chart of Accounts: Link the AP module to the appropriate ledger and chart of accounts. This ensures that all transactions are recorded in the correct financial accounts.

2. Accounting Calendar: Define the accounting periods and fiscal year for your company. This helps in accurate financial reporting and period closing activities.

3. Subledger Accounting Options: Configure subledger accounting options, such as accounting rules, account derivation rules, and journal entry settings. These options control how AP transactions are translated into general ledger entries.

4. Defining Payment and Invoice Options

Payment and invoice options dictate how invoices are processed and payments are made. Important parameters include:

1. Payment Terms: Set up default payment terms that will be applied to vendor invoices. Payment terms define the due date and discount terms for payments.

2. Invoice Matching Options: Configure how invoices are matched to purchase orders and receipts. Options include two-way, three-way, or four-way matching, which help ensure invoice accuracy and prevent overpayments.

3. Automatic Invoice Numbering: Define the rules for automatically generating invoice numbers. This helps in maintaining a consistent numbering scheme and avoiding duplicate invoices.

5. Configuring Tax Options

Tax options are crucial for ensuring compliance with tax regulations and accurate tax reporting. Parameters to set include:

1. Tax Codes and Jurisdictions: Define the tax codes and jurisdictions that apply to your company's transactions. This includes sales tax, VAT, and other applicable taxes.

2. Tax Calculation Rules: Configure rules for calculating taxes on invoices and payments. This may involve setting tax rates, exemptions, and rounding rules.

3. Tax Reporting and Compliance: Set up options for tax reporting and compliance, such as tax filing periods, tax authorities, and reporting formats.

6. Setting Up Approval and Security Settings

Approval and security settings control who can access and approve AP transactions. Key parameters to define are:

1. Approval Hierarchies: Establish approval hierarchies for different types of AP transactions. This ensures that invoices and payments are reviewed and approved by the appropriate personnel.

2. User Roles and Permissions: Assign roles and permissions to users based on their responsibilities. This helps in maintaining security and preventing unauthorized access to sensitive financial data.

3. Segregation of Duties: Implement segregation of duties to ensure that no single individual has control over all aspects of a financial transaction. This helps in preventing fraud and errors.

7. Configuring Reporting and Analytics

Reporting and analytics settings determine how AP data is reported and analyzed. Parameters to configure include:

1. Standard Reports: Set up standard reports for monitoring AP activities, such as aging reports, payment history, and vendor performance reports.

2. Custom Reports: Define custom reporting options to meet specific business requirements. This may involve creating custom report templates, queries, and dashboards.

3. Analytics and BI Integration: Integrate the AP module with business intelligence (BI) tools for advanced analytics and reporting. This helps in gaining deeper insights into AP performance and trends.

8. Testing and Validation

Once all parameters are configured, it's essential to test and validate the setup to ensure everything works as expected. Steps to follow include:

1. Test Transactions: Conduct test transactions, such as creating and processing invoices, making payments, and generating reports. Verify that the transactions are processed correctly and reflect accurately in the financial statements.

2. User Acceptance Testing (UAT): Involve end-users in testing the AP module setup. Gather feedback and make necessary adjustments to ensure the setup meets user requirements.

3. Validation and Documentation: Validate the setup with key stakeholders and document the configuration settings. This helps in maintaining a record of the setup for future reference and audits.

Conclusion

Setting up company parameters for the Accounts Payable module in Oracle ERP is a comprehensive process that involves defining basic company information, accounting parameters, payment and invoice options, tax options, approval and security settings, and reporting and analytics settings. Each step is crucial for ensuring the smooth and efficient operation of the AP module, compliance with legal and regulatory requirements, and accurate financial reporting. By following a structured approach and involving key stakeholders, companies can achieve a robust AP setup that supports their business processes and objectives.

2.1.2 Discuss the different company parameters that can be configured

Configuring company parameters in the Oracle ERP Accounts Payable (AP) module is a critical step in ensuring that the system functions efficiently and meets the specific needs of the organization. These parameters influence how the AP module handles transactions, processes invoices, manages vendors, and integrates with other modules. Below is a detailed discussion of the various company parameters that can be configured within the Accounts Payable module.

1. Operating Unit Configuration

The operating unit is a fundamental configuration parameter that defines the primary operational structure within the Oracle ERP system. It represents a distinct business unit or division within the organization, each with its own set of books and financial reporting requirements.

- Importance: Proper configuration of operating units ensures that transactions are recorded and reported accurately for each business unit, enabling precise financial reporting and compliance.

- Configuration Steps: Define each operating unit with unique identifiers, specify its associated legal entities, and configure its financial calendars and accounting structures.

2. Fiscal Calendar and Accounting Periods

The fiscal calendar defines the financial year and accounting periods within the AP module. This configuration is crucial for accurate financial reporting and period-end processing.

- Importance: Ensuring that the fiscal calendar aligns with the organization's financial year and reporting requirements is vital for timely and accurate financial statements.

- Configuration Steps: Set up the fiscal calendar, define accounting periods (monthly, quarterly, or yearly), and specify the start and end dates for each period.

3. Currency and Exchange Rates

Configuring currencies and exchange rates is essential for organizations that operate in multiple countries or deal with vendors in different currencies.

- Importance: Accurate currency configuration ensures that transactions are recorded in the correct currency and that exchange rate fluctuations are accounted for properly.

- Configuration Steps: Define the functional currency of the organization, set up additional currencies used for transactions, and establish exchange rate types and rates.

4. Payment Terms

Payment terms dictate the conditions under which payments are made to vendors. These terms impact cash flow and vendor relationships.

- Importance: Well-defined payment terms help manage cash flow effectively and maintain good relationships with vendors by ensuring timely payments.

- Configuration Steps: Define various payment terms (e.g., Net 30, Net 45), set discount terms for early payments, and configure default payment terms for vendors.

5. Invoice Processing Controls

Invoice processing controls determine how invoices are validated, approved, and processed within the AP module.

- Importance: Proper configuration ensures that invoices are processed efficiently and accurately, reducing errors and discrepancies.

- Configuration Steps: Set up invoice matching rules (2-way, 3-way matching), configure approval hierarchies, and define tolerances for variances.

6. Tax Configuration

Tax configuration is critical for compliance with tax regulations and accurate financial reporting. It involves setting up tax codes, rates, and jurisdictions.

- Importance: Accurate tax configuration ensures compliance with local and international tax laws and prevents potential penalties.

- Configuration Steps: Define tax codes and rates for different jurisdictions, configure tax accounting rules, and set up tax exemptions where applicable.

7. Bank Accounts and Payment Methods

Configuring bank accounts and payment methods is essential for processing vendor payments. This includes setting up the organization's bank accounts and specifying how payments will be made (e.g., checks, electronic funds transfer).

- Importance: Ensuring that bank accounts and payment methods are configured correctly enables smooth and timely vendor payments.

- Configuration Steps: Set up bank accounts, configure payment methods, and define payment formats (e.g., ACH, wire transfer).

8. Vendor Management Settings

Vendor management settings control how vendor information is stored, managed, and utilized within the AP module.

- Importance: Proper configuration of vendor settings ensures that vendor information is accurate and up-to-date, facilitating effective vendor management.

- Configuration Steps: Define vendor categories, configure vendor approval processes, and set up default values for vendor attributes (e.g., payment terms, tax IDs).

9. Expense Allocation Rules

Expense allocation rules determine how expenses are distributed across different cost centers, departments, or projects.

- Importance: Accurate expense allocation is essential for proper cost management and financial reporting.

- Configuration Steps: Set up allocation rules, define allocation methods (e.g., fixed percentage, direct allocation), and configure allocation cycles.

10. Approval Hierarchies

Approval hierarchies define the levels of authorization required for different types of transactions within the AP module.

- Importance: Configuring approval hierarchies ensures that transactions are reviewed and approved by the appropriate personnel, enhancing internal controls and accountability.

- Configuration Steps: Define approval levels, assign approvers to each level, and configure approval workflows.

11. Expense Report Policies

Expense report policies control how employee expenses are reported, approved, and reimbursed.

- Importance: Well-defined expense report policies ensure that employee expenses are managed effectively and reimbursed in a timely manner.

- Configuration Steps: Define expense categories, set up expense report templates, and configure approval processes for expense reports.

12. Compliance and Audit Settings

Compliance and audit settings determine how the AP module handles regulatory compliance and audit requirements.

- Importance: Proper configuration ensures that the organization meets regulatory requirements and is prepared for audits.

- Configuration Steps: Set up compliance rules, configure audit trails, and define retention periods for financial records.

13. Notifications and Alerts

Notifications and alerts provide timely information to users about important events and actions required within the AP module.

- Importance: Configuring notifications and alerts ensures that users are informed about critical events, such as invoice approvals, payment due dates, and compliance issues.

- Configuration Steps: Set up notification rules, define alert triggers, and configure delivery methods (e.g., email, system alerts).

14. Integration with Other Modules

Integration settings determine how the AP module interacts with other Oracle ERP modules, such as General Ledger, Purchasing, and Inventory.

- Importance: Ensuring seamless integration between modules enhances data consistency and streamlines business processes.

- Configuration Steps: Configure data sharing rules, set up integration points, and define data synchronization schedules.

Conclusion

Configuring company parameters in the Oracle ERP Accounts Payable module is a critical step in setting up the system to meet the organization's specific needs. Each parameter plays a vital role in ensuring accurate transaction processing, effective vendor management, and compliance with regulatory requirements. By carefully defining and configuring these parameters, organizations can optimize their AP operations, improve financial reporting accuracy, and enhance overall operational efficiency.

2.1.3 Emphasize the importance of accurate company parameter setup for proper module operation

Setting up company parameters in the Accounts Payable (AP) module is a foundational task that significantly impacts the module's overall functionality and effectiveness. This section underscores the critical importance of accurate company parameter configuration and explores the potential consequences of incorrect setups, along with best practices to ensure accuracy and efficiency.

Impact on Financial Integrity and Reporting

One of the foremost reasons for ensuring accurate company parameter setup is the direct impact it has on financial integrity and reporting. Company parameters dictate how financial data is recorded, categorized, and reported within the Oracle ERP system. Any inaccuracies at this foundational level can lead to significant discrepancies in financial reports, which can subsequently affect business decisions, stakeholder trust, and regulatory compliance.

For example, incorrect configuration of currency settings or fiscal calendars can lead to misreported financial statements. If the fiscal year is not accurately defined, financial periods may close prematurely or remain open longer than intended, causing confusion and errors in financial tracking. Similarly, misconfigured currency settings can result in erroneous conversion rates, impacting multinational financial consolidation and reporting.

Enhancing Operational Efficiency

Accurate company parameters also enhance operational efficiency. Proper setup ensures that automated processes within the AP module function smoothly. This includes automatic invoice matching, payment processing, and tax calculations. When parameters are correctly configured, the system can accurately match invoices to purchase orders and receipts, reducing the need for manual intervention and minimizing errors.

For instance, when payment terms are accurately defined in the company parameters, the system can automatically calculate due dates for invoices, enabling timely payments and potentially taking advantage of early payment discounts. This not only streamlines the AP process but also improves the company's cash flow management.

Ensuring Compliance with Regulatory Requirements

Compliance with regulatory requirements is another crucial aspect impacted by company parameter setup. Various laws and regulations govern financial transactions, and the AP module must be configured to adhere to these standards. This includes setting up tax codes, jurisdictions, and reporting requirements specific to the regions in which the company operates.

Accurate setup of tax parameters ensures that the correct tax rates are applied to transactions, and appropriate tax reports are generated. Failure to comply with tax regulations can lead to penalties, fines, and legal complications. Thus, meticulous attention to detail during the setup phase can save the company from potential compliance issues and financial losses.

Facilitating Accurate Data Analysis

Data analysis and business intelligence depend heavily on the accuracy of the underlying data. When company parameters are set up correctly, the data captured in the AP module is reliable and can be used confidently for analysis. This, in turn, aids in making informed strategic decisions.

For example, accurate classification of expenses and proper tagging of transactions enable detailed spending analysis. Businesses can track spending patterns, identify cost-saving opportunities, and forecast future financial needs more effectively. Inaccurate data due to poor parameter setup can lead to faulty analysis and misguided business strategies.

Reducing System Downtime and Maintenance Costs

Accurate parameter setup also contributes to reducing system downtime and maintenance costs. Incorrect configurations can lead to frequent system errors and the need for corrective maintenance, which can disrupt business operations and incur additional costs. By ensuring parameters are correctly set from the outset, companies can minimize the need for troubleshooting and maintenance.

Regularly reviewing and updating company parameters as part of system maintenance can also help in adapting to changes in business processes and regulatory requirements. This proactive approach ensures the AP module remains efficient and compliant over time.

Best Practices for Accurate Company Parameter Setup

To achieve accurate company parameter setup, it is essential to follow best practices that ensure precision and reliability:

1. Thorough Planning and Documentation: Before configuring the AP module, conduct thorough planning to understand the specific requirements of the business. Document all necessary parameters, including fiscal calendars, currency settings, tax codes, and payment terms.

2. Involve Key Stakeholders: Engage key stakeholders, including finance, tax, and IT departments, in the setup process. Their input and expertise can help identify critical requirements and potential pitfalls.

3. Leverage Oracle ERP Documentation: Utilize Oracle ERP's comprehensive documentation and support resources. These materials provide detailed guidance on parameter setup and best practices.

4. Conduct Testing: Before finalizing the setup, conduct rigorous testing to ensure that all parameters are functioning as expected. This includes testing various scenarios such as different payment terms, tax calculations, and fiscal period closures.

5. Regular Reviews and Updates: Regularly review and update company parameters to ensure they remain aligned with current business needs and regulatory changes. This proactive approach helps maintain the accuracy and relevance of the setup.

6. Training and Support: Provide training to users responsible for maintaining and updating company parameters. Ensure they understand the importance of accuracy and the potential impact of errors.

Conclusion

Accurate setup of company parameters in the Accounts Payable module is a critical task that lays the foundation for effective financial management within Oracle ERP. It impacts financial integrity, operational efficiency, regulatory compliance, data analysis, and system maintenance. By following best practices and emphasizing accuracy, businesses can ensure that their AP module operates smoothly and delivers reliable financial insights, ultimately supporting informed decision-making and sustainable growth.

2.2 Establishing Vendor Relationships

2.2.1 Describe the steps involved in creating and maintaining vendor records in the Accounts Payable module

Establishing and maintaining vendor relationships is a crucial aspect of managing the Accounts Payable (AP) module in Oracle ERP. Proper vendor management ensures efficient processing of invoices, timely payments, and compliance with procurement policies. This section will detail the steps involved in creating and maintaining vendor records in the Accounts Payable module.

Steps Involved in Creating Vendor Records

1. Accessing the Vendor Management Interface

   - Navigate to the Accounts Payable module.

   - Select the Vendor Management section, often labeled as "Suppliers" or "Vendors."

2. Creating a New Vendor Record

   - Click on the "Create" or "New Vendor" button to initiate a new vendor record.

   - Enter basic vendor details such as Vendor Name, Address, Contact Information, and Tax Identification Number.

3. Entering Vendor General Information

   - Vendor Name: This is the legal name of the vendor as registered.

   - Vendor Type: Specify whether the vendor is a supplier, service provider, or contractor.

   - Vendor Address: Include the complete address for correspondence and shipping.

   - Contact Information: Add primary contact details including phone numbers and email addresses.

   - Tax Identification: Enter the vendor's tax identification number for compliance and reporting purposes.

4. Setting Up Vendor Payment Information

- Bank Account Details: Enter the vendor's bank account information for electronic payments.

- Payment Terms: Define the agreed payment terms, such as Net 30, Net 60, or any custom terms.

- Payment Methods: Specify the preferred payment method (e.g., electronic funds transfer, check, credit card).

5. Defining Vendor Terms and Conditions

- Payment Schedule: Set the payment schedule and frequency.

- Discount Terms: Enter any early payment discounts or special terms agreed upon.

- Freight Terms: Define shipping terms and responsibilities.

6. Adding Vendor Classification and Attributes

- Vendor Category: Categorize the vendor based on goods or services provided.

- Minority Business Classification: If applicable, include any diversity classifications such as minority-owned or women-owned business.

- Risk Assessment: Assess and classify the risk level of the vendor (e.g., low, medium, high).

7. Entering Tax and Compliance Information

- Tax Codes: Assign appropriate tax codes applicable to the vendor.

- Compliance Documents: Attach necessary compliance documents such as W-9 forms or business licenses.

- Insurance Information: Record details of any required insurance coverage.

8. Setting Up Communication Preferences

- Preferred Communication Method: Specify how the vendor prefers to receive communications (e.g., email, postal mail).

- Order Acknowledgments: Set up preferences for receiving order acknowledgments and updates.

- Invoice Submission Preferences: Define how the vendor will submit invoices (e.g., electronically, paper-based).

9. Reviewing and Approving the Vendor Record

  - Review all entered information for accuracy.

  - Submit the vendor record for internal approval if necessary.

  - Once approved, the vendor record is activated and ready for use in transactions.

 Steps Involved in Maintaining Vendor Records

1. Regular Updates and Reviews

  - Periodically review vendor records to ensure all information is up-to-date.

  - Update contact information, address, and payment details as needed.

2. Managing Vendor Performance

  - Monitor vendor performance metrics such as delivery times, product quality, and compliance with terms.

  - Record performance reviews and any corrective actions taken.

3. Handling Vendor Inquiries and Disputes

  - Address vendor inquiries promptly regarding payment status, invoice discrepancies, and contract terms.

  - Record and manage any disputes or issues that arise with vendors.

4. Updating Compliance and Regulatory Information

  - Ensure that all compliance documents are current and renewed as necessary.

  - Update tax codes and regulatory information in accordance with changes in legislation.

5. Vendor Record Deactivation and Archiving

  - If a vendor is no longer used, deactivate the vendor record to prevent future transactions.

- Archive historical data for audit and reference purposes while ensuring it is retained per company policy.

6. Audit and Compliance Checks

- Conduct regular audits of vendor records to ensure compliance with internal policies and external regulations.

- Document audit findings and take corrective actions as required.

7. Vendor Communication and Relationship Management

- Maintain open lines of communication with vendors to foster good relationships.

- Engage in regular meetings or check-ins to discuss performance, future business, and any issues.

8. Integrating Vendor Feedback

- Collect feedback from vendors to improve the relationship and transaction processes.

- Implement changes based on feedback to enhance vendor satisfaction and efficiency.

9. Vendor Risk Management

- Continuously assess and mitigate risks associated with vendors, including financial stability and operational reliability.

- Update risk assessments based on new information and vendor performance.

10. Technology and System Upgrades

- Ensure that vendor management systems are up-to-date with the latest technology and security features.

- Train staff on new features and updates to the vendor management module.

Conclusion

Creating and maintaining vendor records in the Accounts Payable module of Oracle ERP involves a systematic approach to ensure accuracy, compliance, and efficiency. By following these detailed steps, organizations can establish strong vendor relationships that facilitate smooth financial operations and contribute to overall business success. Regular maintenance and updates to vendor records are essential to adapt to changes and ensure ongoing compliance and performance management.

2.2.2 Explain the information required for each vendor record

In Oracle ERP, maintaining accurate and comprehensive vendor records is crucial for efficient accounts payable processing. Vendor records serve as the foundation for managing relationships with suppliers, ensuring timely payments, and maintaining accurate financial records. To achieve this, each vendor record must contain specific information that facilitates seamless interactions and transactions. This section details the essential information required for each vendor record in the Accounts Payable module of Oracle ERP.

1. Basic Vendor Information

 - Vendor Name: The legal name of the vendor. This should be the official name used for all transactions and correspondence.

 - Vendor Number: A unique identifier assigned to each vendor. This number is crucial for tracking and referencing vendor-related activities.

 - Vendor Type: Classification of the vendor based on their business nature (e.g., supplier, contractor, service provider). This helps in categorizing and managing vendors more effectively.

 - Status: Indicates whether the vendor is active or inactive. This is essential for maintaining current and relevant vendor data.

2. Contact Information

 - Primary Contact Name: The main point of contact at the vendor's organization. This individual should be someone who can address queries and issues related to accounts payable.

 - Email Address: A valid email address for communication. Email is often used for sending purchase orders, invoices, and payment notifications.

 - Phone Number: A direct phone number for the primary contact. This ensures quick and direct communication when necessary.

- Fax Number: Though less common today, some transactions may still require fax communication.

- Secondary Contact Information: Details of an alternate contact person, in case the primary contact is unavailable.

3. Address Information

- Remittance Address: The address where payments should be sent. This is critical for ensuring that payments reach the correct location without delays.

- Ordering Address: The address where purchase orders should be sent. This may differ from the remittance address.

- Physical Address: The actual physical location of the vendor. This is useful for site visits or verifying the vendor's existence.

- Billing Address: If different from the remittance address, this is where invoices should be sent for payment processing.

4. Banking Information

- Bank Name: The name of the vendor's bank. This is required for setting up electronic payments.

- Bank Account Number: The vendor's bank account number. This is essential for direct deposit payments.

- Bank Routing Number: The routing number associated with the vendor's bank account. This is necessary for ensuring funds are transferred correctly.

- IBAN/SWIFT Code: For international vendors, these codes are required for cross-border transactions.

5. Tax Information

- Tax Identification Number (TIN): The vendor's tax ID number, which is necessary for tax reporting and compliance.

- VAT/GST Registration Number: If the vendor is registered for Value Added Tax (VAT) or Goods and Services Tax (GST), this number should be recorded.

- Tax Withholding Information: Details regarding any tax withholding requirements. This ensures compliance with local tax regulations.

6. Payment Terms and Conditions

   - Payment Terms: The agreed-upon terms for payment (e.g., Net 30, Net 60). These terms dictate when payments are due and help manage cash flow.

   - Discount Terms: Any discounts offered for early payment. This can incentivize timely payments and improve cash management.

   - Preferred Payment Method: The vendor's preferred method of payment (e.g., check, electronic funds transfer, credit card). This ensures payments are made in a manner convenient for the vendor.

7. Financial Information

   - Credit Limit: The maximum amount of credit extended to the vendor. This helps manage exposure to financial risk.

   - Account Balances: Current and historical account balances, including outstanding invoices and payments. This provides a comprehensive view of the vendor's financial standing.

   - Payment History: A record of past payments, including dates and amounts. This is useful for reviewing the vendor's payment performance.

8. Compliance and Certifications

   - Compliance Documents: Any required compliance documents, such as licenses, certifications, and insurance information. These ensure the vendor meets all necessary regulatory requirements.

   - Contractual Agreements: Copies of any contracts or agreements with the vendor. This ensures that all terms and conditions are clearly documented and accessible.

   - Supplier Code of Conduct: Documentation that the vendor adheres to the organization's supplier code of conduct. This ensures alignment with ethical and operational standards.

9. Notes and Additional Information

   - Internal Notes: Any additional information or notes relevant to the vendor relationship. This could include special instructions, preferences, or historical issues.

   - Attachments: Supporting documents such as scanned contracts, certifications, and correspondence. This centralizes all relevant information in one place.

Importance of Comprehensive Vendor Records

Maintaining comprehensive and accurate vendor records is essential for several reasons:

1. Efficiency in Transactions: Accurate vendor records streamline the processing of purchase orders, invoices, and payments. This reduces errors and delays, ensuring smooth and efficient transactions.

2. Improved Communication: Detailed contact information ensures effective communication with vendors, facilitating prompt resolution of issues and queries.

3. Enhanced Financial Management: Comprehensive financial information helps manage cash flow, credit limits, and payment terms, contributing to better financial planning and control.

4. Regulatory Compliance: Proper documentation of tax information, compliance documents, and certifications ensures adherence to regulatory requirements, reducing the risk of legal issues.

5. Risk Management: Detailed records, including credit limits and payment history, help assess and mitigate financial risk associated with vendor relationships.

6. Strategic Vendor Management: By maintaining detailed and accurate vendor records, organizations can analyze vendor performance, negotiate better terms, and build stronger, more strategic partnerships.

In summary, the information required for each vendor record in the Accounts Payable module of Oracle ERP is extensive and multifaceted. It encompasses basic details, contact information, addresses, banking details, tax information, payment terms, financial data, compliance documents, and additional notes. This comprehensive approach ensures that all necessary information is readily available, facilitating efficient accounts payable processing, enhancing vendor relationships, and supporting overall financial management.

2.2.3 Discuss the importance of maintaining accurate vendor relationships for effective invoice processing

Setting up accurate company parameters is crucial for the seamless operation of the Accounts Payable (AP) module within Oracle ERP. Company parameters serve as the foundational settings that define how the AP module will function, impacting every aspect of vendor relationship management and overall financial operations. Inaccurate or incomplete setup of these parameters can lead to a multitude of issues, including payment delays, compliance problems, and inefficiencies in processing invoices. This section explores the key reasons why precise company parameter setup is essential and provides practical insights into best practices for ensuring accuracy.

1. Ensuring Consistency and Standardization

One of the primary reasons for accurate company parameter setup is to ensure consistency and standardization across all AP operations. When parameters are correctly defined, they create a uniform framework that governs how transactions are processed, how vendor records are maintained, and how payments are handled. This uniformity is critical for maintaining a high level of operational efficiency and minimizing errors that could arise from discrepancies in data entry or procedural inconsistencies.

For example, setting up standardized payment terms ensures that all vendors are paid according to the same criteria, reducing the likelihood of disputes and confusion. Similarly, defining uniform tax codes and jurisdictions helps in maintaining compliance with local and international tax regulations, preventing potential legal issues.

2. Enhancing Data Accuracy and Integrity

Accurate company parameter setup directly contributes to the accuracy and integrity of data within the AP module. When parameters are meticulously configured, they act as control points that validate and verify the information being entered into the system. This reduces the chances of errors and ensures that the data being processed is reliable.

For instance, precise setup of vendor information requirements ensures that all necessary details, such as tax identification numbers, contact information, and payment terms, are captured accurately. This not only facilitates smooth transaction processing but also aids in maintaining a comprehensive and up-to-date vendor database, which is crucial for effective vendor relationship management.

3. Facilitating Compliance and Reporting

Compliance with regulatory requirements is a critical aspect of financial management. Accurate company parameter setup is essential for ensuring that the AP module operates in accordance with relevant laws and regulations. Properly configured parameters help in generating accurate financial reports, which are necessary for both internal management purposes and external audits.

For example, accurate setup of tax codes and jurisdictions enables the system to correctly calculate and apply taxes on transactions, ensuring compliance with tax regulations. This not only prevents potential legal issues but also facilitates the generation of accurate tax reports, which are essential for regulatory filings and audits.

4. Improving Operational Efficiency

Operational efficiency is significantly enhanced when company parameters are accurately set up. Properly defined parameters streamline various processes within the AP module, reducing the time and effort required to complete tasks. This leads to faster processing times, reduced administrative overhead, and improved overall productivity.

For instance, accurate setup of payment terms and options allows for automated payment processing, reducing the need for manual intervention and minimizing the risk of errors. This not only speeds up the payment process but also ensures that vendors are paid promptly, enhancing vendor satisfaction and strengthening business relationships.

5. Enhancing Vendor Relationship Management

Vendor relationship management is a critical component of the AP module, and accurate company parameter setup plays a vital role in this aspect. Properly configured parameters ensure that vendor interactions are smooth and efficient, fostering positive relationships and promoting long-term partnerships.

For example, accurate setup of vendor records, including contact information and payment preferences, ensures that vendors receive timely and accurate payments. This helps in building trust and reliability, encouraging vendors to continue doing business with the organization. Additionally, standardized processes for handling vendor inquiries and resolving issues contribute to a more positive vendor experience, further strengthening the relationship.

6. Mitigating Risks and Reducing Costs

Inaccurate company parameter setup can lead to various risks and increased costs. Errors in payment processing, non-compliance with regulatory requirements, and inefficiencies in vendor management can result in financial losses and damage to the organization's reputation. By ensuring accurate setup of company parameters, these risks can be mitigated, and costs can be reduced.

For example, precise setup of payment terms and options helps in avoiding late payment penalties and taking advantage of early payment discounts, leading to cost savings. Similarly, accurate tax setup prevents potential fines and penalties associated with non-compliance, reducing the financial and reputational risks for the organization.

7. Adapting to Business Changes and Growth

As businesses grow and evolve, their requirements and processes change. Accurate company parameter setup ensures that the AP module can adapt to these changes seamlessly. Properly configured parameters provide the flexibility needed to accommodate new business requirements, such as changes in vendor relationships, tax regulations, or payment terms.

For example, when expanding into new markets, accurate setup of tax codes and jurisdictions ensures compliance with local tax laws, enabling smooth operations in the new regions. Similarly, updating vendor records and payment terms as business relationships evolve helps in maintaining efficient and effective AP processes.

Best Practices for Accurate Company Parameter Setup

To ensure the accuracy of company parameter setup, organizations should follow best practices that include thorough planning, regular review and updates, and continuous monitoring. Here are some key best practices:

1. Thorough Planning and Documentation: Before setting up company parameters, it is essential to conduct thorough planning and document all requirements. This includes identifying the specific needs of the organization, understanding regulatory requirements, and defining standard operating procedures. Proper documentation serves as a reference point for configuring and maintaining parameters.

2. Involvement of Key Stakeholders: Involving key stakeholders, such as finance, procurement, and compliance teams, in the parameter setup process ensures that all requirements are considered. Collaboration between different departments helps in identifying potential issues and addressing them proactively.

3. Regular Review and Updates: Company parameters should be reviewed regularly to ensure they remain accurate and up-to-date. Changes in business processes, regulatory requirements, or vendor relationships may necessitate updates to the parameters. Regular review and updates help in maintaining the relevance and accuracy of the parameters.

4. Continuous Monitoring and Validation: Continuous monitoring and validation of company parameters are essential to ensure their accuracy. This includes periodic audits, data validation checks, and exception reporting. Monitoring helps in identifying discrepancies and addressing them promptly, ensuring the integrity of the AP module.

5. Training and Support: Providing training and support to users involved in setting up and maintaining company parameters is crucial. Proper training ensures that users understand the importance of accurate parameter setup and are equipped with the knowledge and skills to configure and manage parameters effectively.

By following these best practices, organizations can ensure the accuracy of company parameter setup, leading to efficient and effective operation of the AP module within Oracle ERP.

Conclusion

Accurate company parameter setup is the cornerstone of effective Accounts Payable operations within Oracle ERP. It ensures consistency, enhances data accuracy, facilitates compliance, improves operational efficiency, and strengthens vendor relationships. By following best practices for parameter setup and maintenance, organizations can mitigate risks, reduce costs, and adapt to changing business needs. Ultimately, precise company parameter setup contributes to the overall success and efficiency of the AP module, enabling organizations to achieve their financial management goals.

2.3 Configuring Payment Terms and Options

2.3.1 Explain the process of setting up payment terms and options for vendors

Introduction to Payment Terms and Options

Payment terms and options are crucial components of the Accounts Payable (AP) module in Oracle ERP. These settings determine how and when vendors are paid for their goods and services, impacting both cash flow and vendor relationships. Proper configuration ensures that payments are processed efficiently, financial obligations are met promptly, and cash management is optimized.

Understanding Payment Terms

Payment terms define the conditions under which a company will complete a payment for an invoice. These conditions typically include the payment due date, any discount available for early payment, and the specific time frame within which payment must be made. Common examples of payment terms include "Net 30," where payment is due 30 days after the invoice date, or "2/10 Net 30," where a 2% discount is available if payment is made within 10 days, otherwise the full amount is due in 30 days.

Steps to Set Up Payment Terms and Options

1. Access the Payment Terms Configuration

To set up payment terms in Oracle ERP, navigate to the Accounts Payable module. From the main menu, select "Setup" and then "Payment Terms." This will open the Payment Terms configuration screen where you can create, modify, and view existing payment terms.

2. Define New Payment Terms

Click on the "Create" button to define a new payment term. Enter a unique name or code for the payment term, which will be used to identify it in the system. This name should be descriptive enough to convey the essence of the term, such as "Net 30" or "2/10 Net 30."

3. Specify Payment Conditions

In the payment term setup screen, you'll need to specify the details of the payment conditions:

- Days Until Due: Enter the number of days from the invoice date until the payment is due. For example, for a "Net 30" term, you would enter 30 days.

- Discount Percentage: If there is an early payment discount, specify the percentage of the discount available.

- Discount Days: Enter the number of days within which the discount is available. For instance, in "2/10 Net 30," you would enter 10 days.

4. Define Additional Options

Depending on the complexity of your payment terms, you might need to define additional options such as:

- Multiple Installments: If payments are to be made in multiple installments, specify the number of installments and the percentage of the total amount due for each installment.

- Fixed Date: For payment terms based on a fixed date, specify the date on which payment is due, regardless of the invoice date.

5. Save and Validate Payment Terms

Once you have entered all the necessary information, save the new payment term. The system may require validation to ensure there are no conflicts or errors in the setup. This step helps prevent issues during invoice processing.

Configuring Payment Options

Payment options determine how payments are made to vendors, including the method of payment, the currency used, and any specific instructions related to the payment process.

1. Access Payment Options Configuration

Navigate to the Accounts Payable module, select "Setup," and then "Payment Options." This will open the Payment Options configuration screen.

2. Define Payment Methods

Specify the methods of payment that will be used to settle vendor invoices. Common payment methods include:

- Check: Payments are made by issuing checks to vendors.

- Electronic Funds Transfer (EFT): Payments are directly transferred to the vendor's bank account.

- Wire Transfer: Funds are transferred electronically through a bank-to-bank transfer.

- Credit Card: Payments are made using a company credit card.

3. Set Up Payment Currencies

Define the currencies that will be used for vendor payments. If your business operates internationally, you may need to set up multiple currencies and specify exchange rates for each.

4. Specify Bank Accounts

Configure the bank accounts from which payments will be made. This involves entering the details of each bank account, including the account number, bank name, and any routing information required for electronic payments.

5. Define Payment Schedules

Payment schedules determine the frequency and timing of payments. For example, you might configure a schedule to process payments weekly, bi-weekly, or monthly. Specify the day(s) of the week or month when payments should be processed.

6. Set Up Payment Instructions

Payment instructions provide additional details that guide the payment process. This can include:

- Remittance Information: Information that accompanies the payment to help vendors reconcile the payment with their records.

- Payment Approvals: Rules for obtaining approval before payments are processed, ensuring that all payments are authorized by the appropriate personnel.

7. Save and Validate Payment Options

After configuring the payment methods, currencies, bank accounts, schedules, and instructions, save the payment options. Validate the configuration to ensure that all settings are correct and compatible with your business processes.

Impact of Payment Terms on Cash Flow Management

Effective management of payment terms and options directly impacts a company's cash flow. By negotiating favorable payment terms with vendors and setting up efficient payment options, a company can:

- Optimize Cash Flow: Extend payment terms to retain cash longer or take advantage of early payment discounts to reduce costs.

- Improve Vendor Relationships: Consistently meet payment obligations and utilize preferred payment methods to maintain strong vendor partnerships.

- Enhance Financial Planning: Accurately forecast cash outflows based on the defined payment schedules and terms, supporting better financial planning and budgeting.

Conclusion

Configuring payment terms and options in Oracle ERP's Accounts Payable module is a critical step in managing vendor payments efficiently. By following the steps outlined above, businesses can ensure that their payment processes are well-defined, compliant, and optimized for both cash flow management and vendor satisfaction. Accurate setup of these parameters not only streamlines the payment process but also contributes to the overall financial health of the organization.

2.3.2 Discuss the different payment terms and options available

In Oracle ERP's Accounts Payable module, configuring payment terms and options is a crucial step in managing the cash flow and ensuring timely payments to vendors. Payment terms dictate the timeline and conditions under which payments are made to suppliers. The selection and configuration of appropriate payment terms can significantly impact an organization's financial health and vendor relationships. Here, we will discuss the various payment terms and options available within Oracle ERP and how they can be utilized effectively.

Types of Payment Terms

1. Net Payment Terms:

- Net 30/60/90: The most common payment terms are net 30, net 60, and net 90. These terms mean that the full payment is due 30, 60, or 90 days after the invoice date. For instance, if a vendor invoice is dated January 1st and the term is net 30, the payment is due by January 31st.

- End of Month (EOM): Payment is due at the end of the month in which the invoice is received. For example, if an invoice is dated January 15th, the payment is due by January 31st.

2. Discount Terms:

- 2/10 Net 30: This term offers a discount if payment is made within a shorter period. For instance, 2/10 net 30 means that the buyer can take a 2% discount if the invoice is paid within 10 days; otherwise, the full amount is due in 30 days. This incentivizes early payment and can improve the buyer's cash flow management.

- 1/10 Net 45: Similar to 2/10 net 30, but offers a 1% discount if paid within 10 days, with the full amount due in 45 days. This provides a slightly longer timeframe for payment but with a smaller discount.

3. Installment Terms:

- 50% Upon Receipt, 50% After 30 Days: Payment is divided into two installments, with 50% due upon receipt of the invoice and the remaining 50% due after 30 days. This can help in managing cash flow by spreading out the payment.

- 30/60/90: Payments are divided into three equal installments, due in 30, 60, and 90 days. This method helps in distributing the financial burden over a more extended period.

4. Fixed Date Terms:

- Due on the 15th of Each Month: Payment is due on a specific day each month, such as the 15th. This term is helpful for regular, predictable payments.

- Due on the Last Business Day of the Month: Payment is due on the last business day of each month, ensuring that all payments are processed before the month's end.

5. Prox Terms:

- Net 30 Prox: Payment is due 30 days after the end of the month in which the invoice is received. For example, if an invoice is dated January 15th, payment is due by the end of February.

- Net 15 Prox: Similar to net 30 prox but with a 15-day term. This means that if an invoice is received in January, payment is due by mid-February.

Configurable Payment Options in Oracle ERP

1. Multiple Payment Methods:

- Check Payments: Traditional method where a physical check is issued to the vendor.

- Electronic Funds Transfer (EFT): Direct bank transfers that can be processed quickly and reduce the risk of fraud.

- Credit Card Payments: Allows for immediate payment and can be useful for smaller purchases or emergencies.

- Wire Transfers: Often used for international payments, providing a fast and secure way to transfer funds.

2. Payment Schedules:

- Recurring Payments: For regular, ongoing services or contracts, setting up recurring payments ensures timely and consistent disbursement.

- Ad-Hoc Payments: One-time payments that are not part of a regular schedule, often used for unique or infrequent expenses.

3. Early Payment Discounts:

- Configuring early payment discounts in Oracle ERP can automatically apply the discount if the payment is made within the specified timeframe. This setup can encourage early payments and improve vendor relationships.

4. Payment Holds:

- Oracle ERP allows for payment holds on specific invoices if there are disputes or issues that need resolution before payment. This functionality ensures that only approved invoices are paid.

5. Partial Payments:

- The system supports partial payments, where a portion of the invoice amount can be paid while the remaining balance is settled later. This can be beneficial in managing cash flow during tight financial periods.

6. Automatic Clearing:

- This option allows for automatic reconciliation and clearing of payments against outstanding invoices, streamlining the payment process and reducing manual intervention.

Importance of Configuring Payment Terms and Options

1. Cash Flow Management:

- Proper configuration of payment terms helps manage cash flow by aligning outgoing payments with the organization's cash inflows. Early payment discounts can save money, while installment terms can spread out expenses.

2. Vendor Relationships:

- Clear and consistent payment terms build trust with vendors. Timely payments according to agreed terms can strengthen relationships and potentially lead to better terms in future negotiations.

3. Operational Efficiency:

- Automation of payment processes reduces the administrative burden and minimizes errors. Configured terms and options ensure that payments are processed correctly and on time, improving overall efficiency.

4. Financial Planning and Forecasting:

- Accurate payment schedules and terms enable better financial planning and forecasting. Organizations can predict their cash outflows and plan accordingly, avoiding liquidity issues.

5. Compliance and Reporting:

- Adhering to configured payment terms ensures compliance with contractual obligations and internal policies. This adherence is crucial for accurate financial reporting and audit trails.

Best Practices for Configuring Payment Terms and Options

1. Review Vendor Contracts Regularly:

- Periodically review vendor contracts to ensure that the payment terms configured in Oracle ERP match the agreed terms. This practice helps in maintaining accuracy and avoiding disputes.

2. Utilize Early Payment Discounts:

- Take advantage of early payment discounts where possible. These discounts can lead to significant savings over time.

3. Monitor Cash Flow:

- Continuously monitor cash flow to ensure that configured payment terms align with the organization's financial position. Adjust terms as necessary to maintain a healthy cash flow.

4. Train Accounts Payable Staff:

- Ensure that accounts payable staff are well-trained in using Oracle ERP and understand the importance of configured payment terms and options. Proper training helps in effective utilization of the system.

5. Regular Audits and Reconciliation:

- Conduct regular audits and reconciliations of payment terms and transactions to identify any discrepancies and ensure compliance with organizational policies.

By understanding and effectively configuring the various payment terms and options available in Oracle ERP, organizations can optimize their accounts payable processes, enhance vendor relationships, and maintain robust financial health. This detailed approach ensures that all aspects of payment management are aligned with the overall strategic goals of the business.

2.3.3 Emphasize the impact of payment terms on cash flow management

Configuring payment terms and options in the Accounts Payable module is not merely a technical task; it has profound implications for a company's cash flow management. Cash flow is the lifeblood of any organization, and effective management of it ensures that the company can meet its obligations, invest in growth opportunities, and remain solvent during periods of financial strain. Payment terms dictate when a company's obligations to its vendors are due, directly affecting the timing of cash outflows.

Importance of Payment Terms in Cash Flow Management

Payment terms are essentially the conditions under which a buyer will pay a seller for purchased goods and services. Common payment terms include net 30, net 60, and net 90, which indicate that the payment is due 30, 60, or 90 days after the invoice date, respectively. These terms can significantly influence a company's working capital and liquidity.

1. Impact on Working Capital: Working capital is calculated as current assets minus current liabilities. Longer payment terms can improve a company's working capital by delaying cash outflows, thus freeing up more capital to be used for other operational needs.

2. Liquidity Management: Effective liquidity management involves ensuring that the company has enough cash on hand to meet its short-term obligations. Payment terms that extend over a longer period can help maintain higher liquidity levels, allowing the company to better handle unexpected expenses or opportunities.

3. Interest Income and Cost Savings: If a company can delay its payments without incurring late fees or damaging relationships with vendors, it can potentially earn interest on the retained cash. Additionally, by managing payment terms effectively, a company can avoid costly short-term borrowing.

4. Supplier Relationships and Negotiations: While longer payment terms can benefit the buyer's cash flow, it's important to balance this with maintaining healthy supplier relationships. Some suppliers might offer discounts for early payments, which can be a strategic decision for cost savings.

5. Cash Flow Forecasting: Accurate cash flow forecasting is essential for financial planning. Understanding and managing payment terms helps in predicting the exact timing of cash outflows, aiding in better forecasting and financial stability.

Strategies for Optimizing Payment Terms

To leverage payment terms effectively, companies should adopt several strategies:

1. Negotiating Favorable Terms: Companies should negotiate terms that align with their cash flow cycles. For instance, if a company receives payments from its customers every 45 days, negotiating net 60 terms with suppliers can provide a buffer period.

2. Utilizing Early Payment Discounts: Some suppliers offer discounts for early payments. While longer payment terms improve liquidity, taking advantage of early payment discounts can result in significant savings, which should be weighed against the benefits of holding onto the cash longer.

3. Automating Payment Processes: Implementing an automated Accounts Payable system can help ensure that payments are made on the last possible day within the agreed terms, maximizing the benefits of extended terms while avoiding late fees.

4. Dynamic Discounting: This is a flexible approach where the payment terms are adjusted dynamically based on the buyer's cash position and the supplier's cash needs. It allows for negotiated discounts for early payments on an ad-hoc basis.

5. Regular Review and Adjustment of Terms: Payment terms should not be static. Regularly reviewing and adjusting them based on the company's current financial position, market conditions, and supplier relationships can optimize cash flow management.

Case Study: Impact of Payment Terms on Cash Flow

Consider a mid-sized manufacturing company, XYZ Corp., which has an annual revenue of $50 million. XYZ Corp. has traditionally operated with net 30 payment terms with all its suppliers. However, as the company grew, it faced significant cash flow challenges due to the timing mismatch between customer payments and supplier obligations.

Upon reviewing their payment terms, XYZ Corp. negotiated net 60 terms with its major suppliers. This adjustment provided an additional 30 days of cash retention, improving their working capital position. As a result, XYZ Corp. could invest the freed-up capital in expanding its production capacity, leading to a 10% increase in annual revenue.

Moreover, by leveraging early payment discounts selectively, XYZ Corp. managed to save $100,000 annually in procurement costs. This strategic approach not only improved their cash flow but also strengthened relationships with key suppliers, who appreciated the timely payments.

Practical Tips for Managing Payment Terms

1. Understand Supplier Constraints: Not all suppliers can afford to offer extended terms. Understanding the financial health and cash flow needs of suppliers can aid in negotiating mutually beneficial terms.

2. Clear Communication: Transparent communication with suppliers about payment schedules and any changes to terms helps in maintaining trust and avoiding disputes.

3. Monitor Cash Flow Regularly: Regular monitoring of cash flow and adjusting payment schedules accordingly can prevent liquidity crises and optimize cash reserves.

4. Use Technology: Implementing ERP systems like Oracle ERP can automate and streamline the management of payment terms, ensuring compliance and efficiency.

5. Financial Discipline: Adhering to negotiated payment terms and avoiding unnecessary early payments unless strategically beneficial ensures that the company retains control over its cash flow.

Conclusion

The configuration of payment terms and options within the Oracle ERP Accounts Payable module plays a critical role in managing a company's cash flow. By strategically negotiating and managing these terms, companies can enhance their liquidity, optimize working capital, and achieve significant cost savings. Effective cash flow management through thoughtful payment term strategies is not just about delaying payments but involves a delicate balance of maintaining supplier relationships, leveraging discounts, and ensuring financial stability. As businesses navigate through varying economic conditions, the ability to manage cash flow efficiently will be a key determinant of their long-term success and resilience.

2.4 Setting Up Tax Codes and Jurisdictions

In Oracle ERP, setting up tax codes and jurisdictions is a critical component of managing the Accounts Payable module. Proper tax setup ensures compliance with local, state, and international tax regulations, facilitates accurate financial reporting, and helps avoid costly penalties. This section will detail the process of defining tax codes and jurisdictions in the Accounts Payable module, highlighting the steps involved and the considerations to keep in mind for accurate configuration.

2.4.1 Describe the process of defining tax codes and jurisdictions in the Accounts Payable module

Defining tax codes and jurisdictions involves several steps, each crucial for ensuring the correct application of taxes on transactions. The process can be broadly categorized into the following steps:

1. Accessing the Tax Setup Module

2. Defining Tax Codes

3. Setting Up Tax Rates

4. Establishing Tax Jurisdictions

5. Assigning Tax Codes to Vendors

6. Validating Tax Code Configuration

1. Accessing the Tax Setup Module

To begin setting up tax codes and jurisdictions, navigate to the tax setup module within Oracle ERP. This module is typically accessible through the main menu under the Financials or Accounts Payable sections. The exact navigation path may vary based on the version of Oracle ERP you are using.

Steps:

- Log in to Oracle ERP.

- Navigate to Financials or Accounts Payable.

- Select the Tax Setup option.

Considerations:

- Ensure you have the necessary permissions to access and modify tax settings.

- Familiarize yourself with the interface and available options within the tax setup module.

2. Defining Tax Codes

Tax codes represent the specific types of taxes that can be applied to transactions. These codes can vary based on the nature of the transaction and the applicable tax regulations.

Steps:

- In the tax setup module, select the option to create a new tax code.

- Enter a unique identifier for the tax code.

- Provide a description for the tax code, detailing its purpose and applicability.

- Specify the type of tax (e.g., sales tax, VAT, service tax).

Considerations:

- Ensure the tax code identifier is unique and follows any organizational naming conventions.

- The description should be clear and informative to aid users in selecting the appropriate tax code.

3. Setting Up Tax Rates

Tax rates define the percentage or fixed amount of tax to be applied to transactions associated with a specific tax code.

Steps:

- Select the newly created tax code.

- Navigate to the section for defining tax rates.

- Enter the effective date for the tax rate. This determines when the rate becomes applicable.

- Specify the tax rate as a percentage or a fixed amount.

- Optionally, enter an expiration date if the tax rate is temporary.

Considerations:

- Ensure the tax rate is accurate and complies with current tax regulations.

- Keep track of expiration dates for temporary tax rates to update them as needed.

4. Establishing Tax Jurisdictions

Tax jurisdictions represent the geographic regions or entities that impose taxes. These jurisdictions can be at the local, state, or international level.

Steps:

- In the tax setup module, select the option to create a new tax jurisdiction.

- Enter a unique identifier for the jurisdiction.

- Provide a description of the jurisdiction, including its geographic scope and applicable regulations.

- Specify the applicable tax rates for transactions within the jurisdiction.

Considerations:

- Ensure the jurisdiction identifier is unique and follows organizational naming conventions.

- The description should be detailed enough to distinguish between similar jurisdictions.

5. Assigning Tax Codes to Vendors

Vendors may be subject to different tax codes based on their location, the nature of goods or services they provide, and other factors. Assigning the correct tax codes to vendors is essential for accurate tax calculation.

Steps:

- Navigate to the vendor management section within the Accounts Payable module.

- Select the vendor for whom you want to assign tax codes.

- In the vendor's profile, locate the section for tax information.

- Assign the appropriate tax code(s) to the vendor.

Considerations:

- Verify the vendor's tax status and applicable tax regulations before assigning tax codes.

- Regularly review and update vendor tax information to ensure ongoing accuracy.

6. Validating Tax Code Configuration

After setting up tax codes and jurisdictions, it is crucial to validate the configuration to ensure accuracy and compliance.

Steps:

- Perform test transactions using different tax codes and jurisdictions.

- Verify that the correct tax rates are applied to the transactions.

- Review financial reports to ensure taxes are accurately reflected.

Considerations:

- Conduct regular audits of tax configurations to identify and correct any discrepancies.

- Stay informed about changes in tax regulations that may require updates to tax codes and jurisdictions.

Detailed Walkthrough

To provide a comprehensive guide, let's delve deeper into each step with practical examples and additional considerations.

Example Scenario: Setting Up a Sales Tax Code for California

Step 1: Accessing the Tax Setup Module

- Log in to Oracle ERP with administrative privileges.

- Navigate to Financials > Accounts Payable > Tax Setup.

- Select "Create New Tax Code."

Step 2: Defining the Tax Code

- Tax Code Identifier: CA_SALES_TAX

- Description: California Sales Tax

- Type of Tax: Sales Tax

Step 3: Setting Up the Tax Rate

- Select CA_SALES_TAX.

- Effective Date: 01-Jan-2024

- Tax Rate: 7.25% (the current sales tax rate for California)

- Expiration Date: Leave blank (indicating no expiration)

Step 4: Establishing the Tax Jurisdiction

- Create a new jurisdiction.

- Identifier: CA

- Description: State of California

- Assign the CA_SALES_TAX rate to this jurisdiction.

Step 5: Assigning Tax Codes to Vendors

- Navigate to Vendor Management.

- Select a vendor based in California (e.g., Vendor ID: V1234).

- In the tax information section, assign CA_SALES_TAX to this vendor.

Step 6: Validating the Configuration

- Perform a test purchase from Vendor V1234.

- Verify that the invoice includes a 7.25% sales tax.

- Check financial reports to ensure the tax is correctly accounted for.

Additional Considerations

1. Handling Multiple Tax Rates:

  - In cases where different products or services are subject to varying tax rates within the same jurisdiction, create separate tax codes and rates for each category.

  - Example: Create separate tax codes for standard goods and luxury items if they are taxed at different rates.

2. Managing International Taxes:

  - For vendors operating in multiple countries, define tax codes and jurisdictions for each country.

  - Ensure compliance with international tax treaties and regulations.

3. Regular Updates and Maintenance:

  - Tax regulations are subject to change. Regularly review and update tax codes, rates, and jurisdictions to reflect current laws.

  - Implement a process for tracking and applying regulatory updates.

4. Integration with Other Modules:

  - Ensure tax settings in the Accounts Payable module are consistent with those in other modules like Accounts Receivable and General Ledger.

  - Coordinate with other departments to maintain uniform tax configurations across the organization.

5. Training and Documentation:

  - Provide training for users responsible for managing tax settings to ensure they understand the process and its importance.

  - Maintain comprehensive documentation of tax codes, rates, and jurisdictions for reference and audit purposes.

Conclusion

Setting up tax codes and jurisdictions in Oracle ERP's Accounts Payable module is a detailed process that requires careful attention to regulatory compliance and accurate configuration. By following the steps outlined in this section, organizations can ensure their tax setups are robust, compliant, and capable of supporting effective financial management. Regular reviews and updates, along with thorough training and documentation, will help maintain the accuracy and reliability of tax configurations.

2.4.2 Explain the different types of tax codes and jurisdictions supported

Setting up tax codes and jurisdictions in the Accounts Payable (AP) module of Oracle ERP is a critical task that ensures compliance with local, national, and international tax regulations. Oracle ERP supports various types of tax codes and jurisdictions to accommodate the diverse tax requirements encountered by businesses operating in different regions. In this section, we will delve into the different types of tax codes and jurisdictions supported by the Accounts Payable module, providing an in-depth understanding of their configuration and usage.

Types of Tax Codes Supported

1. Sales Tax Codes

Sales tax codes are used to calculate taxes on goods and services sold within a particular jurisdiction. These codes are essential for businesses that sell taxable goods or services and need to charge and collect sales tax from customers. Oracle ERP allows for the configuration of multiple sales tax codes to account for different tax rates applicable in various regions or states. Sales tax codes typically include information such as the tax rate, the jurisdiction to which the tax applies, and any exemptions or special conditions.

2. Use Tax Codes

Use tax codes are designed for situations where goods are purchased without paying sales tax but are subsequently used in a jurisdiction that imposes a tax on the use of such goods. This often occurs when a business purchases goods from out-of-state vendors who do not charge sales tax. The use tax code ensures that the appropriate tax is calculated and remitted to the local tax authority. Configuring use tax codes in Oracle ERP involves defining the tax rate, applicability, and the jurisdictions where the tax must be reported.

3. Value-Added Tax (VAT) Codes

Value-Added Tax (VAT) is a type of consumption tax that is prevalent in many countries around the world. VAT codes in Oracle ERP are used to calculate taxes on the value added at each stage of production and distribution of goods and services. VAT codes are complex as they often involve multiple rates for different types of goods and services, exemptions, and special schemes for certain industries. Oracle ERP allows for detailed configuration of VAT codes, including standard rates, reduced rates, zero rates, and exempt transactions.

4. Goods and Services Tax (GST) Codes

Goods and Services Tax (GST) is similar to VAT but is specifically used in countries like Australia, Canada, and India. GST codes in Oracle ERP are used to manage the tax on the supply of goods and services. These codes help in calculating the correct amount of GST payable or receivable based on the nature of the transaction. Oracle ERP supports various GST rates, including standard, reduced, and zero rates, and provides mechanisms to handle GST credits and adjustments.

5. Excise Tax Codes

Excise taxes are specific taxes levied on certain goods, such as alcohol, tobacco, and fuel. These taxes are often imposed at the federal or state level and are based on the quantity of the product rather than its value. In Oracle ERP, excise tax codes are configured to calculate the appropriate tax based on the type and quantity of goods subject to excise tax. This configuration ensures that businesses comply with excise tax regulations and accurately report their tax liabilities.

6. Service Tax Codes

Service tax codes are used to calculate taxes on services rendered by businesses. These taxes are applicable in jurisdictions where the government imposes a tax on the provision of services. Oracle ERP allows for the creation of service tax codes that specify the tax rate, applicable services, and any exemptions. This ensures that businesses providing taxable services can accurately calculate and remit service tax.

7. Withholding Tax Codes

Withholding tax codes are used to calculate the amount of tax that must be withheld from payments made to vendors, employees, or contractors. These taxes are typically required by government authorities to ensure that tax liabilities are met at the source of income. Oracle ERP supports the configuration of various withholding tax codes, including those for domestic and international transactions. This feature helps businesses comply with withholding tax regulations and ensures that the correct amount of tax is withheld and remitted to the tax authorities.

Types of Tax Jurisdictions Supported

1. Federal Tax Jurisdictions

Federal tax jurisdictions refer to the national level of tax authority that imposes taxes on income, sales, goods, and services. In Oracle ERP, federal tax jurisdictions are configured to manage taxes that are imposed by the central government. This includes defining the tax rates, reporting requirements, and any specific rules or exemptions that apply at the federal level. Federal tax jurisdictions are essential for businesses that operate across multiple states or regions but are subject to nationwide tax regulations.

2. State or Provincial Tax Jurisdictions

State or provincial tax jurisdictions refer to the regional level of tax authority within a country. These jurisdictions have their own tax laws and rates, which may differ from the federal regulations. In Oracle ERP, state or provincial tax jurisdictions are configured to manage taxes that are imposed by the state or province. This includes setting up sales tax, use tax, and other regional taxes that apply to transactions within the state or province. Accurate configuration of state tax jurisdictions ensures compliance with regional tax laws and facilitates proper tax reporting.

3. Local Tax Jurisdictions

Local tax jurisdictions refer to the municipal or city level of tax authority that imposes taxes on specific geographic areas within a state or province. These jurisdictions often have their own tax rates and regulations for sales, property, and other local taxes. In Oracle ERP, local tax jurisdictions are configured to manage taxes that apply to transactions within a specific locality. This includes defining the tax rates, applicability, and reporting requirements for local taxes. Proper setup of local tax jurisdictions ensures that businesses comply with local tax laws and accurately calculate their tax liabilities.

4. International Tax Jurisdictions

International tax jurisdictions refer to the tax authorities in different countries where a business operates. These jurisdictions have their own tax laws, rates, and reporting requirements for transactions conducted within their borders. In Oracle ERP, international tax jurisdictions are configured to manage taxes for cross-border transactions. This includes setting up VAT, GST, and other international taxes that apply to imports, exports, and foreign sales. Accurate configuration of international tax jurisdictions ensures compliance with global tax regulations and facilitates smooth international operations.

5. Special Tax Jurisdictions

Special tax jurisdictions refer to specific areas or zones within a country that have unique tax rules and incentives. These may include free trade zones, economic development zones, or other special tax districts that offer reduced tax rates or exemptions to encourage business investment. In Oracle ERP, special tax jurisdictions are configured to manage the specific tax rules and incentives that apply to these areas. This includes defining the tax rates, eligibility criteria, and reporting requirements for special tax jurisdictions. Proper setup of special tax jurisdictions ensures that businesses can take advantage of tax incentives and comply with the specific rules of these areas.

Configuring Tax Codes and Jurisdictions in Oracle ERP

1. Defining Tax Codes

To define tax codes in Oracle ERP, businesses must first identify the types of taxes that apply to their operations. This involves understanding the tax regulations in the jurisdictions where they operate and determining the applicable tax rates, exemptions, and special conditions. Once the tax types are identified, businesses can create tax codes in the ERP system by specifying the tax rate, applicability, and any special rules. This process ensures that the tax codes accurately reflect the tax obligations of the business.

2. Mapping Tax Jurisdictions

Mapping tax jurisdictions in Oracle ERP involves defining the geographic areas where each tax code applies. This includes specifying the federal, state, local, international, and special tax jurisdictions relevant to the business. By accurately mapping tax jurisdictions, businesses ensure that the correct tax rates are applied to transactions based on their location. This mapping process also facilitates accurate tax reporting and compliance with regional tax laws.

3. Configuring Tax Calculation Rules

Tax calculation rules in Oracle ERP determine how taxes are calculated for different types of transactions. This includes defining the order of tax calculation, handling tax exemptions, and applying special conditions. Businesses must configure these rules to ensure that the ERP system accurately calculates taxes based on the defined tax codes and jurisdictions. Proper configuration of tax calculation rules ensures that the business complies with tax regulations and minimizes the risk of errors in tax calculations.

4. Setting Up Tax Reporting

Tax reporting in Oracle ERP involves generating reports that detail the tax liabilities and payments for different jurisdictions. This includes creating reports for federal, state, local, international, and special tax jurisdictions. Businesses must set up tax reporting to ensure that they can accurately track and report their tax obligations. This setup includes defining the format, frequency, and content of tax reports to meet the requirements of tax authorities.

5. Maintaining Tax Codes and Jurisdictions

Maintaining tax codes and jurisdictions in Oracle ERP is an ongoing process that involves regularly updating the tax rates, rules, and jurisdictions to reflect changes in tax regulations. This includes monitoring changes in tax laws, adjusting tax codes and jurisdictions, and ensuring that the ERP system is up-to-date. Regular maintenance of tax codes and jurisdictions ensures that businesses remain compliant with tax regulations and avoid penalties for non-compliance.

Conclusion

Setting up tax codes and jurisdictions in the Accounts Payable module of Oracle ERP is a complex but essential task that ensures compliance with various tax regulations. By understanding the different types of tax codes and jurisdictions supported by Oracle ERP, businesses can accurately configure their tax settings to meet their tax obligations. Proper configuration and maintenance of tax codes and jurisdictions help businesses manage their tax liabilities, ensure compliance with tax laws, and facilitate accurate tax reporting.

2.4.3 Discuss the importance of accurate tax setup for compliance and reporting

The accurate setup of tax codes and jurisdictions within the Accounts Payable (AP) module of Oracle ERP is a critical task that underpins the compliance and financial reporting of an organization. Properly configured tax codes ensure that the organization adheres to legal requirements and avoids the pitfalls of non-compliance, which can result in significant financial penalties and reputational damage. Moreover, accurate tax setup facilitates seamless financial reporting, providing a clear and precise picture of the company's tax liabilities and payments. This section will delve into the various facets of why accurate tax setup is essential, covering legal compliance, financial accuracy, audit readiness, and overall operational efficiency.

Legal Compliance

One of the primary reasons for accurate tax setup is to ensure compliance with local, regional, and international tax laws. Each jurisdiction may have distinct tax rates, rules, and reporting requirements. An organization operating in multiple regions must configure tax codes to reflect these differences accurately. Failure to comply with tax regulations can lead to severe consequences, including hefty fines, legal action, and even business closure.

1. Local Tax Regulations: Local governments often impose specific taxes that are unique to their jurisdictions. These may include city taxes, municipal taxes, or special district taxes. Accurately setting up tax codes ensures that the organization correctly calculates and remits these taxes, thus maintaining compliance with local laws.

2. Regional and Federal Tax Laws: In addition to local taxes, companies must adhere to regional and federal tax laws. These laws can encompass value-added tax (VAT), goods and services tax (GST), sales tax, and more. Accurate tax code setup ensures that these taxes are correctly applied to transactions, avoiding discrepancies that could trigger audits or penalties.

3. International Tax Compliance: For companies operating globally, international tax compliance is paramount. Different countries have varying tax treaties, double taxation agreements, and withholding tax requirements. Accurate tax setup within Oracle ERP helps manage these complexities, ensuring that the company remains compliant with international tax obligations.

Financial Accuracy

Accurate tax setup is crucial for maintaining the financial accuracy of an organization. It ensures that all transactions are recorded with the correct tax implications, leading to precise financial statements and reports. This accuracy is vital for several reasons:

1. Correct Tax Calculation: Properly configured tax codes ensure that taxes are calculated correctly on all transactions. This accuracy prevents underpayment or overpayment of taxes, both of which can have financial ramifications.

2. Accurate Financial Statements: Financial statements must reflect true and fair values, including the correct tax liabilities and expenses. Accurate tax setup ensures that these statements are reliable, providing stakeholders with confidence in the financial health of the organization.

3. Budgeting and Forecasting: Accurate tax data is essential for effective budgeting and forecasting. It allows the organization to predict tax liabilities accurately and allocate resources accordingly, leading to better financial planning and decision-making.

Audit Readiness

Being prepared for audits is another critical aspect of accurate tax setup. Tax authorities may conduct audits to verify compliance with tax laws. An organization with well-configured tax codes and jurisdictions is better positioned to pass these audits without issues. Here's why:

1. Transparent Records: Accurate tax setup ensures that all tax-related transactions are recorded transparently. This transparency is vital during an audit, as it allows auditors to trace transactions and verify that taxes have been correctly calculated and remitted.

2. Documentation and Reporting: Proper tax setup facilitates the generation of accurate tax reports and documentation. These documents are crucial during audits, providing evidence that the organization has complied with tax laws and regulations.

3. Reduced Audit Risk: An organization with a robust tax setup is less likely to trigger red flags during an audit. This reduces the risk of extended audits, fines, or penalties, ensuring smoother and less disruptive audit processes.

Operational Efficiency

Accurate tax setup also contributes to the overall operational efficiency of the organization. It streamlines processes, reduces manual interventions, and minimizes errors, leading to more efficient and cost-effective operations.

1. Automation of Tax Calculations: With accurate tax codes configured in Oracle ERP, tax calculations can be automated. This automation reduces the need for manual calculations, saving time and reducing the risk of human error.

2. Streamlined Reporting: Accurate tax setup allows for the generation of precise tax reports with minimal effort. These reports are essential for compliance and financial analysis, and their accuracy ensures that decision-makers have reliable data at their disposal.

3. Consistent Processes: Proper tax setup ensures consistency in how taxes are applied across the organization. This consistency is crucial for maintaining standard operating procedures and ensuring that all departments and business units follow the same tax rules.

Risk Mitigation

Proper tax setup helps mitigate various risks associated with tax compliance and financial reporting. These risks include legal risks, financial risks, and reputational risks. Accurate tax setup addresses these risks in several ways:

1. Legal Risk Mitigation: Accurate tax setup ensures compliance with all relevant tax laws and regulations, reducing the risk of legal penalties and sanctions. It also helps the organization stay up-to-date with any changes in tax laws, ensuring continuous compliance.

2. Financial Risk Mitigation: By ensuring correct tax calculations and reporting, accurate tax setup prevents financial discrepancies that could lead to significant losses. It also helps in avoiding unexpected tax liabilities that could impact the organization's financial stability.

3. Reputational Risk Mitigation: Non-compliance with tax laws can damage an organization's reputation. Accurate tax setup ensures that the organization maintains a positive reputation by demonstrating its commitment to legal and financial integrity.

Enhanced Decision-Making

Accurate tax setup provides reliable data that enhances decision-making across the organization. Decision-makers rely on accurate financial data to make informed choices about investments, expansions, and other strategic initiatives. Accurate tax setup contributes to this by providing:

1. Reliable Tax Data: Accurate tax setup ensures that tax data used in financial analysis and decision-making is reliable. This reliability is crucial for making informed decisions that align with the organization's financial goals and compliance requirements.

2. Clear Financial Insights: Accurate tax setup provides clear insights into the organization's tax liabilities and expenses. These insights are essential for financial planning, budgeting, and forecasting, helping the organization allocate resources effectively.

3. Informed Strategic Planning: With accurate tax data, decision-makers can better understand the tax implications of various strategic initiatives. This understanding helps in evaluating the feasibility and potential impact of these initiatives, leading to more informed strategic planning.

Conclusion

Accurate tax setup within the Accounts Payable module of Oracle ERP is a cornerstone of compliance and financial integrity. It ensures that the organization adheres to all relevant tax laws, maintains financial accuracy, and is prepared for audits. Furthermore, it enhances operational efficiency, mitigates various risks, and provides reliable data for informed decision-making. By prioritizing accurate tax setup, organizations can safeguard their financial health, maintain compliance, and support their long-term strategic objectives.

CHAPTER III
Processing Invoice Transactions

3.1 Creating and Entering Invoices

3.1.1 Explain the different methods for creating and entering invoices into the Accounts Payable module

Creating and entering invoices into the Accounts Payable (AP) module of Oracle ERP is a critical function for ensuring timely and accurate payment processing. There are several methods available for creating and entering invoices, each catering to different business needs and preferences. This section delves into these methods, providing detailed insights into their processes, benefits, and best practices.

Manual Entry

Manual entry is the most straightforward method of invoice creation, often used for low volumes of invoices or when invoices are received in paper format. In this process, an accounts payable clerk manually inputs the invoice data into the system.

Steps for Manual Entry:

1. Gather Invoice Information:

   - Collect the physical or digital copy of the invoice from the vendor.

   - Ensure that all required information is present, such as vendor details, invoice number, date, line items, quantities, unit prices, and total amounts.

2. Log into the Accounts Payable Module:

  - Access the AP module within Oracle ERP using secure login credentials.

3. Navigate to Invoice Entry Screen:

  - Go to the Invoice Entry section, typically found under the Transactions or Invoices menu.

4. Enter Invoice Data:

  - Input the invoice details into the corresponding fields.

  - Double-check for accuracy, ensuring that all mandatory fields are filled.

5. Save and Validate:

  - Save the invoice record.

  - Perform validation checks to ensure data integrity and compliance with company policies.

Benefits:

- Control and Customization: Manual entry allows for a high level of control and customization, making it suitable for handling complex invoices.

- Flexibility: Adaptable to various types of invoices, including those with special terms or conditions.

Challenges:

- Time-Consuming: Manual entry can be time-consuming and labor-intensive, especially with a high volume of invoices.

- Error-Prone: Increased risk of human error, leading to potential discrepancies and processing delays.

Electronic Data Interchange (EDI)

EDI is an automated method for creating and entering invoices, commonly used by businesses with high transaction volumes. EDI facilitates the electronic exchange of standardized business documents between trading partners.

Steps for EDI Invoice Processing:

1. Set Up EDI Integration:

   - Configure EDI settings within Oracle ERP.

   - Establish connections with vendors who support EDI transactions.

2. Receive EDI Invoice:

   - The vendor sends the invoice electronically in an agreed-upon format (e.g., ANSI X12, EDIFACT).

3. Import Invoice Data:

   - Oracle ERP automatically imports the EDI invoice data into the AP module.

   - Perform automated validation checks to ensure data accuracy.

4. Review and Approve:

   - Accounts payable staff review the imported invoices for any discrepancies.

   - Approve the invoices for payment processing.

Benefits:

- Efficiency: Significantly reduces manual data entry, speeding up the invoice processing cycle.

- Accuracy: Minimizes human error, ensuring high data accuracy and integrity.

- Cost Savings: Reduces paper usage and administrative overhead.

Challenges:

- Initial Setup: Requires initial setup and configuration of EDI standards and connections.

- Vendor Coordination: Both trading partners must support and agree on the EDI format and protocols.

Invoice Imaging and OCR

Invoice imaging and Optical Character Recognition (OCR) technology enable the digitization and automated processing of paper invoices. This method combines manual and automated processes to improve efficiency and accuracy.

Steps for Invoice Imaging and OCR:

1. Scan Paper Invoices:

  - Use a high-resolution scanner to create digital images of paper invoices.

2. Upload Images to OCR System:

  - Upload the scanned images to the OCR system integrated with Oracle ERP.

3. Extract Invoice Data:

  - The OCR software extracts key data fields from the invoice images, such as vendor name, invoice number, date, and line items.

4. Validate and Correct:

  - Review the extracted data for accuracy.

  - Correct any errors or missing information identified by the OCR system.

5. Import into AP Module:

  - Import the validated invoice data into the Accounts Payable module for further processing.

Benefits:

- Automation: Automates data extraction, reducing manual entry effort.

- Accuracy: Enhances data accuracy with advanced recognition algorithms.

- Document Management: Facilitates electronic storage and retrieval of invoice documents.

Challenges:

- Image Quality: OCR accuracy depends on the quality of the scanned images.

- Exception Handling: Requires manual intervention for handling exceptions and errors in data extraction.

Self-Billing and Evaluated Receipt Settlement (ERS)

Self-billing and Evaluated Receipt Settlement (ERS) are advanced methods where the buyer generates the invoice on behalf of the supplier. These methods are typically used in supply chain and procurement processes where purchase orders and receipts are matched automatically.

Steps for Self-Billing and ERS:

1. Create Purchase Order:

  - The buyer creates a purchase order (PO) in Oracle ERP.

2. Receive Goods/Services:

  - The supplier delivers the goods or services, and the buyer records the receipt in the system.

3. Generate Self-Bill Invoice:

  - Based on the receipt and PO details, Oracle ERP automatically generates an invoice for the received items.

4. Review and Approve:

  - Accounts payable staff review the self-bill invoice for accuracy and approve it for payment.

Benefits:

- Streamlined Process: Eliminates the need for suppliers to send invoices, streamlining the invoicing process.

- Accuracy and Control: Ensures accurate matching of PO, receipt, and invoice data.

- Efficiency: Reduces administrative workload and accelerates the payment cycle.

Challenges:

- Supplier Agreement: Requires agreement and collaboration with suppliers to adopt self-billing or ERS practices.

- System Integration: Necessitates robust system integration to handle automated invoice generation and matching.

Supplier Portal

A supplier portal is an online platform that allows suppliers to submit invoices directly into the buyer's Accounts Payable system. This method promotes transparency and collaboration between buyers and suppliers.

Steps for Supplier Portal Invoicing:

1. Supplier Access:

   - Suppliers log into the supplier portal using secure credentials.

2. Invoice Submission:

   - Suppliers enter invoice details directly into the portal, attaching supporting documents if needed.

3. System Validation:

   - The portal performs automated validation checks on the submitted invoices.

4. Import into AP Module:

   - Validated invoices are imported into Oracle ERP's Accounts Payable module for processing.

Benefits:

- Real-Time Submission: Enables real-time submission and tracking of invoices.

- Reduced Errors: Minimizes data entry errors through supplier input.

- Improved Collaboration: Enhances communication and collaboration with suppliers.

Challenges:

- Portal Adoption: Requires suppliers to adopt and regularly use the portal.

- Training: May necessitate training for suppliers on how to use the portal effectively.

Automated Invoice Matching

Automated invoice matching involves the use of advanced algorithms to match invoices with corresponding purchase orders and receipts. This method is often integrated with other invoicing methods to ensure accuracy and control.

Steps for Automated Invoice Matching:

1. Receive Invoice:

  - The invoice is received via EDI, OCR, or manual entry.

2. Match Invoice Data:

  - Oracle ERP's automated matching engine compares the invoice data with purchase orders and receipts.

3. Identify Discrepancies:

  - The system flags any discrepancies or mismatches for further review.

4. Approve and Release:

  - Accounts payable staff review and approve the matched invoices for payment processing.

Benefits:

- Accuracy: Ensures high accuracy in invoice matching, reducing errors.

- Efficiency: Speeds up the invoice processing cycle by automating matching tasks.

- Control: Enhances control over the procurement-to-payment process.

Challenges:

- Complexity: Requires sophisticated algorithms and system configuration.

- Exception Management: Needs effective handling of exceptions and mismatches.

Conclusion

The Accounts Payable module in Oracle ERP offers various methods for creating and entering invoices, each with its unique benefits and challenges. Businesses can choose the method that best suits their needs based on transaction volumes, complexity, and available resources. By leveraging these methods effectively, organizations can enhance their invoice processing efficiency, accuracy, and overall financial management.

3.1.2 Discuss the information required for each invoice record

Creating and entering invoices in the Accounts Payable (AP) module is a critical function that ensures vendors are paid accurately and on time. This process requires meticulous attention to detail and the inclusion of essential information for each invoice record. The completeness and accuracy of this data not only streamline the AP process but also enhance the reliability of financial reporting and compliance. Here, we will discuss the key pieces of information required for each invoice record within the Oracle ERP Accounts Payable module.

Invoice Number

The invoice number is a unique identifier assigned by the vendor to each invoice. It is crucial for tracking and referencing specific transactions. In the Oracle ERP system, the invoice number helps to avoid duplicate payments and supports audit trails. It is essential that the invoice number is entered correctly to ensure the accuracy of records and facilitate seamless communication with vendors.

Invoice Date

The invoice date is the date the invoice was issued by the vendor. This date is significant as it often determines the due date for payment based on the agreed payment terms. The invoice date also affects financial reporting periods, making it critical for accurate accounting and financial analysis. Incorrect invoice dates can lead to misaligned financial statements and potential cash flow issues.

Vendor Information

Vendor information includes the vendor name, address, and contact details. This information is used to identify the supplier from whom goods or services were procured. In Oracle ERP, each vendor should have a unique vendor ID that links to their detailed profile within the system. Accurate vendor information ensures that payments are directed to the correct recipient and that any correspondence regarding the invoice can be managed effectively.

Purchase Order Number

The purchase order (PO) number is a unique identifier for the order placed with the vendor. Including the PO number on the invoice allows for easy matching and verification of the goods or services received against the original order. This matching process helps to prevent discrepancies and unauthorized payments. The PO number also facilitates efficient reconciliation and auditing processes.

Description of Goods or Services

A detailed description of the goods or services provided is essential for verifying that the invoice aligns with what was ordered and received. This description should be clear and concise, outlining quantities, unit prices, and any relevant specifications or terms. In Oracle ERP, this information supports the validation process and helps to ensure that the invoice is processed accurately and promptly.

Quantity and Unit of Measure

The quantity of goods or services provided and the corresponding unit of measure (e.g., pieces, hours, kilograms) must be specified. This information is crucial for verifying that the quantities billed match those received and ordered. Accurate quantity information helps to prevent overpayments and ensures that inventory records are updated correctly in the system.

Unit Price and Total Amount

The unit price is the cost per individual unit of goods or services, while the total amount is the aggregate cost for all units provided. Both the unit price and total amount need to be verified against the purchase order and receiving documents. Ensuring that these figures are correct is vital for accurate financial reporting and budgeting. In Oracle ERP, the system can automatically calculate the total amount based on the unit price and quantity, reducing the risk of manual errors.

Tax Information

Tax information includes any applicable sales tax, VAT, or other taxes associated with the transaction. The tax rate and the total tax amount should be clearly indicated on the invoice. Accurate tax information is necessary for compliance with tax regulations and for proper accounting in the financial statements. Oracle ERP allows for the configuration of various tax codes and jurisdictions to ensure that tax calculations are performed correctly.

Payment Terms

Payment terms define the conditions under which the invoice is to be paid, such as net 30 days, 2/10 net 30 (2% discount if paid within 10 days), or other agreed-upon terms. These terms affect the due date of the invoice and any potential discounts for early payment. Correctly entered payment terms help manage cash flow and optimize working capital. In Oracle ERP, payment terms can be configured to automate due date calculations and alert users to upcoming payment deadlines.

Discounts and Allowances

Any discounts or allowances provided by the vendor should be clearly indicated on the invoice. This includes early payment discounts, volume discounts, or other negotiated reductions. Accurate entry of discounts ensures that the company benefits from all available savings and avoids overpaying. Oracle ERP can automate the application of discounts based on predefined criteria, streamlining the invoice processing workflow.

Freight and Shipping Charges

Freight and shipping charges should be included if they are billed separately from the goods or services. These charges are often listed as separate line items on the invoice. Accurate entry of these costs ensures that the total payable amount reflects all incurred expenses. In Oracle ERP, freight and shipping charges can be allocated to specific cost centers or projects, facilitating precise cost tracking and allocation.

Payment Method

The payment method indicates how the invoice will be paid, such as by check, electronic funds transfer (EFT), or credit card. Specifying the payment method helps ensure that the payment process aligns with both the vendor's preferences and the company's payment policies. Oracle ERP supports various payment methods, allowing for flexibility and efficiency in managing vendor payments.

Approval and Authorization

The invoice should include information on who has reviewed and approved it for payment. This could be a digital signature, approval stamp, or an authorization code. Proper approval and authorization ensure that only valid and legitimate invoices are processed for payment. Oracle ERP includes workflow functionalities that can route invoices through the necessary approval hierarchies, ensuring compliance with internal controls and policies.

Supporting Documentation

Supporting documentation may include receipts, delivery notes, contracts, or any other relevant documents that substantiate the invoice. These documents help verify the accuracy and legitimacy of the invoice and are often required for audit purposes. In Oracle ERP, supporting documentation can be attached to the invoice record electronically, providing easy access for review and approval.

Cost Allocation

Cost allocation details specify how the invoice amount is to be distributed across different accounts, departments, or projects. This allocation is crucial for accurate financial reporting and budgeting. Oracle ERP allows for detailed cost allocation entries, enabling precise tracking of expenses and ensuring that costs are charged to the appropriate cost centers.

Currency

The currency in which the invoice is issued should be clearly indicated. This is especially important for international transactions where currency exchange rates may apply. Oracle ERP supports multi-currency transactions and can automatically convert amounts to the base currency using current exchange rates, ensuring accurate financial reporting.

Payment Schedule

For invoices that are to be paid in installments or on a specific schedule, the payment schedule should be outlined. This includes the dates and amounts for each payment. Clear payment schedules help manage cash flow and ensure timely payments. Oracle ERP can track and manage payment schedules, sending reminders for upcoming payments and ensuring compliance with the agreed terms.

Notes and Special Instructions

Any additional notes or special instructions from the vendor should be included on the invoice. This might include delivery instructions, specific payment handling requests, or other relevant information. Including these details ensures that all parties are aware of and can adhere to any special requirements.

In summary, the accuracy and completeness of the information entered for each invoice record are paramount to efficient and effective invoice processing in Oracle ERP. By ensuring that all required details are meticulously captured and verified, organizations can streamline their AP processes, enhance financial control, and maintain strong vendor relationships.

3.1.3 Emphasize the importance of data accuracy and completeness for invoice processing

In the Accounts Payable module of Oracle ERP, the accuracy and completeness of invoice data are paramount for efficient and error-free processing. Accurate and complete data ensures that the entire invoice lifecycle—from entry to payment—is seamless, minimizing the risk of errors, discrepancies, and delays. This section delves into why data accuracy and completeness are crucial, the potential consequences of inaccuracies, and best practices for maintaining high data integrity in invoice processing.

1. Ensuring Accurate Payments

Accurate invoice data directly impacts the accuracy of payments. Incorrect or incomplete data can lead to overpayments, underpayments, or payments to the wrong vendors. Overpayments can strain cash flow and may be difficult to recover, while underpayments can harm vendor relationships and disrupt the supply chain. Ensuring that all invoice data is correct helps prevent such issues, facilitating timely and accurate payments to vendors.

2. Enhancing Financial Reporting and Compliance

Financial reporting relies heavily on the accuracy of data recorded in the Accounts Payable module. Inaccurate invoice data can lead to erroneous financial statements, affecting decision-making and regulatory compliance. Complete and accurate data ensures that financial reports reflect the true financial position of the organization, aiding in compliance with accounting standards and regulatory requirements. This is particularly important for audits, where accurate records are crucial for demonstrating compliance and avoiding penalties.

3. Streamlining the Audit Process

Accurate and complete invoice data simplifies the audit process. Auditors require detailed records to verify the legitimacy of transactions and the accuracy of financial statements. If invoice data is accurate and complete, it reduces the time and effort needed for audits, leading to a smoother and more efficient audit process. Incomplete or inaccurate data, on the other hand, can raise red flags and result in more extensive audits, consuming valuable resources and potentially uncovering further issues.

4. Improving Vendor Relationships

Vendors are critical stakeholders in the supply chain, and maintaining positive relationships with them is essential. Accurate invoice data helps ensure that vendors are paid correctly and on time, fostering trust and reliability. Errors in invoice data can lead to payment delays, disputes, and strained relationships. By prioritizing data accuracy, organizations can build and maintain strong, collaborative relationships with their vendors, which can lead to better terms and services.

5. Reducing Manual Interventions and Increasing Efficiency

Inaccurate invoice data often requires manual intervention to correct errors, which can be time-consuming and labor-intensive. This not only slows down the invoice processing cycle but also increases the risk of further errors. Complete and accurate data entry reduces the need for manual corrections, streamlining the entire process and allowing Accounts Payable staff to focus on more value-added activities. Automation can further enhance efficiency, but it relies on high-quality data to be effective.

6. Minimizing Fraud Risk

Fraudulent activities can be mitigated by ensuring data accuracy and completeness. Inaccurate data can provide opportunities for fraud, such as duplicate payments or payments to fictitious vendors. Implementing strict data entry protocols and regular audits can help detect and prevent fraudulent activities. Accurate and complete data makes it easier to spot irregularities and take corrective action promptly.

7. Facilitating Effective Cash Flow Management

Accurate invoice data is essential for effective cash flow management. Organizations need precise information about their payables to manage their cash flow effectively, plan for future expenses, and ensure they have sufficient funds available for critical operations. Inaccurate data can lead to cash flow mismanagement, resulting in liquidity issues or missed opportunities for investment. By maintaining accurate and complete invoice data, organizations can better forecast and manage their cash flow.

Best Practices for Ensuring Data Accuracy and Completeness

To achieve high data accuracy and completeness, organizations should implement the following best practices:

1. Standardize Data Entry Procedures

Establishing standardized data entry procedures ensures consistency and reduces the likelihood of errors. This includes using standardized templates, validation rules, and automated checks to ensure that all required fields are completed accurately.

2. Train Accounts Payable Staff

Regular training for Accounts Payable staff on the importance of data accuracy and the correct data entry procedures is crucial. Well-trained staff are more likely to enter data accurately and recognize potential issues before they become problematic.

3. Utilize Automated Solutions

Leveraging automated solutions for invoice processing, such as Optical Character Recognition (OCR) and e-invoicing, can significantly reduce manual data entry errors. Automated solutions can capture data directly from invoices, validate it against purchase orders and receipts, and flag discrepancies for review.

4. Implement Data Validation Checks

Implementing data validation checks within the Accounts Payable module helps catch errors at the point of entry. These checks can include verifying vendor information, ensuring invoice amounts match purchase orders, and confirming that all required fields are completed.

5. Conduct Regular Audits and Reviews

Regular audits and reviews of invoice data help identify and correct inaccuracies. Periodic checks can uncover systemic issues in data entry processes and provide an opportunity to reinforce best practices and training.

6. Foster a Culture of Accuracy

Creating a culture that values data accuracy and completeness can have a significant impact. Encouraging staff to double-check their work, rewarding accuracy, and emphasizing the importance of accurate data in achieving organizational goals can foster a commitment to high data quality.

7. Use Integrated Systems

Using integrated systems where data flows seamlessly between different modules of the ERP system reduces the risk of data discrepancies. For example, integrating the Accounts Payable module with the Procurement and Inventory modules ensures that data entered in one module is consistent and accurate across the system.

Conclusion

Data accuracy and completeness in the Accounts Payable module are not just operational necessities but are critical components of overall financial health and operational efficiency. By emphasizing the importance of accurate and complete invoice data, organizations can enhance their financial reporting, improve vendor relationships, streamline operations, and reduce the risk of fraud. Implementing best practices for data entry and validation, coupled with regular training and audits, ensures that the Accounts Payable function operates smoothly and contributes positively to the organization's financial management.

3.2 Matching Invoices to Purchase Orders

3.2.1 Describe the process of matching invoices to purchase orders in the Accounts Payable module

The process of matching invoices to purchase orders (POs) in the Accounts Payable (AP) module is a critical step in ensuring accuracy, control, and efficiency in the procurement and payment cycle. This process involves verifying that the details on an invoice align with the corresponding purchase order and, often, the goods receipt. Matching helps to ensure that organizations pay only for the goods and services they have actually received and at the agreed-upon prices. This section will detail the steps involved in this process within the Oracle ERP Accounts Payable module.

Step 1: Invoice Receipt and Entry

The first step in the matching process is the receipt and entry of the invoice into the AP module. Invoices can be received through various channels, such as email, postal mail, or electronic data interchange (EDI). Once an invoice is received, it is entered into the system. The data entry process involves capturing essential details from the invoice, including:

- Invoice number

- Invoice date

- Vendor name and address

- Purchase order number

- Description of goods or services

- Quantity and unit of measure

- Unit price and total amount

- Payment terms

The accuracy and completeness of this data are crucial for the subsequent matching process.

Step 2: Initial Validation

Before the matching process begins, the system performs an initial validation to ensure that the invoice is eligible for matching. This validation includes checking that:

- The purchase order number on the invoice exists in the system.

- The invoice has not been previously processed.

- The invoice data is consistent with the purchase order data in terms of vendor details and basic invoice information.

If the invoice passes these initial checks, it moves to the matching stage. If any discrepancies are found, they must be resolved before proceeding.

Step 3: Two-Way, Three-Way, and Four-Way Matching

Oracle ERP supports different types of matching based on organizational needs and the nature of the transaction. The most common types are:

Two-Way Matching:

- Compares the invoice to the purchase order.

- Verifies that the price and quantity billed match the purchase order.

- Typically used for services or direct purchases without a goods receipt.

Three-Way Matching:

- Compares the invoice to both the purchase order and the goods receipt.

- Ensures that the quantity and price billed match both the purchase order and the goods receipt.

- Commonly used for material purchases where a goods receipt is required.

Four-Way Matching:

- Adds a fourth layer of verification by comparing the invoice to the purchase order, goods receipt, and inspection records.

- Ensures that the items received meet quality standards and specifications before payment.

- Used for high-value or sensitive purchases requiring stringent quality checks.

Step 4: Matching Execution

The matching process is executed within the AP module. The system automatically compares the invoice details to the corresponding purchase order and, if applicable, the goods receipt and inspection records. Key elements checked during matching include:

- Quantity: Ensuring the quantity billed matches the quantity ordered and received.

- Price: Verifying the unit price on the invoice matches the purchase order.

- Terms: Confirming that payment terms and conditions align with the purchase order.

The system flags any discrepancies for review and resolution.

Step 5: Handling Matching Discrepancies

Discrepancies identified during the matching process need to be addressed promptly to avoid payment delays and maintain supplier relationships. Common types of discrepancies include:

- Quantity Discrepancies: The invoice quantity exceeds or falls short of the quantity received.

- Price Discrepancies: The invoice price does not match the agreed-upon price on the purchase order.

- Receipt Discrepancies: The invoice references items not yet received or already fully invoiced.

The resolution process involves investigating the root cause of the discrepancy, which may include communication with the vendor, review of receiving documentation, or adjustment of purchase order details. Once resolved, the invoice can proceed to approval.

Step 6: Invoice Approval and Payment

After successful matching and resolution of any discrepancies, the invoice moves to the approval stage. Approval workflows within Oracle ERP ensure that invoices are reviewed and authorized according to organizational policies. The workflow typically involves:

- Verification by the purchasing department

- Approval by designated managers or department heads

- Final review by the finance team

Once approved, the invoice is scheduled for payment based on the agreed payment terms.

Step 7: Record Keeping and Audit Trail

Oracle ERP maintains a comprehensive audit trail of all matching activities, approvals, and communications related to the invoice. This audit trail is essential for compliance, internal controls, and future reference. Detailed records include:

- Date and time stamps of matching and approval actions

- User IDs of individuals involved in the process

- Documentation of discrepancies and resolutions

Benefits of Effective Matching

The matching process provides several benefits to organizations, including:

- Accuracy: Ensures that payments are made only for goods and services received at the agreed prices.

- Control: Strengthens internal controls by enforcing compliance with procurement policies.

- Efficiency: Automates invoice processing and reduces manual intervention.

- Transparency: Enhances visibility into the procurement and payment cycle.

- Compliance: Supports regulatory and audit requirements through detailed record-keeping.

In conclusion, the process of matching invoices to purchase orders in the Oracle ERP Accounts Payable module is a critical component of effective financial management. By ensuring accuracy, control, and efficiency, this process helps organizations maintain strong supplier relationships, optimize cash flow, and uphold robust internal controls.

3.2.2 Explain the benefits of matching invoices to purchase orders for accuracy and control

Matching invoices to purchase orders is a fundamental process in the Accounts Payable module within Oracle ERP, offering numerous benefits for accuracy and control in financial management. This matching process ensures that invoices are validated against the purchase orders (POs) and receiving documents, enhancing the accuracy of payments and streamlining the workflow. The practice of matching invoices to POs is crucial for maintaining financial integrity, controlling costs, and ensuring compliance with internal policies and external regulations.

Ensuring Accurate Payments

One of the primary benefits of matching invoices to purchase orders is the assurance of accurate payments. By verifying that the details on the invoice match the corresponding PO and the receipt of goods or services, organizations can avoid overpayments, duplicate payments, and payments for goods or services not received. This accuracy is vital for maintaining the financial health of the organization and preventing unnecessary cash outflows.

For example, when an invoice is received, the Accounts Payable team can check the invoice amount, quantities, and unit prices against the original PO. If there are discrepancies, such as an overcharge or a mismatch in the quantities received, these can be identified and rectified before payment is made. This verification process helps in ensuring that the company only pays for what was actually ordered and received, thereby safeguarding the organization's financial resources.

Enhancing Financial Control

Matching invoices to purchase orders enhances financial control by providing a systematic way to validate transactions before they are recorded in the financial system. This control mechanism helps in preventing fraud and unauthorized transactions, as it requires multiple steps of verification before any payment is processed. Each step in the matching process acts as a checkpoint, ensuring that all details align with the company's procurement policies and contractual agreements with suppliers.

Moreover, this matching process supports better financial forecasting and budgeting. By having accurate and validated data on expenses, organizations can make more informed decisions about future expenditures and cash flow management. This improved control over financial data leads to more reliable financial statements and reports, which are crucial for internal decision-making and external reporting to stakeholders.

Streamlining Workflow and Efficiency

The process of matching invoices to purchase orders contributes to streamlining the workflow in the Accounts Payable department. Automated matching systems within Oracle ERP can significantly reduce the time and effort required for manual verification. These systems can automatically match invoices to POs and receipts, flagging any discrepancies for further review. This automation not only speeds up the invoice processing time but also reduces the likelihood of human error.

By implementing automated matching, organizations can handle a higher volume of transactions with the same or fewer resources, leading to increased efficiency and productivity. Employees can focus on resolving exceptions and discrepancies rather than spending time on routine matching tasks. This efficiency gains can be particularly beneficial during peak processing times, such as at the end of the financial period when the volume of transactions typically increases.

Improving Supplier Relationships

Accurate and timely payments facilitated by the matching process can lead to improved relationships with suppliers. When suppliers are confident that they will be paid correctly and on time, they are more likely to offer favorable terms and conditions, such as discounts for early payment or extended credit terms. This reliability can also result in a more collaborative and trusting relationship between the organization and its suppliers.

In addition, by minimizing payment errors and delays, organizations can avoid disputes and the administrative burden associated with resolving payment issues. This smoother payment process can enhance the overall efficiency of the supply chain and contribute to better supplier performance and satisfaction.

Supporting Compliance and Audit Requirements

Matching invoices to purchase orders is also essential for ensuring compliance with internal controls and external audit requirements. This process provides a clear audit trail that demonstrates the organization's adherence to its procurement policies and procedures. During an audit, the ability to show that each invoice has been matched to a corresponding PO and receipt can provide evidence of proper financial management and internal control.

Furthermore, compliance with regulatory requirements, such as those related to Sarbanes-Oxley (SOX) in the United States, often necessitates stringent controls over financial transactions. The matching process helps in meeting these regulatory standards by ensuring that all payments are properly authorized and documented. This compliance not only avoids potential legal and financial penalties but also enhances the organization's reputation and credibility with stakeholders.

Reducing Risk of Fraud

The matching process reduces the risk of fraud by ensuring that payments are made only for valid and authorized transactions. By requiring invoices to match POs and receipts, the organization can prevent fraudulent activities such as fake invoices, overbilling, or unauthorized purchases. This verification process acts as a deterrent to internal and external fraudsters, as it increases the likelihood that any fraudulent attempts will be detected and stopped.

Implementing robust matching controls within the Oracle ERP system further strengthens the organization's defenses against fraud. These controls can include automated alerts for discrepancies, segregation of duties to ensure that no single individual has control over the entire transaction process, and regular audits to review and validate the matching process.

Enhancing Data Accuracy and Integrity

Accurate matching of invoices to purchase orders contributes to the overall data accuracy and integrity within the Oracle ERP system. By ensuring that all transactions are validated and recorded correctly, organizations can maintain high-quality financial data. This accurate data is essential for reliable financial reporting, effective decision-making, and strategic planning.

High data integrity also supports other business processes that rely on accurate financial information, such as inventory management, procurement planning, and cost control. By maintaining accurate records through the matching process, organizations can improve their overall operational efficiency and effectiveness.

Facilitating Dispute Resolution

In cases where discrepancies arise between invoices, POs, and receipts, the matching process provides a structured approach to resolving these issues. By having detailed records of each transaction, including the original PO and receipt documentation, the Accounts Payable team can quickly identify and investigate the source of the discrepancy. This prompt resolution of issues helps in maintaining smooth operations and avoiding delays in payment.

Effective dispute resolution also contributes to maintaining good relationships with suppliers. By addressing and resolving discrepancies promptly and fairly, organizations can demonstrate their commitment to accuracy and transparency, which can enhance trust and collaboration with suppliers.

Conclusion

Matching invoices to purchase orders is a critical process within the Accounts Payable module of Oracle ERP, offering numerous benefits for accuracy and control. By ensuring accurate payments, enhancing financial control, streamlining workflow, improving supplier relationships, supporting compliance and audit requirements, reducing fraud risk, enhancing data accuracy and integrity, and facilitating dispute resolution, this matching process plays a vital role in effective financial management. Organizations that implement robust matching controls can achieve greater efficiency, reduce costs, and maintain strong financial health, ultimately contributing to their overall success and sustainability.

3.2.3 Discuss the different methods for matching invoices to purchase orders

Matching invoices to purchase orders (POs) is a crucial task in the Accounts Payable module of Oracle ERP, ensuring that payments are made only for goods and services that have been received and approved. This process helps maintain financial accuracy, control over expenditures, and compliance with corporate policies. There are several methods for matching invoices to purchase orders, each with its own advantages and best-use scenarios. In this section, we will discuss the primary methods of matching invoices to purchase orders: two-way matching, three-way matching, and four-way matching.

Two-Way Matching

Definition:

Two-way matching involves comparing the invoice with the purchase order. This method ensures that the details on the invoice correspond to what was agreed upon in the purchase order.

Process:

1. Invoice Entry: When an invoice is received, it is entered into the Accounts Payable module.

2. PO Comparison: The system automatically compares the invoice details, such as item descriptions, quantities, and prices, with the corresponding purchase order.

3. Approval: If the invoice matches the purchase order, it is approved for payment. Discrepancies may trigger a review process.

Advantages:

- Simplicity: This method is straightforward and less time-consuming.

- Efficiency: Suitable for companies with simple procurement processes or where goods and services are consistent and predictable.

Best Use Cases:

- Service Contracts: Where services are billed periodically, and quantities or units are not a concern.

- Recurring Purchases: For office supplies or routine items where quantities and prices are well-established.

Disadvantages:

- Limited Verification: Two-way matching does not verify receipt of goods, which can lead to potential discrepancies if goods are not received as expected.

Three-Way Matching

Definition:

Three-way matching adds an additional layer of verification by including a goods receipt note (GRN). This method matches the invoice, purchase order, and the receipt of goods.

Process:

1. Invoice Entry: The invoice is entered into the Accounts Payable module.

2. PO and GRN Comparison: The system compares the invoice details with both the purchase order and the goods receipt note.

3. Approval: The invoice is approved for payment only if it matches both the purchase order and the receipt note. Discrepancies initiate an investigation.

Advantages:

- Enhanced Control: This method provides a higher level of accuracy and control by ensuring that the goods or services invoiced have been received.

- Error Reduction: Minimizes the risk of paying for goods not received, thereby reducing fraud and errors.

Best Use Cases:

- Physical Goods: Ideal for companies dealing with physical goods where the receipt of items needs to be verified.

- Complex Purchases: Suitable for high-value or complex procurement processes where additional verification is necessary.

Disadvantages:

- Complexity: Involves more steps and documentation, which can increase processing time and administrative workload.

- Resource Intensive: Requires coordination between multiple departments, such as purchasing, receiving, and accounts payable.

Four-Way Matching

Definition:

Four-way matching further extends the verification process by including an inspection or quality check report. This method matches the invoice, purchase order, goods receipt note, and inspection report.

Process:

1. Invoice Entry: The invoice is entered into the Accounts Payable module.

2. PO, GRN, and Inspection Report Comparison: The system compares the invoice details with the purchase order, goods receipt note, and inspection report.

3. Approval: The invoice is approved for payment only if it matches the purchase order, receipt note, and inspection report. Any discrepancies are flagged for resolution.

Advantages:

- Maximum Accuracy: Provides the highest level of accuracy and control by ensuring that received goods are not only accounted for but also meet quality standards.

- Risk Mitigation: Reduces the risk of paying for defective or substandard goods.

Best Use Cases:

- High-Value Items: Suitable for industries where product quality is critical, such as manufacturing, pharmaceuticals, and electronics.

- Regulated Industries: Ideal for sectors with strict regulatory requirements where quality assurance is paramount.

Disadvantages:

- Time-Consuming: The most time-intensive method, requiring multiple checks and approvals.

- Resource Demands: Requires significant coordination and documentation, involving several departments and possibly additional software integrations.

Choosing the Right Matching Method

The choice of matching method depends on various factors, including the nature of the business, the types of goods and services purchased, and the company's internal controls and policies. Here are some considerations to help determine the most appropriate matching method:

Nature of Transactions:

- Routine Purchases: For routine, low-value purchases, two-way matching might suffice.

- Significant Purchases: For higher-value or more significant purchases, three-way or four-way matching is recommended to ensure accuracy and accountability.

Internal Controls:

- Control Environment: Companies with robust internal controls and a high level of trust in their purchasing and receiving processes may opt for simpler matching methods.

- Risk Management: Organizations with stringent risk management practices may prefer more comprehensive matching methods.

Regulatory Requirements:

- Compliance: Industries with stringent regulatory requirements, such as pharmaceuticals or aerospace, may require four-way matching to comply with quality assurance and regulatory standards.

Resource Availability:

- Staffing and Technology: The availability of staff and technology to support the matching process is crucial. More complex methods require more resources and advanced software capabilities.

Transaction Volume:

- High Volume: Companies with a high volume of transactions may need to balance accuracy with efficiency, potentially using a combination of matching methods depending on transaction value and risk.

Implementation in Oracle ERP

Oracle ERP provides robust capabilities to support all three matching methods. Here's how these processes can be implemented within the Oracle Accounts Payable module:

Configuration:

- Setup Matching Rules: Administrators can configure matching rules based on the company's policies and requirements.

- Automation: The system can be set up to automatically perform matching and flag discrepancies for review.

Workflow Integration:

- Seamless Integration: Oracle ERP integrates seamlessly with purchasing, inventory, and quality control modules to ensure that all relevant data is available for matching.

- Workflow Automation: Automated workflows can be established for invoice approval, discrepancy resolution, and payment processing.

Reporting and Analytics:

- Real-Time Reporting: Real-time reporting and dashboards provide visibility into the matching process, helping identify trends, issues, and opportunities for improvement.

- Audit Trails: Comprehensive audit trails ensure that all actions are logged and traceable, supporting compliance and accountability.

User Training:

- Training Programs: Regular training programs for users involved in the matching process ensure that they are familiar with the system and its capabilities.

- Continuous Improvement: Feedback loops and continuous improvement initiatives help refine processes and enhance efficiency.

Conclusion

Matching invoices to purchase orders is a fundamental process in managing accounts payable, ensuring financial accuracy and control. By understanding the different methods—two-way, three-way, and four-way matching—and their respective advantages and disadvantages, organizations can choose the most suitable approach for their needs. Implementing these methods effectively within Oracle ERP involves configuring the system, integrating workflows, leveraging reporting tools, and training users. By doing so, companies can achieve a high level of accuracy, control, and efficiency in their accounts payable processes.

3.3 Approving and Releasing Invoices

3.3.1 Explain the workflow for approving and releasing invoices in the Accounts Payable module

Approving and releasing invoices in the Accounts Payable (AP) module is a critical process to ensure that only valid and authorized payments are made. This workflow involves several steps and checks to maintain accuracy, control, and compliance. Here's a detailed look at the workflow for approving and releasing invoices:

1. Invoice Entry:

   - Data Entry: The process begins with the entry of invoice data into the AP module. This can be done manually by entering invoice details into the system or automatically through electronic data interchange (EDI), email, or other automated methods.

   - Invoice Scanning and OCR: For paper invoices, scanning and optical character recognition (OCR) technology can be used to digitize and extract invoice information automatically.

2. Initial Validation:

   - Data Validation: Once the invoice is entered into the system, initial validation checks are performed. These checks include verifying the vendor information, invoice date, amount, purchase order (PO) number, and other required fields.

   - Duplicate Check: The system checks for duplicate invoices by comparing key fields such as invoice number, vendor, and date. Duplicate invoices are flagged for review.

3. Invoice Matching:

   - Three-Way Matching: Invoices are matched against the corresponding purchase orders and goods receipts. This three-way matching ensures that the invoice details (price, quantity) match the PO and receipt records. Any discrepancies are flagged for further review.

- Two-Way Matching: For services or contracts without goods receipts, a two-way matching process is used, comparing the invoice with the PO.

4. Invoice Approval Workflow:

  - Approval Routing: Invoices that pass the initial validation and matching steps are routed for approval. The approval workflow can be configured based on various criteria such as invoice amount, department, or vendor.

  - Approval Levels: The workflow may involve multiple levels of approval, depending on the organization's policies. For example, lower-value invoices might require a single approval, while higher-value invoices may need multiple approvals from different levels of management.

5. Review and Approval:

  - Approver Notification: Approvers are notified of pending invoices through email alerts, dashboard notifications, or in-system messages.

  - Invoice Review: Approvers review the invoice details, ensuring that all information is accurate and that the goods or services have been received satisfactorily. They may also check supporting documents attached to the invoice.

  - Approval Actions: Approvers can either approve, reject, or request additional information. Approved invoices move to the next step, while rejected invoices are returned to the AP team for further action.

6. Final Validation:

  - Compliance Checks: Before releasing the payment, final compliance checks are performed. These checks include verifying tax codes, payment terms, and ensuring that the invoice adheres to the company's policies and regulatory requirements.

  - Hold and Release: Invoices can be placed on hold for various reasons (e.g., pending receipt of goods, awaiting further approval). Once the hold reasons are resolved, the invoices are released for payment.

7. Payment Processing:

- Payment Scheduling: Approved invoices are scheduled for payment based on the payment terms and due dates. The AP module generates a payment batch, which can be reviewed and adjusted if necessary.

- Payment Methods: Payments can be made using various methods such as electronic funds transfer (EFT), checks, or corporate credit cards. The chosen payment method is based on the vendor's preference and the company's policies.

- Payment Authorization: The final payment authorization involves a review by authorized personnel to ensure that the payment batch is accurate and complete.

8. Payment Execution:

- Payment Generation: Once authorized, the system generates the payment instructions. For EFT, the instructions are sent to the bank, while for checks, the system prints the checks and prepares them for mailing.

- Payment Posting: After the payment is executed, the system automatically posts the payment to the vendor's account, updating the AP ledger and reducing the outstanding liability.

9. Record Keeping and Reporting:

- Audit Trail: The AP module maintains a detailed audit trail of all actions taken during the invoice approval and payment process. This includes timestamps, user actions, and comments.

- Reporting: Various reports can be generated to track the status of invoices, approvals, and payments. These reports help in monitoring the AP process, identifying bottlenecks, and ensuring compliance.

10. Exception Handling:

- Discrepancies and Disputes: Any discrepancies or disputes identified during the approval process are handled through predefined procedures. This may involve communication with vendors, internal departments, or further investigation.

- Escalation: Issues that cannot be resolved at the initial level are escalated to higher management for resolution.

Importance of the Workflow

The workflow for approving and releasing invoices in the Accounts Payable module is designed to ensure:

- Accuracy: By validating data and performing matching checks, the workflow minimizes errors and ensures that only accurate invoices are processed.

- Control: The approval workflow provides control over the payment process, ensuring that only authorized personnel can approve and release invoices.

- Compliance: Compliance checks ensure adherence to company policies, tax regulations, and other legal requirements.

- Efficiency: Automation of the approval workflow reduces manual intervention, speeds up the process, and enhances efficiency.

- Transparency: The audit trail and reporting features provide transparency and accountability, allowing for effective monitoring and auditing of the AP process.

Implementing a robust invoice approval and release workflow in the Accounts Payable module is essential for maintaining financial control, reducing errors, and ensuring timely and accurate payments to vendors. This workflow not only enhances the efficiency of the AP process but also contributes to the overall financial health and operational efficiency of the organization.

3.3.2 Discuss the roles and responsibilities involved in the approval process

The approval and release of invoices within the Accounts Payable (AP) module of Oracle ERP is a critical component of the financial management process. Ensuring that invoices are accurately approved and released involves multiple roles and responsibilities within an organization. This section outlines the key stakeholders and their respective responsibilities in the invoice approval process.

1. Accounts Payable Clerk

The Accounts Payable (AP) Clerk plays a foundational role in the initial stages of the invoice approval process. Their primary responsibilities include:

- Invoice Entry and Verification: The AP Clerk is responsible for entering invoices into the system and verifying their accuracy. This involves checking for correct vendor details, invoice amounts, and applicable taxes.

- Initial Validation: Before forwarding invoices for approval, the AP Clerk ensures that all necessary documentation is attached and that the invoice complies with company policies and procedures.

- Coding Invoices: Assigning the correct general ledger (GL) codes to invoices to ensure proper accounting and reporting.

2. Invoice Approver

Invoice Approvers are typically managers or supervisors responsible for reviewing and authorizing invoices before payment. Their key duties include:

- Review for Accuracy: Approvers meticulously review each invoice to confirm that the goods or services were received as described, and the pricing matches the terms agreed upon with the vendor.

- Compliance Check: Ensuring that the invoice adheres to internal policies, contractual terms, and relevant regulations.

- Approval Authorization: Approvers give the final authorization for payment by signing off on the invoice electronically or physically, depending on the organization's workflow.

3. Department Manager

The Department Manager oversees the budget and expenses for their specific department. Their responsibilities in the invoice approval process include:

- Budgetary Oversight: Reviewing invoices to ensure that expenses align with the department's budget and that funds are available for payment.

- Expense Justification: Ensuring that all expenses are necessary and justified, and that they contribute to the department's operational goals.

- Approval or Rejection: Based on their review, Department Managers either approve the invoice for payment or reject it, providing reasons and suggesting necessary corrections.

4. Finance Manager

The Finance Manager ensures that the organization's financial transactions are accurately recorded and reported. Their role in the invoice approval process includes:

- Financial Review: Conducting a final review of invoices to ensure they are accurately coded and comply with accounting standards.

- Cash Flow Management: Assessing the impact of invoice payments on the company's cash flow and making decisions about payment scheduling.

- Policy Enforcement: Ensuring that all invoices adhere to the company's financial policies and procedures.

5. Controller

The Controller oversees the overall accounting operations, including the AP function. Their responsibilities include:

- Internal Controls: Implementing and maintaining robust internal controls to prevent fraud and ensure the accuracy of financial records.

- Audit Preparation: Ensuring that all invoices and approval processes are documented correctly for internal and external audits.

- Policy Development: Developing and updating policies and procedures related to the AP process to improve efficiency and compliance.

6. Chief Financial Officer (CFO)

The CFO has the ultimate responsibility for the financial health of the organization. Their involvement in the invoice approval process is typically high-level but crucial:

- Strategic Oversight: Ensuring that all financial activities, including AP processes, align with the organization's strategic goals.

- Risk Management: Identifying and mitigating risks related to invoice processing and financial transactions.

- Final Approval: In some cases, the CFO may be required to provide the final approval for large or critical payments.

7. Internal Auditor

Internal Auditors play a vital role in maintaining the integrity of the AP process. Their responsibilities include:

- Process Review: Regularly reviewing the invoice approval process to ensure compliance with internal controls and regulatory requirements.

- Fraud Detection: Identifying and investigating any discrepancies or irregularities in the invoice approval process.

- Audit Reporting: Providing detailed reports on the findings of their audits and recommending improvements.

8. Information Technology (IT) Department

The IT Department supports the AP process by maintaining and managing the Oracle ERP system. Their responsibilities include:

- System Maintenance: Ensuring the AP module is functioning correctly and efficiently.

- User Support: Providing technical support to AP staff and other users involved in the invoice approval process.

- Security Management: Implementing security measures to protect sensitive financial data and ensure compliance with data protection regulations.

Workflow of the Approval Process

The workflow for approving and releasing invoices typically follows a structured sequence to ensure accuracy, compliance, and efficiency. Here's an overview of a typical approval workflow:

1. Invoice Receipt and Entry: The AP Clerk receives the invoice, verifies its details, and enters it into the Oracle ERP system.

2. Initial Validation: The AP Clerk performs initial validation checks, including verifying vendor information, checking invoice amounts, and ensuring supporting documentation is attached.

3. Forwarding for Approval: The invoice is forwarded to the designated Invoice Approver or Department Manager for review.

4. Review and Authorization: The Approver or Department Manager reviews the invoice for accuracy, compliance, and budgetary alignment. If everything is in order, they approve the invoice.

5. Final Review by Finance Manager: The Finance Manager conducts a final review to ensure proper coding and compliance with accounting standards.

6. Payment Scheduling: The Finance Manager or Controller schedules the payment based on the company's cash flow and payment terms.

7. Release of Payment: Once all approvals are in place, the payment is processed and released to the vendor.

Importance of Proper Authorization and Review

Proper authorization and review of invoices are crucial for several reasons:

- Accuracy: Ensuring that the invoice amounts and details are accurate prevents overpayments and financial discrepancies.

- Compliance: Adhering to internal policies and regulatory requirements minimizes the risk of non-compliance penalties and legal issues.

- Fraud Prevention: Implementing robust approval processes helps detect and prevent fraudulent activities.

- Financial Control: Maintaining control over expenses and cash flow ensures the organization's financial stability.

- Operational Efficiency: Streamlining the approval process improves operational efficiency and reduces delays in payment processing.

Conclusion

The roles and responsibilities involved in the invoice approval process are diverse and interconnected. Each stakeholder, from the AP Clerk to the CFO, plays a vital role in ensuring the accuracy, compliance, and efficiency of invoice processing. By clearly defining these roles and implementing a structured approval workflow, organizations can enhance their financial management processes and maintain strong financial control.

3.3.3 Emphasize the importance of proper authorization and review for invoice payments

In the realm of Accounts Payable (AP), the processes of approving and releasing invoices are critical stages that ensure the accuracy, legitimacy, and timeliness of payments. Proper authorization and review mechanisms play an indispensable role in maintaining financial integrity, mitigating fraud, and ensuring compliance with internal and external financial policies.

1. Ensuring Financial Accuracy and Integrity

Proper authorization is crucial in verifying that invoices are accurate and correspond to the actual goods or services received. This step involves cross-checking invoice details such as amounts, dates, vendor information, and the items or services billed against purchase orders and delivery receipts. A meticulous review helps identify any discrepancies that could lead to overpayments, duplicate payments, or payments for unreceived goods.

For instance, an authorized approver should verify that the invoiced amount matches the agreed-upon terms in the purchase order. Any deviations should be investigated and resolved before payment is processed. This attention to detail helps maintain the financial accuracy of the organization's records, ensuring that the expenses reported are correct and reflective of actual transactions.

2. Mitigating Fraud and Unapproved Transactions

Authorization serves as a critical control point for preventing fraudulent activities and unauthorized transactions. By implementing a structured approval workflow, organizations can ensure that only legitimate and verified invoices are processed for payment. This reduces the risk of fraudulent invoices being paid, which could otherwise lead to significant financial losses and damage to the company's reputation.

Segregation of duties is a fundamental aspect of fraud prevention. It ensures that no single individual has control over all aspects of the AP process. For example, the person responsible for entering invoices should not be the same individual approving the payments. This separation creates a system of checks and balances, making it more difficult for fraudulent activities to go undetected.

3. Compliance with Internal and External Policies

Organizations must comply with various internal policies and external regulations regarding financial transactions. Proper authorization and review of invoices ensure adherence to these guidelines, reducing the risk of regulatory breaches and associated penalties.

Internal policies may include specific approval hierarchies, expenditure limits, and documentation requirements. External regulations could involve tax compliance, anti-corruption laws, and industry-specific financial reporting standards. By enforcing a robust approval process, organizations demonstrate their commitment to governance and regulatory compliance.

4. Enhancing Operational Efficiency

A well-defined authorization process contributes to operational efficiency by streamlining invoice approvals and reducing delays in payment processing. Timely payments are essential for maintaining good relationships with suppliers, avoiding late fees, and taking advantage of early payment discounts.

Effective invoice approval workflows typically involve automated systems that route invoices to the appropriate approvers based on predefined criteria such as department, vendor, or invoice amount. These systems can send reminders and notifications to approvers, ensuring that invoices are reviewed and authorized promptly. Automation reduces the administrative burden on staff and minimizes the risk of human error, further enhancing efficiency.

5. Establishing Accountability and Transparency

Authorization and review processes establish clear accountability within the organization. Approvers are responsible for validating the accuracy and legitimacy of invoices, ensuring that payments are justified and necessary. This accountability fosters a culture of responsibility and diligence among employees, promoting transparency in financial operations.

Detailed audit trails are an integral part of this process, recording who approved each invoice and when. These records provide a transparent view of the approval history, making it easier to investigate any issues or discrepancies that may arise. Audit trails are also valuable during internal and external audits, demonstrating the organization's adherence to proper financial controls.

6. Addressing and Resolving Invoice Discrepancies

During the approval process, any discrepancies identified in the invoices must be addressed and resolved before payments are made. Discrepancies can arise from various issues such as incorrect pricing, quantity mismatches, or billing errors. Approvers play a critical role in investigating these discrepancies, collaborating with vendors and internal departments to rectify them.

For example, if an invoice reflects a higher amount than the purchase order, the approver should contact the vendor to clarify the discrepancy. This may involve providing supporting documentation or adjusting the invoice to match the agreed terms. Resolving discrepancies at this stage prevents disputes and ensures that payments are accurate and justified.

7. Leveraging Technology for Enhanced Control

Modern AP systems leverage technology to enhance the authorization and review process. These systems often include features such as automated workflows, digital signatures, and real-time tracking, providing greater control and visibility over invoice approvals.

Automated workflows route invoices to the appropriate approvers based on predefined rules, reducing the likelihood of bottlenecks and ensuring timely reviews. Digital signatures offer a secure and efficient method for approving invoices, eliminating the need for physical signatures and paperwork. Real-time tracking allows finance teams to monitor the status of invoices throughout the approval process, providing insights into potential delays and areas for improvement.

8. Training and Empowering Employees

Training employees on the importance of proper authorization and review is essential for maintaining robust AP processes. Approvers should be well-versed in the organization's policies, procedures, and best practices for invoice verification. Regular training sessions and updates ensure that staff members are aware of any changes in policies or regulatory requirements.

Empowering employees with the knowledge and tools they need to perform their roles effectively fosters a proactive approach to financial management. It also encourages a culture of continuous improvement, where employees actively seek ways to enhance the efficiency and accuracy of the AP process.

Conclusion

Proper authorization and review of invoice payments are fundamental to the integrity and efficiency of the Accounts Payable process. By ensuring financial accuracy, mitigating fraud, complying with policies, enhancing operational efficiency, establishing accountability, addressing discrepancies, leveraging technology, and training employees, organizations can create a robust framework for managing invoice transactions. This framework not only protects the organization's financial assets but also fosters trust and transparency in its financial operations.

3.4 Handling Invoice Discrepancies

Handling invoice discrepancies is a critical part of managing accounts payable efficiently. Invoice discrepancies occur when there is a mismatch between the invoice details and the corresponding purchase order, receipt, or contract. These discrepancies need to be addressed promptly to ensure smooth payment processes and maintain good vendor relationships. This section outlines the procedures for identifying and resolving invoice discrepancies within the Oracle ERP Accounts Payable module.

3.4.1 Describe the procedures for identifying and resolving invoice discrepancies

Identifying Invoice Discrepancies

1. Automated Matching Processes:

   - Three-Way Matching: Oracle ERP's three-way matching process compares the invoice with the purchase order and the goods receipt. This automated process helps in quickly identifying discrepancies in quantity, price, and terms.

   - Two-Way Matching: This process involves matching the invoice with the purchase order only. It is typically used when goods receipt information is not available or applicable.

2. Manual Review:

   - Visual Inspection: Accounts payable staff can manually review invoices against purchase orders and receipts. This involves checking quantities, prices, dates, and terms to identify any mismatches.

   - Cross-Referencing: Verifying the details in the invoice against the corresponding purchase order and delivery receipts to ensure accuracy.

3. Automated Alerts and Notifications:

   - System Alerts: Oracle ERP can be configured to generate alerts for discrepancies. These alerts notify the responsible personnel immediately when a discrepancy is detected.

- Dashboard Reports: Regularly reviewing dashboard reports that highlight discrepancies can help in quickly identifying problematic invoices.

4. Regular Audits:

- Internal Audits: Conducting regular internal audits to review a sample of invoices can help in identifying discrepancies that might have been missed during routine processing.

- External Audits: Engaging third-party auditors to review the accounts payable process can provide an additional layer of scrutiny and help in uncovering discrepancies.

Resolving Invoice Discrepancies

1. Documenting Discrepancies:

- Discrepancy Log: Maintain a log of all discrepancies identified. This log should include details such as the invoice number, vendor name, nature of the discrepancy, and steps taken to resolve it.

- Communication Records: Keep records of all communications with vendors and internal stakeholders regarding the discrepancy. This ensures transparency and accountability.

2. Communication with Vendors:

- Initial Notification: Contact the vendor immediately upon identifying a discrepancy. Provide details of the discrepancy and request clarification or a corrected invoice.

- Follow-Up: Regularly follow up with the vendor until the issue is resolved. This may involve multiple communications and escalations if necessary.

3. Internal Review and Approval:

- Review by Purchasing Department: Forward the discrepancy to the purchasing department for review. They can verify if the goods or services were received as per the purchase order and if there were any agreed-upon changes that were not documented.

- Approval from Management: In case of significant discrepancies, obtain approval from senior management before making any adjustments. This ensures that any financial impact is carefully considered.

4. Corrective Actions:

- Adjustments: If the discrepancy is minor and can be resolved with an adjustment, update the invoice records in the ERP system accordingly. This might involve adjusting quantities, prices, or discount terms.

- Issuing Credit/Debit Memos: For significant discrepancies, issue a credit or debit memo. This document adjusts the financial records to reflect the correct amounts.

- Invoice Rejection: If the discrepancy cannot be resolved, reject the invoice. Communicate the rejection to the vendor, explaining the reasons, and request a new, corrected invoice.

5. Updating ERP Records:

- Invoice Adjustment: Make necessary adjustments in the Oracle ERP system to correct the invoice details. Ensure that these adjustments are accurately recorded and reflected in financial reports.

- Transaction History: Update the transaction history to reflect the actions taken to resolve the discrepancy. This provides a clear audit trail for future reference.

6. Preventive Measures:

- Vendor Training: Provide training and guidelines to vendors on the proper way to issue invoices. This can help in reducing the occurrence of discrepancies.

- System Improvements: Regularly review and improve the matching algorithms and discrepancy detection processes in the Oracle ERP system to enhance accuracy.

- Policy Updates: Update internal policies and procedures based on common discrepancy issues to prevent them from recurring. This might involve changes in purchase order creation, receipt documentation, and invoice processing practices.

By following these procedures, organizations can effectively manage invoice discrepancies, ensuring that they are resolved promptly and accurately. This not only maintains good relationships with vendors but also ensures that financial records are accurate and compliant with accounting standards.

3.4.2 Discuss the different types of invoice discrepancies that may occur

records. 3.4 Handling Invoice Discrepancies

b. Discuss the Different Types of Invoice Discrepancies That May Occur

Invoice discrepancies are variances between the details on an invoice and the corresponding purchase order, receipt, or contract. These discrepancies can disrupt the payment process, cause delays, and impact financial reporting. Understanding the various types of invoice discrepancies that may occur is essential for effectively managing and resolving them. Below are the primary types of invoice discrepancies that businesses may encounter in the Accounts Payable (AP) module of Oracle ERP:

1. Quantity Discrepancies:

  - Over-Quantity: This occurs when the invoice reflects a higher quantity of goods or services than what was actually received or ordered. This can happen due to clerical errors, supplier mistakes, or intentional overbilling. Over-quantity discrepancies can lead to overpayments if not identified and corrected.

  - Under-Quantity: This is when the invoice shows a lower quantity than what was received or ordered. This can result in underpayment to suppliers and may cause issues in inventory management. It can also affect future orders and supplier relationships.

2. Price Discrepancies:

  - Overpricing: When the invoice price per unit is higher than the price agreed upon in the purchase order or contract, it is considered overpricing. This discrepancy can arise from price changes that were not communicated, errors in pricing, or intentional overcharges by the supplier.

- Underpricing: This occurs when the invoice price per unit is lower than the agreed price. While this might seem advantageous, it can lead to complications in reconciling accounts and may indicate errors that need to be investigated and corrected.

3. Tax Discrepancies:

- Incorrect Tax Rates: Invoices may reflect incorrect tax rates due to errors in tax calculation, changes in tax legislation that were not updated, or misinterpretation of tax rules. This can lead to incorrect tax payments and potential legal and compliance issues.

- Tax Code Errors: Using the wrong tax codes can result in discrepancies between the invoice and the expected tax amounts. This can affect financial reporting and compliance with tax authorities.

4. Discount Discrepancies:

- Missed Discounts: Suppliers may offer early payment discounts or other types of discounts that are not reflected on the invoice. Missing these discounts can lead to higher costs for the company.

- Incorrect Discount Application: Sometimes, discounts may be applied incorrectly on the invoice, either overstated or understated, leading to discrepancies that need adjustment.

5. Freight and Shipping Discrepancies:

- Incorrect Freight Charges: Invoices may contain incorrect freight charges due to miscommunication, errors in calculation, or changes in shipping costs. These discrepancies need to be reconciled to ensure accurate payment.

- Missing or Additional Freight Charges: Sometimes, freight charges might be missing from the invoice or additional charges may be included without prior agreement. These need to be identified and verified against the purchase order and delivery terms.

6. Payment Terms Discrepancies:

- Mismatched Payment Terms: If the payment terms on the invoice differ from those agreed upon in the purchase order or contract, it can lead to disputes and delays in payment. This includes discrepancies in due dates, early payment discounts, and penalties for late payments.

7. Currency Discrepancies:

- Exchange Rate Differences: For international transactions, discrepancies can arise due to differences in exchange rates used by the supplier and the company. This can affect the final payment amount and needs to be reconciled accurately.

- Currency Code Errors: Incorrect currency codes on the invoice can lead to significant discrepancies in the payable amount, requiring careful review and correction.

8. Invoice Duplication:

- Duplicate Invoices: Receiving duplicate invoices for the same goods or services can result from errors in the supplier's billing system or miscommunication. Duplicate invoices need to be identified to prevent double payment.

- Partial Invoicing: Sometimes, suppliers may send multiple invoices for partial deliveries. This can lead to confusion and discrepancies if not managed correctly.

9. Incorrect Supplier Information:

- Wrong Supplier Details: Invoices with incorrect supplier details such as name, address, or tax identification number can cause discrepancies that delay payment processing. Verifying supplier information is crucial to avoid such issues.

10. Service Date Discrepancies:

- Incorrect Service Dates: Invoices for services rendered may contain incorrect service dates that do not match the purchase order or contract. This can affect the recognition of expenses and the timing of payments.

11. Missing or Incorrect PO References:

- Missing PO Numbers: Invoices without reference to the purchase order number can cause delays in matching and processing. It is essential to ensure that all invoices reference the correct PO number.

- Incorrect PO Numbers: Using the wrong PO number on an invoice can lead to mismatches and discrepancies, requiring additional time and effort to resolve.

12. Handling Fees and Additional Charges:

- Unexpected Charges: Invoices may include handling fees or additional charges that were not agreed upon. These need to be reviewed and verified before processing the payment.

- Discrepancies in Agreed Fees: Sometimes, the handling fees or additional charges on the invoice may differ from those agreed upon in the contract or purchase order, leading to discrepancies.

13. Item Description Discrepancies:

- Mismatched Descriptions: Differences in the description of items or services between the invoice and the purchase order can lead to confusion and delays in processing. Accurate item descriptions are essential for proper matching and verification.

14. Incomplete Invoices:

- Missing Information: Invoices that lack necessary details such as item descriptions, quantities, prices, or supplier information are considered incomplete and can cause delays in processing. Ensuring that all required information is present is crucial for efficient invoice handling.

15. Contractual Discrepancies:

- Terms of Contract Not Met: Invoices that do not adhere to the terms outlined in the contract, such as delivery timelines, quality standards, or payment schedules, can lead to disputes and require resolution before payment can be made.

Each type of invoice discrepancy requires a specific approach for resolution. The Accounts Payable team must be equipped with robust processes and tools to identify, investigate, and correct these discrepancies efficiently. Effective discrepancy management involves regular training, clear communication with suppliers, and the use of advanced features in the Oracle ERP system to automate and streamline the process. By addressing invoice discrepancies promptly and accurately, organizations can maintain healthy supplier relationships, ensure compliance, and optimize their financial operations.

3.4.3 Explain the methods for investigating and correcting invoice discrepancies

Invoice discrepancies can disrupt the smooth processing of transactions within the Accounts Payable module, leading to potential delays, financial inaccuracies, and strained vendor relationships. Effective investigation and correction methods are crucial for maintaining the integrity of financial records and ensuring timely payments. This section will explore various techniques and best practices for identifying, investigating, and resolving invoice discrepancies.

Identifying Invoice Discrepancies

Before addressing the methods for correcting invoice discrepancies, it is essential to establish how these discrepancies are identified. Common indicators of discrepancies include:

1. Mismatch with Purchase Orders: Differences between the invoice and the associated purchase order (PO) in terms of quantity, price, or item details.

2. Discrepancies in Receiving Reports: Variances between the invoice and the receiving report, which details the actual items and quantities received.

3. Duplicate Invoices: Invoices that have been entered multiple times for the same goods or services.

4. Incorrect or Missing Information: Errors such as incorrect vendor details, invoice numbers, dates, or missing critical information.

5. Discrepancies in Payment Terms: Differences between the agreed payment terms and those listed on the invoice.

Methods for Investigating Invoice Discrepancies

1. Review Supporting Documents:

  - Purchase Orders (POs): Compare the invoice with the original PO to verify quantities, prices, and terms. This step helps identify any discrepancies in the agreed-upon terms and actual invoiced amounts.

  - Receiving Reports: Check the receiving reports to ensure that the goods or services listed on the invoice match what was actually received. This step is crucial for identifying discrepancies in quantities or items.

  - Contracts and Agreements: Review any relevant contracts or agreements to verify the terms and conditions agreed upon with the vendor. This can help identify discrepancies related to pricing, payment terms, or other contractual obligations.

2. Engage with Stakeholders:

  - Internal Departments: Collaborate with relevant departments such as procurement, receiving, and finance to gather additional information and insights. These departments can provide context and clarity regarding the discrepancies.

  - Vendors: Communicate directly with vendors to address any discrepancies. This step involves verifying details, discussing potential errors, and negotiating corrections.

3. Use Automated Tools:

  - Invoice Matching Software: Utilize automated invoice matching tools that compare invoices with POs and receiving reports. These tools can quickly identify discrepancies and flag them for review.

- Error Detection Algorithms: Implement algorithms that detect common discrepancies, such as duplicate invoices or mismatched quantities, and alert the Accounts Payable team for further investigation.

4. Perform Root Cause Analysis:

- Identify Patterns: Look for patterns in discrepancies to identify systemic issues. For example, repeated discrepancies from a particular vendor may indicate a need for improved communication or process adjustments.

- Analyze Processes: Examine internal processes to identify potential areas of improvement. This analysis can help prevent future discrepancies by addressing root causes such as inadequate training, unclear procedures, or system limitations.

Methods for Correcting Invoice Discrepancies

1. Update Invoice Records:

- Manual Corrections: Make necessary corrections directly in the Accounts Payable system. This may involve updating quantities, prices, or other details to match the PO or receiving report.

- Issue Credit or Debit Memos: If the discrepancy results in an overpayment or underpayment, issue a credit or debit memo to adjust the invoice amount accordingly.

2. Adjust Purchase Orders:

- Modify POs: In some cases, it may be necessary to adjust the original PO to reflect the correct quantities, prices, or terms. This step ensures that future invoices match the revised PO details.

- Close Out POs: For discrepancies that cannot be resolved, consider closing out the original PO and issuing a new one with accurate details.

3. Reconcile Receiving Reports:

- Update Receiving Records: Ensure that receiving records accurately reflect the goods or services received. This may involve correcting quantities, item descriptions, or other details.

- Resolve Receiving Discrepancies: Work with the receiving department to address any discrepancies in receiving reports. This step may involve verifying deliveries, inspecting goods, or updating records.

4. Communicate with Vendors:

- Request Corrected Invoices: Ask vendors to issue corrected invoices that accurately reflect the agreed-upon terms and received quantities. This step helps ensure that future transactions are processed without discrepancies.

- Negotiate Resolutions: In cases where discrepancies are disputed, negotiate with vendors to reach a mutually acceptable resolution. This may involve agreeing on revised terms, issuing partial payments, or other adjustments.

5. Implement Process Improvements:

- Standardize Procedures: Develop and implement standardized procedures for invoice processing, including clear guidelines for matching invoices to POs and receiving reports. This step helps prevent discrepancies by ensuring consistency and accuracy.

- Training and Education: Provide training for Accounts Payable staff and other relevant departments to ensure they understand best practices for invoice processing and discrepancy resolution.

- Continuous Monitoring: Establish ongoing monitoring and review processes to identify and address discrepancies promptly. This may involve regular audits, performance metrics, and feedback mechanisms.

Conclusion

Handling invoice discrepancies effectively is crucial for maintaining the accuracy and integrity of financial records within the Accounts Payable module. By implementing robust investigation and correction methods, organizations can minimize the impact of discrepancies, ensure timely payments, and maintain strong vendor relationships. The strategies outlined in this section provide a comprehensive approach to identifying, investigating, and resolving invoice discrepancies, ultimately contributing to more efficient and reliable accounts payable processes.

CHAPTER IV
Managing Payments and Adjustments

4.1 Processing Manual Payments

4.1.1 Explain the process of creating and processing manual payments in the Accounts Payable module

Processing manual payments within the Oracle ERP Accounts Payable module involves several critical steps to ensure accuracy, proper authorization, and documentation. This section will outline these steps in detail, providing a comprehensive guide for users.

Step 1: Accessing the Manual Payments Functionality

To begin the process of creating and processing manual payments, users must first navigate to the appropriate section within the Accounts Payable module. Typically, this involves the following steps:

1. Login to Oracle ERP: Access the Oracle ERP system using your credentials.

2. Navigate to the Accounts Payable Module: From the main dashboard, select the Accounts Payable module.

3. Select the Payments Work Area: Within the Accounts Payable module, locate and select the Payments work area, which houses all payment-related functionalities.

4. Initiate a Manual Payment: Look for the option to create a new manual payment. This is usually labeled as "Create Manual Payment" or similar.

Step 2: Entering Payment Information

Once you have accessed the manual payment functionality, the next step is to enter the payment details. This involves several key pieces of information:

1. Payment Date: Enter the date on which the payment will be issued.

2. Supplier Information: Select the supplier to whom the payment will be made. This can be done by searching for the supplier name or supplier number.

3. Invoice Selection: Choose the invoices that the payment will cover. This step involves selecting from a list of outstanding invoices for the chosen supplier.

4. Payment Amount: Enter the amount to be paid. This can either be the full amount of the selected invoices or a partial payment.

5. Payment Method: Specify the method of payment, such as check, electronic funds transfer (EFT), or wire transfer.

6. Payment Reference: Include any necessary references or notes for the payment, such as an internal payment reference number or a brief description of the payment purpose.

Step 3: Payment Authorization

Before a manual payment can be processed, it must go through an authorization process to ensure that it is legitimate and properly approved. This typically involves the following steps:

1. Review and Approval: The payment details entered in the previous step are reviewed by an authorized approver. This individual verifies that the payment is accurate and valid.

2. Approval Workflow: The payment request might be routed through an approval workflow within Oracle ERP, where multiple levels of authorization may be required based on the payment amount and company policies.

3. Authorization: Once all required approvals are obtained, the payment is authorized. This step is crucial for maintaining internal controls and preventing unauthorized payments.

Step 4: Generating the Payment Document

After authorization, the next step is to generate the actual payment document. The steps involved vary depending on the payment method chosen:

1. Check Payment: If the payment method is a check, the system will generate a check document that can be printed and sent to the supplier. This involves:

  - Printing the check using the designated check printer and check stock.

  - Ensuring that the printed check includes all necessary details, such as the payee name, payment amount, and check number.

  - Storing a copy of the check for record-keeping purposes.

2. Electronic Funds Transfer (EFT): For EFT payments, the system will generate an electronic payment file that can be sent to the bank for processing. This involves:

  - Creating the EFT file in the format required by the bank.

  - Uploading the file to the bank's portal or sending it via a secure electronic channel.

  - Confirming receipt and processing of the payment by the bank.

3. Wire Transfer: If a wire transfer is chosen, the system will generate a wire transfer instruction that can be sent to the bank. This involves:

  - Entering the wire transfer details, such as the beneficiary bank account number, SWIFT code, and beneficiary name.

  - Sending the wire transfer instruction to the bank, usually via a secure banking platform.

  - Confirming the successful execution of the wire transfer.

Step 5: Recording the Payment

Once the payment document is generated and sent, it is essential to record the payment in the Accounts Payable module to update the accounting records and ensure accurate financial reporting. This involves:

1. Updating the Invoice Status: Mark the selected invoices as paid in the system. This step ensures that the invoices are no longer listed as outstanding liabilities.

2. Posting to the General Ledger: Create the necessary journal entries to reflect the payment in the general ledger. This typically involves:

- Debiting the Accounts Payable account to reduce the liability.

- Crediting the Cash or Bank account to reflect the payment outflow.

3. Recording Payment Details: Store all relevant payment details, including the payment method, date, and amount, for future reference and audit purposes.

Step 6: Handling Payment Discrepancies

In some cases, discrepancies may arise during the manual payment process. It is crucial to have procedures in place to address these issues promptly. Common discrepancies include:

1. Payment Amount Mismatch: If the payment amount does not match the invoice amount, investigate the discrepancy and take corrective action, such as adjusting the payment amount or correcting the invoice.

2. Payment Method Errors: If the wrong payment method is used, void the incorrect payment and reissue the payment using the correct method.

3. Payment Authorization Issues: If the payment is not properly authorized, halt the payment process, and obtain the necessary approvals before proceeding.

Step 7: Ensuring Compliance and Documentation

Finally, ensuring compliance with internal controls and maintaining proper documentation is critical for audit purposes and internal control. Key activities include:

1. Maintaining Payment Records: Store copies of all payment documents, including checks, EFT files, and wire transfer instructions, in an organized manner.

2. Compliance Checks: Regularly review payment processes to ensure compliance with company policies and regulatory requirements.

3. Audit Trails: Ensure that all payment activities are recorded in the system, creating a clear audit trail for future reference.

Conclusion

Processing manual payments within the Oracle ERP Accounts Payable module involves a structured and meticulous process. By following these detailed steps, users can ensure that payments are made accurately, authorized appropriately, and documented thoroughly. This not only enhances the efficiency of the Accounts Payable function but also strengthens internal controls and supports effective cash flow management.

4.1.2 Discuss the different payment methods supported

When processing manual payments in the Oracle ERP Accounts Payable module, it is crucial to understand the various payment methods supported. The choice of payment method can impact efficiency, cost, and the accuracy of financial records. Below is an in-depth discussion of the different payment methods supported by Oracle ERP:

1. Checks

Overview:

Checks are a traditional and widely used method of payment. They involve the physical issuance of a paper document that instructs a bank to pay a specified sum from the payer's account to the payee.

Process:

Creating checks in Oracle ERP involves generating a payment batch or individual check. The system allows for printing checks with the necessary details such as the payee's name, amount, and date.

Advantages:

- Wide Acceptance: Most vendors accept checks.

- Record Keeping: Physical checks provide a tangible record of payment.

- Control: Issuing checks manually allows for direct oversight and authorization.

Disadvantages:

- Time-Consuming: The process of printing, signing, and mailing checks can be slow.

- Risk of Fraud: Physical checks can be altered or forged.

- Cost: Printing and mailing checks involve additional costs.

Best Practices:

- Secure Storage: Keep check stock in a secure location to prevent unauthorized access.

- Authorization Controls: Implement a robust check authorization process to mitigate fraud risks.

- Reconciliation: Regularly reconcile issued checks with bank statements to ensure accuracy.

2. Electronic Funds Transfer (EFT)

Overview:

EFT is a digital payment method where funds are transferred electronically from one bank account to another. This method includes various types such as ACH (Automated Clearing House) payments, wire transfers, and direct deposits.

Process:

In Oracle ERP, setting up EFT involves configuring bank account details and payment templates. The system can generate an electronic payment file that is transmitted to the bank for processing.

Advantages:

- Speed: EFTs are processed quickly, often within the same day.

- Cost-Effective: Lower transaction costs compared to issuing checks.

- Security: Reduced risk of fraud as there are no physical documents to manipulate.

Disadvantages:

- Setup Complexity: Initial setup of EFT can be complex and require accurate bank details.

- Dependence on Bank Systems: The process is reliant on the bank's electronic systems and any issues with the bank can delay payments.

Best Practices:

- Accurate Setup: Ensure bank details and payment templates are correctly configured.

- Authorization Controls: Implement strict authorization processes for initiating EFTs.

- Audit Trails: Maintain detailed records of all electronic transactions for auditing purposes.

3. Credit Cards

Overview:

Paying vendors via credit cards is becoming increasingly popular due to convenience and the potential for rewards or cash back.

Process:

Oracle ERP allows for the setup of credit card payment options. This involves entering the credit card details and selecting it as a payment method during the payment process.

Advantages:

- Convenience: Simplifies the payment process, especially for smaller or urgent transactions.

- Rewards: Companies can earn rewards points or cash back.

- Cash Flow Management: Delays the actual cash outflow, providing short-term cash flow benefits.

Disadvantages:

- Fees: Credit card transactions can incur higher fees.

- Limits: Credit cards often have transaction limits that may not be suitable for larger payments.

- Security Risks: Increased risk of fraud and misuse if credit card information is not securely handled.

Best Practices:

- Limit Usage: Use credit cards for smaller or urgent payments where the convenience outweighs the cost.

- Secure Handling: Ensure credit card information is stored securely and only accessible to authorized personnel.

- Regular Monitoring: Frequently monitor credit card transactions for any unauthorized or fraudulent activity.

4. Wire Transfers

Overview:

Wire transfers are a form of EFT but are typically used for high-value transactions or international payments due to their speed and reliability.

Process:

Oracle ERP can generate wire transfer instructions, which are then sent to the bank for processing. This involves providing the payee's bank details and ensuring all information is accurate to avoid delays.

Advantages:

- Speed: Wire transfers are one of the fastest methods for transferring funds, often completed within hours.

- Reliability: Highly reliable and suitable for large transactions.

- Global Reach: Ideal for international payments where other methods might not be feasible.

Disadvantages:

- Cost: Wire transfers can be expensive, with higher fees compared to other methods.

- Complexity: Requires precise information to avoid errors or delays.

- Irreversibility: Once a wire transfer is initiated, it is challenging to reverse, making accuracy critical.

Best Practices:

- Double-Check Details: Verify all recipient bank details to avoid costly mistakes.

- Authorization: Implement strict authorization protocols for wire transfers.

- Documentation: Keep detailed records of all wire transfers, including confirmation receipts and transaction IDs.

5. Cash Payments

Overview:

Though less common in a corporate setting, cash payments might still be used for certain transactions, particularly small or immediate needs.

Process:

Oracle ERP can record cash payments made to vendors. This involves manually entering the payment details and ensuring they are accurately reflected in the system.

Advantages:

- Immediate Settlement: Cash payments provide immediate settlement of transactions.

- Simplicity: Straightforward for small, on-the-spot transactions.

Disadvantages:

- Security: Handling large amounts of cash poses significant security risks.

- Lack of Traceability: Cash payments are harder to trace and audit.

- Limited Use: Not practical for large transactions or vendors that prefer electronic payments.

Best Practices:

- Minimize Use: Use cash payments only when necessary and for small amounts.

- Secure Handling: Ensure cash is handled securely and stored in a safe location until it can be deposited.

- Detailed Records: Keep detailed records of all cash payments for auditing purposes.

6. Bank Drafts

Overview:

Bank drafts, also known as cashier's checks, are issued by a bank and guaranteed by the bank's funds, making them a secure form of payment.

Process:

In Oracle ERP, bank drafts can be requested and recorded similarly to checks. The funds are withdrawn from the company's account and the bank issues the draft to the payee.

Advantages:

- Security: Bank drafts are less prone to fraud since they are backed by the bank.

- Certainty of Payment: Ensures the payee that the funds are available.

- Widely Accepted: Often used for large or important transactions.

Disadvantages:

- Cost: Banks may charge fees for issuing drafts.

- Time-Consuming: Obtaining a bank draft requires a visit to the bank.

- Inflexibility: Once issued, the draft cannot be easily canceled or altered.

Best Practices:

- Plan Ahead: Request bank drafts in advance to avoid delays.

- Keep Records: Maintain detailed records of all bank drafts issued and ensure they are properly documented in the ERP system.

- Secure Storage: Handle bank drafts securely to prevent loss or theft.

Conclusion

Understanding and utilizing the different payment methods supported by Oracle ERP is essential for efficient and effective financial management within the Accounts Payable module. Each payment method has its advantages and disadvantages, and choosing the right one depends on various factors, including transaction size, urgency, cost, and security considerations. By implementing best practices and maintaining strict controls, organizations can ensure that their payment processes are smooth, secure, and accurately reflected in their financial records.

4.1.3 Emphasize the importance of payment authorization and documentation

Payment authorization and documentation are crucial elements in the Accounts Payable (AP) module of Oracle ERP. Properly managing these aspects ensures financial accuracy, compliance, and accountability within an organization. Here, we delve into why these processes are indispensable and how they can be effectively managed in Oracle ERP.

1. Ensuring Financial Control and Accuracy

Payment authorization is the first line of defense against errors and fraud. By requiring multiple levels of approval, organizations can ensure that only legitimate and accurate payments are processed. This involves setting up workflows where each payment must be reviewed and authorized by designated personnel before execution. In Oracle ERP, this can be configured using approval hierarchies and automated workflows, which help maintain a robust internal control system.

Documentation serves as a record of all financial transactions, providing a trail that can be audited at any time. Each manual payment should be accompanied by supporting documents, such as invoices, receipts, and purchase orders. Oracle ERP allows users to attach these documents directly to the payment records, ensuring that all necessary information is stored in a centralized location for easy access and review.

2. Enhancing Compliance and Auditability

Compliance with internal policies and external regulations is another critical reason for rigorous payment authorization and documentation. Organizations must adhere to regulatory requirements such as the Sarbanes-Oxley Act (SOX) in the United States, which mandates stringent internal controls and documentation for financial transactions.

Oracle ERP supports compliance by enabling detailed audit trails for all payments. Every action taken within the system, from payment initiation to final authorization, is logged with timestamps and user details. This level of transparency ensures that organizations can demonstrate compliance during internal and external audits, mitigating the risk of regulatory penalties.

3. Reducing Fraud and Operational Risks

Fraud prevention is a significant benefit of enforcing strict payment authorization protocols. By requiring multiple approvals, the likelihood of unauthorized or fraudulent payments is significantly reduced. In Oracle ERP, segregation of duties can be implemented to ensure that no single individual has control over all aspects of the payment process. For instance, one person may be responsible for entering the payment details, while another person must approve the payment.

Documentation further mitigates fraud risk by providing evidence for every transaction. In cases of discrepancies or suspected fraud, the documentation can be reviewed to identify any irregularities or unauthorized actions. Oracle ERP's document management features allow for secure storage and easy retrieval of all supporting documents, enhancing the overall security of the payment process.

4. Facilitating Dispute Resolution and Accountability

Disputes may arise regarding payments, whether from suppliers questioning payment amounts or internal stakeholders seeking clarification on transactions. Comprehensive documentation helps resolve these disputes swiftly and accurately. By maintaining detailed records, organizations can provide evidence to support their payment decisions, ensuring transparency and accountability.

Oracle ERP's centralized document repository and audit trail features facilitate efficient dispute resolution. Authorized users can quickly access relevant documents and transaction histories to address any queries or issues. This capability not only improves relationships with suppliers but also reinforces accountability within the organization.

5. Streamlining Financial Reporting and Analysis

Accurate and thorough documentation is essential for reliable financial reporting. Payment records, along with their supporting documents, provide the data needed for various financial reports, such as cash flow statements and expense analyses. These reports are crucial for strategic decision-making and financial planning.

Oracle ERP's reporting tools can generate comprehensive financial reports based on the documented payment transactions. By ensuring that all payments are properly authorized and documented, organizations can trust the integrity of their financial data, leading to more informed and effective decision-making.

Implementing Effective Authorization and Documentation Practices in Oracle ERP

To maximize the benefits of payment authorization and documentation, organizations should implement best practices within Oracle ERP:

- Define Clear Approval Workflows: Establish and configure approval hierarchies that align with organizational policies. Ensure that workflows require multiple levels of approval for payments above certain thresholds.

- Centralize Documentation: Utilize Oracle ERP's document management capabilities to attach and store all supporting documents related to payments. This centralization ensures that documentation is complete and easily accessible.

- Enforce Segregation of Duties: Implement role-based access controls to segregate duties among employees. Ensure that individuals responsible for initiating payments are not the same as those approving them.

- Regular Audits and Reviews: Conduct periodic audits of payment transactions and documentation to identify and address any discrepancies or compliance issues. Use Oracle ERP's audit trail features to facilitate these reviews.

- Training and Awareness: Educate employees on the importance of payment authorization and documentation. Provide training on using Oracle ERP's features to ensure compliance with internal controls and regulatory requirements.

Conclusion

The importance of payment authorization and documentation in the Accounts Payable module cannot be overstated. These practices ensure financial control, compliance, fraud prevention, dispute resolution, and accurate financial reporting. By leveraging the capabilities of Oracle ERP, organizations can implement robust authorization workflows and centralized documentation processes, safeguarding their financial integrity and operational efficiency.

4.2 Setting Up and Running Automatic Payments

4.2.1 Describe the process of setting up and running automatic payments in the Accounts Payable module

Setting up and running automatic payments in the Accounts Payable (AP) module of Oracle ERP involves several critical steps. These steps are designed to ensure efficiency, accuracy, and compliance with organizational policies and vendor agreements. Below is a detailed description of this process.

1. Configuring Payment Methods:

The first step in setting up automatic payments is to configure the payment methods that your organization will use. Oracle ERP supports various payment methods, including electronic funds transfer (EFT), checks, and wire transfers.

- Electronic Funds Transfer (EFT): EFT is the most common method for automatic payments due to its efficiency and reduced processing time. To configure EFT, you need to set up bank accounts and define payment formats compatible with your bank.

- Checks: For organizations that still use checks, it's essential to configure the check printing process and ensure that checks are printed accurately and securely.

- Wire Transfers: Wire transfers are often used for high-value or international payments. Configuring wire transfers involves setting up the necessary bank details and ensuring that the process complies with banking regulations.

2. Defining Payment Terms and Schedules:

Once the payment methods are configured, the next step is to define the payment terms and schedules. Payment terms specify when invoices are due for payment, and they can include early payment discounts or late payment penalties.

- Payment Terms: Set up payment terms based on vendor agreements. Common payment terms include Net 30 (payment due in 30 days) or Net 60 (payment due in 60 days). Ensure that these terms are accurately reflected in the AP module.

- Payment Schedules: Define payment schedules to determine how often payments are processed. For example, you might schedule payments to run weekly, bi-weekly, or monthly. This schedule ensures that payments are made on time without manual intervention.

3. Creating Payment Batches:

After configuring payment methods and defining payment terms, the next step is to create payment batches. Payment batches group multiple invoices for payment processing, which streamlines the payment process.

- Batch Creation: Create payment batches based on criteria such as due date, payment method, or vendor. This grouping ensures that all due invoices are processed together, reducing the administrative burden.

- Batch Review: Review payment batches for accuracy before processing. This review includes verifying invoice amounts, checking for duplicate invoices, and ensuring that all necessary approvals are in place.

4. Setting Up Approval Workflows:

Approval workflows are essential to ensure that all payments are authorized before processing. These workflows help prevent fraudulent payments and ensure compliance with organizational policies.

- Approval Hierarchies: Define approval hierarchies based on the organization's structure. For example, payments above a certain threshold may require additional approvals from senior management.

- Workflow Configuration: Configure the AP module to route payment batches through the appropriate approval workflows. This configuration ensures that payments are only processed after receiving the necessary approvals.

5. Running the Automatic Payment Process:

With all configurations in place, the next step is to run the automatic payment process. This process involves several stages, including selecting invoices, generating payment files, and transmitting payments.

- Invoice Selection: The AP module automatically selects invoices for payment based on the defined payment terms and schedules. Ensure that all selected invoices are due for payment and meet the criteria set during batch creation.

- Payment File Generation: Generate payment files based on the configured payment methods. For EFT payments, the system creates a file that can be uploaded to the bank for processing. For checks, the system generates a file for check printing.

- Payment Transmission: Transmit the payment files to the bank for processing. Ensure that all necessary security measures are in place to protect the payment information during transmission.

6. Monitoring and Reconciliation:

After running the automatic payment process, it's crucial to monitor and reconcile the payments. This step ensures that all payments are processed correctly and that any issues are promptly addressed.

- Monitoring: Use the AP module's monitoring tools to track the status of payments. These tools provide real-time updates on payment processing and highlight any errors or issues.

- Reconciliation: Reconcile the payments with bank statements to ensure that all payments are processed accurately. This reconciliation involves comparing the payment records in the AP module with the bank's records and addressing any discrepancies.

7. Handling Payment Exceptions:

During the payment process, exceptions may occur, such as payment rejections or insufficient funds. It's essential to have procedures in place to handle these exceptions efficiently.

- Payment Rejections: If a payment is rejected by the bank, identify the reason for the rejection and take corrective action. Common reasons for rejection include incorrect bank details or insufficient funds.

- Insufficient Funds: If there are insufficient funds in the bank account, prioritize payments based on criticality and communicate with vendors about potential delays.

8. Reporting and Documentation:

Finally, ensure that all payment processes are well-documented and that comprehensive reports are generated for audit and compliance purposes.

- Documentation: Maintain detailed records of all payment configurations, approval workflows, and payment batches. This documentation is essential for audit trails and future reference.

- Reporting: Generate reports on payment activity, including the total amount paid, payment methods used, and any exceptions encountered. These reports provide valuable insights into the organization's payment processes and help identify areas for improvement.

Conclusion:

Setting up and running automatic payments in the Accounts Payable module of Oracle ERP involves a series of well-defined steps. By configuring payment methods, defining payment terms, creating payment batches, setting up approval workflows, running the payment process, monitoring and reconciling payments, handling exceptions, and maintaining thorough documentation and reporting, organizations can achieve efficient, accurate, and compliant payment processing. This streamlined approach not only saves time and reduces errors but also ensures that vendor relationships are maintained and cash flow is managed effectively..

4.2.2 Explain the benefits of using automatic payments for efficiency and timeliness

processes. 4.2 Setting Up and Running Automatic Payments

 b. Explain the Benefits of Using Automatic Payments for Efficiency and Timeliness

The implementation of automatic payments in the Accounts Payable (AP) module of Oracle ERP offers several significant benefits, particularly in terms of efficiency and timeliness. These benefits are vital for streamlining financial operations, enhancing cash flow management, and ensuring timely payments to vendors. The following points detail the key advantages of using automatic payments within the AP module:

1. Increased Operational Efficiency

  - Automation of Routine Tasks: By automating the payment process, organizations can reduce the manual effort required to process payments. This allows accounts payable staff to focus on more strategic activities, such as analyzing spending patterns and negotiating better terms with suppliers.

  - Reduction of Errors: Manual payment processing is prone to human errors, such as incorrect data entry or miscalculation. Automatic payments minimize these errors by ensuring that data is consistently and accurately handled according to predefined rules and workflows.

2. Timeliness of Payments

  - Adherence to Payment Schedules: Automatic payments ensure that invoices are paid on time according to the terms agreed upon with vendors. This not only helps in maintaining good supplier relationships but also avoids late payment penalties.

  - Improved Cash Flow Management: With automatic payments, organizations can better manage their cash flow by scheduling payments to optimize the use of available funds. This can prevent overdrafts and ensure that sufficient liquidity is maintained for other operational needs.

3. Cost Savings

  - Reduction in Processing Costs: Automating the payment process reduces the administrative costs associated with manual payment handling, including the costs of printing and mailing checks. Additionally, electronic payments are often less expensive than paper checks.

- Avoidance of Late Fees and Penalties: By ensuring that payments are made on time, automatic payments help organizations avoid late fees and penalties, which can accumulate and become a significant financial burden.

4. Enhanced Security and Control

- Secure Payment Transactions: Automatic payments often utilize secure electronic payment methods, such as Automated Clearing House (ACH) transfers or electronic funds transfers (EFTs), which reduce the risk of fraud associated with paper checks.

- Consistent Payment Authorization: The AP module can be configured to follow strict authorization protocols for automatic payments, ensuring that only approved invoices are paid. This provides an added layer of control and compliance with internal financial policies.

5. Improved Vendor Relationships

- Reliable Payment Practices: Consistent and timely payments demonstrate reliability to vendors, fostering stronger business relationships. This can lead to more favorable terms, discounts, and a more collaborative partnership.

- Streamlined Communication: Automatic payments reduce the need for frequent follow-ups and queries from vendors regarding payment status, leading to smoother and more efficient communication.

6. Scalability

- Handling High Volumes: As businesses grow, the volume of invoices and payments increases. Automatic payment systems can easily scale to handle larger volumes without a corresponding increase in manual effort, ensuring that the payment process remains efficient and effective.

- Adaptability to Business Needs: The flexibility of automatic payment systems allows organizations to adapt their payment processes to changing business needs, such as new payment methods, different currencies, and varying payment terms.

7. Enhanced Reporting and Compliance

 - Accurate Financial Reporting: Automated payment processes provide accurate and real-time data on payment statuses, cash outflows, and vendor balances. This enhances the accuracy of financial reporting and supports better decision-making.

 - Regulatory Compliance: Automatic payments can be configured to comply with various regulatory requirements, such as tax reporting and audit trails. This ensures that organizations remain compliant with relevant laws and regulations, reducing the risk of fines and penalties.

8. Resource Optimization

 - Optimized Use of Human Resources: By reducing the manual workload associated with payment processing, automatic payments allow finance teams to allocate their resources more effectively. Staff can focus on higher-value tasks that contribute to the organization's strategic goals.

 - Efficiency in Managing Multiple Accounts: For organizations with multiple bank accounts or subsidiaries, automatic payments simplify the management of payments across different entities, ensuring that funds are appropriately allocated and managed.

9. Integration with Other Systems

 - Seamless Integration: Automatic payments can be integrated with other financial systems and modules within Oracle ERP, such as General Ledger (GL), Cash Management, and Procurement. This integration ensures that payment data is consistently and accurately reflected across all financial records.

 - Real-Time Updates: Integration with other systems provides real-time updates on payment statuses, account balances, and vendor information, enhancing the overall visibility and control of financial operations.

10. Strategic Financial Planning

 - Data-Driven Insights: The data generated from automatic payment processes can be used for strategic financial planning and analysis. Organizations can gain insights into spending patterns, vendor performance, and cash flow trends, supporting more informed decision-making.

- Forecasting and Budgeting: Automatic payments contribute to more accurate forecasting and budgeting by providing reliable data on expected cash outflows. This helps organizations plan their finances more effectively and allocate resources where they are needed most.

In conclusion, the adoption of automatic payments within the Accounts Payable module of Oracle ERP offers substantial benefits in terms of efficiency and timeliness. By streamlining payment processes, reducing errors, and ensuring timely payments, organizations can improve their financial operations, enhance vendor relationships, and achieve significant cost savings. Furthermore, the enhanced security, scalability, and integration capabilities of automatic payments support better compliance and strategic financial planning, making it a critical component of modern financial management.

4.2.3 Discuss the different options for scheduling and managing automatic payments

In the Oracle ERP Accounts Payable module, the ability to set up and run automatic payments is crucial for maintaining efficiency and ensuring timely payments to vendors. Automatic payments streamline the process, reduce manual intervention, and help maintain a good relationship with suppliers. In this section, we will delve into the various options available for scheduling and managing automatic payments, highlighting their features, benefits, and implementation steps.

Scheduling Options for Automatic Payments

1. Fixed Schedule Payments

- Description: Fixed schedule payments are set up to occur at regular, predefined intervals. This could be daily, weekly, bi-weekly, monthly, or any other consistent timeframe.

- Benefits: Provides predictability and consistency, ensuring that payments are always made on time. It helps in managing cash flow efficiently as the outflows are predictable.

- Implementation Steps:

1. Navigate to the Automatic Payments Setup Screen: Access the Accounts Payable module and locate the setup for automatic payments.

2. Define Payment Frequency: Specify the frequency of the payments. For example, select "monthly" for monthly payments.

3. Select Payment Date: Choose a specific date or day of the week when the payments should be processed.

4. Assign Vendors: Link the appropriate vendors to this payment schedule.

5. Save and Activate Schedule: Confirm the details and activate the schedule to ensure it runs as specified.

2. Ad-Hoc or One-Time Payments

- Description: These payments are scheduled on an as-needed basis rather than at regular intervals. They are typically used for unique or unexpected payment needs.

- Benefits: Provides flexibility to handle non-recurring payments without disrupting the regular payment cycle.

- Implementation Steps:

1. Access the Payment Scheduling Interface: Go to the Accounts Payable module and find the option for scheduling ad-hoc payments.

2. Select Payment Date: Choose the specific date on which the payment should be processed.

3. Enter Vendor Details: Input the necessary details for the vendor who will receive the payment.

4. Confirm and Schedule: Verify the payment details and schedule the payment.

3. Milestone-Based Payments

- Description: Payments are scheduled based on the achievement of specific milestones. This is common in project-based work where payments are tied to the completion of certain tasks or phases.

- Benefits: Ensures that payments are aligned with project progress, providing financial control and ensuring accountability.

- Implementation Steps:

1. Identify Project Milestones: Define the key milestones that will trigger payments.

2. Configure Milestone Payment Schedule: Set up the automatic payment to be triggered upon the completion of each milestone.

3. Link to Project Management Module: Integrate the payment schedule with the project management module to automatically recognize milestone completion.

4. Activate and Monitor: Activate the schedule and monitor the milestone achievements to ensure timely payments.

4. Threshold-Based Payments

- Description: Payments are triggered when certain financial thresholds are met, such as reaching a minimum invoice amount.

- Benefits: Helps manage cash flow by ensuring payments are made only when necessary thresholds are met, preventing frequent small payments.

- Implementation Steps:

1. Set Financial Thresholds: Define the minimum invoice amount or other financial criteria that will trigger a payment.

2. Configure Payment Triggers: Set up the system to automatically schedule payments when these thresholds are reached.

3. Assign Vendors and Invoices: Link the relevant vendors and their invoices to this payment setup.

4. Activate and Review: Activate the threshold-based payment schedule and periodically review to ensure it operates as expected.

Managing Automatic Payments

1. Payment Batch Management

- Description: Automatic payments can be grouped into batches for easier management and processing. This is especially useful for organizations handling a large volume of transactions.

- Benefits: Simplifies the payment process by allowing multiple payments to be processed together, reducing administrative overhead.

- Implementation Steps:

1. Create Payment Batches: Set up payment batches within the Accounts Payable module.

2. Assign Payments to Batches: Link individual payments to the appropriate batch based on criteria such as due date or vendor.

3. Review and Approve Batches: Periodically review the batches to ensure all included payments are accurate and necessary.

4. Process Batches: Initiate the processing of the payment batches as per the schedule.

2. Payment Approvals Workflow

- Description: Implementing a workflow for payment approvals ensures that all automatic payments undergo a review process before being processed.

- Benefits: Adds a layer of oversight and control, reducing the risk of errors or unauthorized payments.

- Implementation Steps:

1. Define Approval Workflow: Set up the approval workflow within the Accounts Payable module, specifying the stages and approvers.

2. Assign Roles and Responsibilities: Designate the individuals responsible for each stage of the approval process.

3. Configure Notification Alerts: Set up notifications to alert approvers when payments are pending approval.

4. Monitor and Audit: Continuously monitor the approval process and conduct regular audits to ensure compliance.

3. Integration with Banking Systems

- Description: Integrating the Accounts Payable module with banking systems allows for seamless execution of automatic payments.

- Benefits: Reduces manual intervention, minimizes errors, and ensures timely payment execution.

- Implementation Steps:

1. Set Up Bank Integration: Configure the integration between the Oracle ERP system and the organization's banking systems.

2. Test Integration: Conduct thorough testing to ensure data flows correctly between the systems.

3. Automate Payment File Transfers: Set up automatic transfers of payment files to the bank.

4. Monitor Transactions: Regularly monitor the transactions to ensure they are processed correctly and timely.

4. Reconciliation and Reporting

- Description: Regular reconciliation and reporting are essential to ensure the accuracy of automatic payments and to provide visibility into the organization's cash flow.

- Benefits: Ensures financial accuracy, supports auditing requirements, and provides insights into payment trends and cash flow.

- Implementation Steps:

1. Set Up Reconciliation Processes: Define the processes for reconciling payments with bank statements and other financial records.

2. Generate Regular Reports: Schedule regular reports that detail all automatic payments, including any discrepancies.

3. Review and Adjust: Periodically review the reconciliation reports and make any necessary adjustments to the payment schedules.

4. Audit and Compliance: Ensure that the reconciliation and reporting processes meet all audit and compliance requirements.

5. Handling Payment Exceptions

- Description: Not all payments go as planned; exceptions can occur due to various reasons such as insufficient funds, vendor disputes, or system errors. Managing these exceptions is crucial.

- Benefits: Helps in identifying and resolving issues promptly, ensuring that vendors are paid correctly and on time.

- Implementation Steps:

1. Define Exception Handling Procedures: Establish procedures for identifying, recording, and resolving payment exceptions.

2. Implement Alert Mechanisms: Set up alerts to notify relevant personnel when exceptions occur.

3. Resolve Exceptions Promptly: Assign responsibility for resolving exceptions and ensure they are addressed in a timely manner.

4. Track and Report: Maintain records of all exceptions and their resolutions, and generate reports to identify trends and areas for improvement.

6. Vendor Communication and Support

- Description: Keeping vendors informed about their payment status is essential for maintaining good relationships and ensuring smooth operations.

- Benefits: Enhances vendor satisfaction, reduces inquiries, and supports transparency.

- Implementation Steps:

1. Automate Vendor Notifications: Set up automated notifications to inform vendors about payment schedules, status, and any changes.

2. Provide Self-Service Portals: Offer vendors access to self-service portals where they can view their payment status and history.

3. Establish Support Channels: Ensure that vendors have access to support channels for any payment-related inquiries or issues.

4. Monitor Vendor Feedback: Regularly collect and review feedback from vendors to improve the payment process.

Best Practices for Managing Automatic Payments

1. Regular Review and Optimization

- Conduct regular reviews of the automatic payment schedules and processes to identify areas for optimization.

- Ensure that the schedules align with current business needs and cash flow requirements.

2. Maintain Up-to-Date Vendor Information

- Keep vendor records current to avoid payment delays or errors.

- Regularly update vendor contact information, banking details, and payment terms.

3. Implement Robust Security Measures

- Protect sensitive payment information through encryption, secure access controls, and regular security audits.

- Ensure compliance with data protection regulations and industry standards.

4. Training and Documentation

- Provide comprehensive training for staff involved in managing automatic payments to ensure they understand the processes and best practices.

- Maintain detailed

documentation of all payment schedules, processes, and procedures for reference and audit purposes.

5. Leverage Technology and Automation

- Utilize the full capabilities of the Oracle ERP system to automate as much of the payment process as possible.

- Explore additional tools and integrations that can enhance the efficiency and accuracy of automatic payments.

By carefully scheduling and managing automatic payments in the Oracle ERP Accounts Payable module, organizations can significantly improve their financial operations. The different options for scheduling—fixed, ad-hoc, milestone-based, and threshold-based—offer flexibility to cater to various business needs. Effective management through batch processing, approval workflows, bank integration, reconciliation, exception handling, and vendor communication ensures that payments are processed smoothly and accurately, supporting overall financial health and vendor relationships.

4.3 Applying Prepayments and Credits

4.3.1 Explain the process of applying prepayments and credits to invoices in the Accounts Payable module

In the Oracle ERP Accounts Payable module, applying prepayments and credits to invoices is a crucial process that helps in managing cash flow and ensuring accurate financial records. This section will provide a detailed explanation of the steps involved in applying prepayments and credits.

Understanding Prepayments and Credits

Before diving into the process, it's essential to understand what prepayments and credits are in the context of Accounts Payable:

- Prepayments: These are payments made to vendors before the receipt of goods or services. Prepayments are typically made when a vendor requires advance payment or as a part of contractual agreements. Once the goods or services are received, the prepayment amount is applied to the invoice.

- Credits: These are amounts that reduce the balance of an invoice. Credits can arise from various situations such as returned goods, overpayments, or adjustments due to errors in the original invoice.

Steps to Apply Prepayments and Credits

The process of applying prepayments and credits involves several steps, which are outlined below:

1. Create the Prepayment or Credit Memo:

   - To apply a prepayment, you first need to create a prepayment invoice. This is done by entering an invoice in the Accounts Payable module and specifying it as a prepayment. You will enter the amount, vendor details, and other relevant information.

   - For credits, you need to create a credit memo. A credit memo is created by entering a negative amount invoice that references the original invoice number.

2. Matching Prepayments or Credits to Invoices:

- Once the prepayment or credit memo is created, you need to match it to the corresponding invoice. This is done through the "Match Invoices" window in Oracle ERP. You will select the invoice that you want to apply the prepayment or credit to and then select the appropriate prepayment or credit memo.

3. Applying the Prepayment or Credit:

- After matching, the next step is to apply the prepayment or credit. In the "Apply" window, you will specify the amount to be applied. For prepayments, you can apply the full amount or a partial amount depending on the total invoice value.

- Similarly, for credits, you can apply the credit amount to reduce the invoice balance.

4. Updating the Payment Schedule:

- Once the prepayment or credit is applied, the payment schedule for the invoice is updated. This ensures that the remaining balance, if any, is correctly reflected in the Accounts Payable ledger.

5. Reviewing and Approving the Application:

- It's important to review the application of prepayments and credits to ensure accuracy. This involves checking the vendor account, the invoice balance, and the applied amounts.

- Once reviewed, the application needs to be approved. Approval workflows can be configured in Oracle ERP to ensure that appropriate checks are in place.

6. Recording the Transaction:

- Finally, the transaction needs to be recorded in the general ledger. This involves posting the applied amounts to the appropriate accounts. For prepayments, this typically means moving the amount from a prepayment account to an expense account. For credits, the reduction is applied to the accounts payable balance.

Detailed Example: Applying a Prepayment

To illustrate the process, let's go through a detailed example of applying a prepayment:

Scenario:

A company, ABC Corp, has made a prepayment of $10,000 to a vendor, XYZ Ltd, for the supply of office furniture. The total invoice amount for the furniture is $15,000.

Step-by-Step Process:

1. Creating the Prepayment Invoice:

   - Navigate to the "Invoices" section in the Accounts Payable module.

   - Create a new invoice and select the type as "Prepayment."

   - Enter the vendor details (XYZ Ltd), amount ($10,000), and other required information.

   - Save and submit the prepayment invoice.

2. Receiving the Goods and Creating the Invoice:

   - Once the furniture is received, create a standard invoice for the total amount ($15,000) in the Accounts Payable module.

   - Ensure that all the details such as quantity, price, and vendor information are accurately entered.

3. Matching and Applying the Prepayment:

   - Navigate to the "Match Invoices" window.

   - Select the standard invoice ($15,000) and the prepayment invoice ($10,000).

   - In the "Apply" window, enter the amount to be applied ($10,000).

   - Confirm the application.

4. Updating the Payment Schedule:

   - The remaining balance on the invoice ($5,000) is updated in the payment schedule.

   - Ensure that the payment terms and due date are correctly reflected.

5. Review and Approval:

   - Review the vendor account to ensure that the prepayment has been correctly applied.

   - Follow the configured approval workflow to approve the application.

6. Recording the Transaction:

 - Post the transaction to the general ledger.

 - The $10,000 prepayment is moved from the prepayment account to the office furniture expense account.

 - The remaining $5,000 is recorded as an outstanding payable.

Detailed Example: Applying a Credit

Now, let's look at an example of applying a credit:

Scenario:

A company, ABC Corp, has received a credit memo of $500 from a vendor, XYZ Ltd, due to overbilling on a previous invoice. The original invoice amount was $2,000.

Step-by-Step Process:

1. Creating the Credit Memo:

 - Navigate to the "Invoices" section in the Accounts Payable module.

 - Create a new invoice and select the type as "Credit Memo."

 - Enter the vendor details (XYZ Ltd), amount (-$500), and reference the original invoice number.

 - Save and submit the credit memo.

2. Matching and Applying the Credit:

 - Navigate to the "Match Invoices" window.

 - Select the original invoice ($2,000) and the credit memo (-$500).

 - In the "Apply" window, enter the amount to be applied ($500).

 - Confirm the application.

3. Updating the Payment Schedule:

 - The remaining balance on the original invoice ($1,500) is updated in the payment schedule.

 - Ensure that the payment terms and due date are correctly reflected.

4. Review and Approval:

  - Review the vendor account to ensure that the credit has been correctly applied.

  - Follow the configured approval workflow to approve the application.

5. Recording the Transaction:

  - Post the transaction to the general ledger.

  - The $500 credit is recorded as a reduction in the accounts payable balance.

  - The remaining $1,500 is recorded as an outstanding payable.

 Best Practices for Applying Prepayments and Credits

1. Accurate Documentation:

 - Ensure that all prepayments and credits are accurately documented. This includes maintaining records of vendor agreements, payment terms, and credit memos.

2. Regular Reconciliation:

 - Regularly reconcile vendor accounts to ensure that prepayments and credits are correctly applied and reflected in the financial records.

3. Approval Workflows:

 - Implement robust approval workflows to ensure that prepayments and credits are authorized and reviewed before being applied.

4. Vendor Communication:

 - Maintain clear communication with vendors regarding prepayments and credits. Ensure that vendors are informed about the application of prepayments and any discrepancies are promptly addressed.

5. Training and Support:

 - Provide training and support to Accounts Payable staff on the process of applying prepayments and credits. This ensures consistency and accuracy in the application process.

In conclusion, applying prepayments and credits in the Oracle ERP Accounts Payable module is a detailed process that requires careful attention to detail and proper documentation. By following the outlined steps and best practices, organizations can effectively manage their payables and maintain accurate financial records.

4.3.2 Discuss the different types of prepayments and credits

In the Accounts Payable (AP) module of Oracle ERP, managing prepayments and credits is crucial for maintaining accurate financial records and optimizing cash flow. Understanding the various types of prepayments and credits and their application to invoices ensures that organizations can efficiently handle their payables and maintain a healthy financial status. This section explores the different types of prepayments and credits commonly encountered in the AP module, their characteristics, and their significance in financial management.

 Types of Prepayments

1. Advance Payments:

 - Definition: Advance payments are payments made to vendors before the receipt of goods or services. These are often required to secure orders, especially for large or custom orders.

 - Characteristics: Advance payments are typically made based on a purchase order or a contractual agreement. They are recorded in the AP module as a prepayment and are applied against future invoices.

 - Significance: Advance payments help establish trust with vendors and may be necessary to initiate production or procurement processes. They also affect cash flow since funds are disbursed before receiving the corresponding goods or services.

2. Deposit Payments:

   - Definition: Deposit payments are similar to advance payments but are specifically used to secure a portion of the total cost of goods or services. These are often used in industries where significant upfront costs are incurred by the vendor.

   - Characteristics: Deposits are usually a percentage of the total order value and are applied to the final invoice upon completion of the order. They are recorded as a liability until the corresponding goods or services are received.

   - Significance: Deposits ensure commitment from both parties and help vendors manage their initial costs. They are crucial for managing cash flow and budgeting for both the vendor and the purchasing organization.

3. Retainer Payments:

   - Definition: Retainer payments are advance payments made to secure the availability of services from a vendor or contractor. These are common in professional services, legal, and consultancy sectors.

   - Characteristics: Retainers are recorded as prepayments and are typically applied against the invoices for services rendered over a specified period.

   - Significance: Retainer payments guarantee the availability of specialized services when needed and help in managing long-term relationships with service providers. They also impact cash flow and financial planning.

 Types of Credits

1. Credit Memos:

   - Definition: Credit memos are documents issued by vendors to reduce the amount owed by the purchasing organization. These are often provided as compensation for returned goods, overpayments, or billing errors.

   - Characteristics: Credit memos are recorded in the AP module and can be applied against future invoices from the same vendor. They reduce the outstanding payable amount and are essential for accurate financial reporting.

- Significance: Credit memos ensure that the purchasing organization is not overcharged and help maintain accurate financial records. They also improve vendor relationships by providing a mechanism for resolving billing discrepancies.

2. Debit Memos:

- Definition: Debit memos are issued by the purchasing organization to the vendor, requesting a reduction in the payable amount. These are used when goods are returned, or services are not fully rendered as per the agreement.

- Characteristics: Debit memos are recorded in the AP module as reductions in the outstanding payable amount. They require vendor approval and subsequent issuance of a corresponding credit memo.

- Significance: Debit memos provide a formal method for requesting adjustments to payable amounts, ensuring that the purchasing organization pays only for received and accepted goods or services. They also facilitate effective vendor communication and dispute resolution.

3. Prepayment Credits:

- Definition: Prepayment credits are credits applied to invoices based on previously made advance or deposit payments. These credits are used to offset the total payable amount when the final invoice is issued.

- Characteristics: Prepayment credits are recorded in the AP module and are automatically applied to the corresponding invoices. They reduce the amount payable and are essential for accurate financial accounting.

- Significance: Prepayment credits ensure that advance and deposit payments are appropriately accounted for, reducing the risk of overpayment. They also streamline the payment process and improve cash flow management.

4. Discount Credits:

- Definition: Discount credits are credits offered by vendors for early payment of invoices. These are often part of negotiated payment terms to incentivize timely payments.

- Characteristics: Discount credits are recorded in the AP module and applied when payments are made within the discount period. They reduce the payable amount and provide financial benefits to the purchasing organization.

- Significance: Discount credits encourage timely payments, improving vendor relationships and resulting in cost savings for the purchasing organization. They also enhance cash flow management by reducing the total amount payable.

Practical Applications of Prepayments and Credits

1. Applying Prepayments to Invoices:

- Process: Prepayments are applied to invoices by matching the prepayment records with the corresponding invoices. This is done in the AP module by selecting the prepayment and applying it to the open invoice.

- Example: If a company made an advance payment of $10,000 for an order, this amount would be recorded as a prepayment. When the invoice for the order is received, the prepayment is applied, reducing the payable amount by $10,000.

2. Managing Credit Memos:

- Process: Credit memos are managed by recording them in the AP module and applying them to open invoices. This ensures that the payable amount is accurately reduced based on the credit memo amount.

- Example: If a vendor issues a credit memo for $500 due to returned goods, this amount is applied to the next invoice, reducing the amount payable by $500.

3. Utilizing Discount Credits:

- Process: Discount credits are applied when payments are made within the discount period. The AP module calculates the discount based on the payment terms and reduces the payable amount accordingly.

- Example: If an invoice of $1,000 offers a 2% discount for payment within 10 days, and the payment is made within this period, a discount credit of $20 is applied, reducing the payable amount to $980.

Impact of Prepayments and Credits on Cash Flow Management

Effective management of prepayments and credits significantly impacts cash flow management. By understanding the different types of prepayments and credits and their application, organizations can:

1. Optimize Cash Flow: Proper application of prepayments and credits ensures that funds are not tied up unnecessarily, improving overall cash flow. This enables organizations to manage their financial resources more effectively.

2. Enhance Financial Accuracy: Accurate recording and application of prepayments and credits ensure that financial records reflect the true financial position of the organization. This enhances financial reporting and compliance with accounting standards.

3. Improve Vendor Relationships: Timely and accurate application of prepayments and credits fosters trust and reliability in vendor relationships. It ensures that vendors are paid correctly and any discrepancies are resolved promptly.

4. Streamline Payment Processes: Efficient handling of prepayments and credits simplifies the payment process, reducing administrative overhead and minimizing errors. This leads to more efficient accounts payable operations.

5. Leverage Discounts: By taking advantage of discount credits, organizations can achieve cost savings and improve their bottom line. Timely payments within discount periods result in direct financial benefits.

Conclusion

In the AP module of Oracle ERP, understanding and managing the different types of prepayments and credits is crucial for maintaining accurate financial records and optimizing cash flow. Advance payments, deposit payments, and retainer payments serve as essential tools for securing orders and services, while credit memos, debit memos, prepayment credits, and discount credits provide mechanisms for adjusting payable amounts. Proper application of these prepayments and credits ensures efficient accounts payable processes, enhances financial accuracy, and improves vendor relationships, ultimately contributing to the overall financial health of the organization.

4.3.3 Emphasize the impact of prepayments and credits on cash flow management

In the context of Accounts Payable (AP) management, prepayments and credits play a critical role in influencing an organization's cash flow. Understanding and effectively managing these elements is essential for maintaining healthy financial operations and ensuring efficient cash flow management.

1. Enhancing Liquidity Management

Prepayments, or advance payments made to suppliers, can significantly affect an organization's liquidity. By making prepayments, companies temporarily reduce their available cash reserves. However, this practice might be necessary to secure favorable terms or to establish strong relationships with key suppliers. Managing prepayments involves careful planning to ensure that the company's liquidity remains sufficient to cover other operational expenses. Balancing the timing and amount of prepayments is crucial to avoid cash shortages and ensure continuous business operations.

2. Optimizing Working Capital

Credits received from suppliers, on the other hand, provide an opportunity to optimize working capital. When suppliers offer credits, companies can delay payments without incurring penalties. This delay allows the organization to use the available cash for other critical needs, such as investing in inventory, paying off short-term liabilities, or seizing new business opportunities. Efficiently managing supplier credits helps improve the company's working capital position, which is a key indicator of financial health.

3. Managing Cash Flow Timing

The timing of prepayments and credits directly impacts cash flow cycles. Prepayments require careful scheduling to align with the company's cash flow forecasts. Making prepayments too early can strain the cash flow, while delaying them may lead to missed opportunities or strained supplier relationships. Conversely, effectively utilizing credits requires monitoring due dates and ensuring that payments are made just in time to avoid penalties while maximizing cash on hand. Proper timing ensures a smooth cash flow cycle, reducing the risk of liquidity issues.

4. Negotiating Favorable Terms

Negotiating favorable payment terms with suppliers is a strategic approach to managing prepayments and credits. Companies can leverage their financial stability and purchasing volume to negotiate extended credit terms, discounts for early payments, or other beneficial arrangements. These negotiations can lead to improved cash flow management by allowing the organization to retain cash for longer periods or benefit from cost savings through early payment discounts. Effective negotiation skills are essential for finance and procurement teams to optimize cash flow.

5. Impact on Financial Planning and Forecasting

Accurate financial planning and forecasting depend on the precise management of prepayments and credits. Prepayments must be accounted for in financial projections to ensure that cash flow forecasts reflect the actual cash outflows. Similarly, credits should be tracked to anticipate future cash outflows accurately. Incorporating these elements into financial models helps organizations make informed decisions, plan for future cash needs, and avoid unexpected cash flow disruptions. Regularly updating forecasts based on actual prepayments and credits ensures that financial plans remain relevant and reliable.

6. Compliance and Reporting

Properly managing prepayments and credits is crucial for compliance with accounting standards and regulatory requirements. Prepayments must be accurately recorded as assets on the balance sheet until the corresponding goods or services are received. Similarly, credits should be correctly documented to reflect the company's liabilities accurately. Ensuring compliance with accounting standards helps maintain the integrity of financial statements and provides stakeholders with a clear and accurate picture of the organization's financial position. Transparent reporting of prepayments and credits also facilitates external audits and regulatory reviews.

7. Reducing the Risk of Fraud

Effective management of prepayments and credits can mitigate the risk of fraud. Implementing robust controls and approval processes for prepayments ensures that only authorized transactions are executed. Regular reconciliation of supplier credits helps detect any discrepancies or unauthorized adjustments. By maintaining a strong internal control environment, organizations can safeguard against fraudulent activities and ensure that prepayments and credits are accurately recorded and utilized for legitimate business purposes.

8. Enhancing Supplier Relationships

Proactive management of prepayments and credits can strengthen supplier relationships. Timely prepayments demonstrate a company's commitment to fulfilling its obligations, fostering trust and reliability. Suppliers are more likely to offer favorable terms, prioritize orders, and provide better service to companies that consistently meet their payment commitments. Positive supplier relationships can lead to preferential treatment, better pricing, and increased collaboration, ultimately benefiting the organization's cash flow and overall business operations.

9. Cash Flow Management Strategies

To effectively manage prepayments and credits, organizations should implement comprehensive cash flow management strategies. These strategies may include:

- Cash Flow Forecasting: Regularly updating cash flow forecasts to reflect anticipated prepayments and credits, allowing for proactive cash management.

- Payment Scheduling: Establishing a schedule for prepayments and credit utilization that aligns with cash flow needs and supplier terms.

- Credit Utilization Policies: Defining policies for the optimal use of supplier credits, including criteria for selecting which credits to utilize and when.

- Monitoring and Reporting: Implementing systems to monitor prepayments and credits, track their impact on cash flow, and generate regular reports for management review.

10. Case Studies and Best Practices

Examining case studies and industry best practices can provide valuable insights into the effective management of prepayments and credits. Learning from organizations that have successfully optimized their cash flow through strategic prepayment and credit management can inspire new approaches and solutions. Best practices may include leveraging technology for automated payment processing, establishing clear communication channels with suppliers, and continuously reviewing and adjusting cash flow management strategies.

11. Technology and Automation

Leveraging technology and automation can significantly enhance the management of prepayments and credits. Advanced ERP systems like Oracle ERP offer features that streamline the tracking, processing, and reporting of prepayments and credits. Automation reduces manual errors, accelerates payment processes, and provides real-time visibility into cash flow positions. Implementing these technologies allows finance teams to focus on strategic cash flow management rather than administrative tasks, ultimately improving efficiency and accuracy.

12. Continuous Improvement

Effective cash flow management through prepayments and credits requires continuous improvement and adaptation. Regularly reviewing and refining cash flow management practices based on changing business needs, market conditions, and supplier dynamics ensures that organizations remain agile and resilient. Continuous improvement efforts may involve conducting cash flow analysis, seeking feedback from suppliers, and staying informed about industry trends and best practices.

Conclusion

In conclusion, the impact of prepayments and credits on cash flow management cannot be overstated. Properly managing these elements enhances liquidity, optimizes working capital, improves financial planning, ensures compliance, reduces fraud risk, and strengthens supplier relationships. By implementing strategic cash flow management practices, leveraging technology, and continuously improving processes, organizations can achieve a balanced and efficient cash flow, supporting sustainable growth and financial stability.

4.4 Issuing Adjustments and Refunds

4.4.1 Describe the process of issuing adjustments and refunds for invoices in the Accounts Payable module

Issuing adjustments and refunds for invoices in the Accounts Payable (AP) module of Oracle ERP is a critical process that ensures financial accuracy and compliance. Adjustments and refunds can arise due to various reasons such as overpayments, returned goods, pricing errors, or duplicate payments. Here, we will outline the detailed steps involved in issuing adjustments and refunds, the types of adjustments, and how they impact the accounting records.

1. Identifying the Need for an Adjustment or Refund

The first step in issuing adjustments and refunds is identifying the need for such actions. This usually occurs during the invoice reconciliation process, where discrepancies between the invoice and the actual goods received or services rendered are discovered. Common scenarios include:

- Overpayments: When a payment exceeds the invoice amount.

- Returned Goods: When goods are returned to the supplier after payment.

- Pricing Errors: When there is a discrepancy in the pricing agreed upon and the amount invoiced.

- Duplicate Payments: When an invoice is accidentally paid more than once.

2. Authorization and Documentation

Before proceeding with adjustments or refunds, it is crucial to obtain the necessary approvals according to the company's internal controls and policies. This ensures that all adjustments and refunds are legitimate and properly documented. Key steps include:

- Approval Workflow: Routing the adjustment/refund request through the appropriate approval workflow in Oracle ERP.

- Supporting Documentation: Collecting and attaching all relevant supporting documents, such as the original invoice, proof of return, and any correspondence with the supplier.

3. Entering Adjustments in Oracle ERP

Once the need for an adjustment is identified and authorized, it is entered into the AP module. The process involves the following steps:

- Navigate to the Invoices Workbench: Access the Invoices Workbench in Oracle ERP, which is the primary interface for managing invoices.

- Select the Invoice: Identify and select the invoice that requires adjustment.

- Create Adjustment: Use the "Create Adjustment" option to enter the adjustment details. This includes specifying the type of adjustment (e.g., credit memo, debit memo) and the amount.

- Specify Reason: Clearly state the reason for the adjustment to ensure transparency and traceability.

4. Processing Refunds

If a refund is necessary, the process involves coordinating with the supplier to issue the refund. The steps include:

- Request Refund: Initiate a refund request to the supplier, providing all necessary details and supporting documentation.

- Record Refund Receipt: Once the refund is received, record the refund in the AP module. This involves creating a receipt entry that credits the supplier's account and debits the cash account.

- Reconcile with Bank Statement: Ensure that the refund is reflected in the bank statement and reconcile it with the AP records to maintain accuracy.

5. Adjusting Payment Records

After entering the adjustment or refund, it is essential to update the payment records to reflect the changes accurately. This includes:

- Update Payment Status: Modify the payment status of the affected invoice to reflect the adjustment or refund.

- Recalculate Balances: Recalculate the outstanding balances to ensure that the supplier's account accurately reflects the current amount due.

6. Impact on Financial Statements

Adjustments and refunds have a direct impact on the company's financial statements. It is crucial to understand and accurately record these impacts to maintain financial integrity. The impacts include:

- Accounts Payable: Adjustments reduce the liability in the Accounts Payable account.

- Expense Accounts: Refunds may reduce the expenses recorded, depending on the nature of the original transaction.

- Cash Flow: Both adjustments and refunds impact the cash flow statements by reflecting changes in cash outflows.

7. Reporting and Audit Trail

Maintaining a robust audit trail and generating accurate reports are vital for transparency and compliance. Steps include:

- Generate Adjustment Reports: Use Oracle ERP's reporting tools to generate detailed reports of all adjustments and refunds processed.

- Audit Trail: Ensure that each adjustment and refund entry is linked with the appropriate supporting documentation and approval records. This creates a clear audit trail that can be reviewed during internal and external audits.

8. Best Practices for Issuing Adjustments and Refunds

Adhering to best practices ensures the efficiency and accuracy of adjustments and refunds:

- Regular Reconciliation: Conduct regular reconciliation of supplier accounts to identify discrepancies early.

- Automated Workflows: Utilize automated approval workflows within Oracle ERP to streamline the authorization process.

- Training and Awareness: Train AP staff on the correct procedures and the importance of accurate adjustments and refunds.

- Supplier Communication: Maintain clear and open communication with suppliers to resolve discrepancies promptly and amicably.

9. Handling Common Issues

Several common issues can arise during the adjustment and refund process. Understanding and addressing these issues proactively can help maintain smooth operations:

- Delayed Approvals: Delays in obtaining approvals can slow down the adjustment process. Implementing automated workflows can mitigate this issue.

- Incorrect Entries: Incorrectly entered adjustments or refunds can lead to accounting discrepancies. Implementing validation checks within Oracle ERP can reduce the likelihood of errors.

- Supplier Disputes: Disputes with suppliers regarding adjustments or refunds can be challenging. Maintaining detailed records and clear communication helps in resolving such disputes effectively.

Conclusion

Issuing adjustments and refunds in the Accounts Payable module of Oracle ERP is a vital process for maintaining financial accuracy and compliance. By following a systematic approach that includes identification, authorization, entry, and reconciliation, businesses can ensure that their financial records accurately reflect their transactions. Leveraging Oracle ERP's robust features and adhering to best practices helps streamline the process, minimize errors, and enhance overall financial management.

4.4.2 Explain the different types of adjustments and refunds

In the Accounts Payable (AP) module of Oracle ERP, managing adjustments and refunds efficiently is crucial for maintaining accurate financial records and ensuring proper cash flow management. There are various types of adjustments and refunds that can be processed in the AP module, each serving a specific purpose and addressing different scenarios that may arise during the invoice lifecycle. This section provides a comprehensive explanation of the different types of adjustments and refunds that can be issued, emphasizing their significance and the impact they have on the overall accounting and financial management processes.

Types of Adjustments

Adjustments in the AP module are modifications made to previously recorded transactions to correct errors, update information, or account for changes in the business environment. There are several types of adjustments that can be made, including:

1. Invoice Adjustments

 - Price Adjustments: These occur when there is a discrepancy between the invoiced amount and the agreed-upon price. Price adjustments ensure that the vendor is paid the correct amount based on the purchase order or contract terms. This can happen due to pricing errors, discounts, or negotiated changes.

 - Quantity Adjustments: Quantity adjustments are made when the actual quantity of goods or services received differs from what was initially invoiced. This type of adjustment ensures that the invoice reflects the accurate number of items received.

 - Tax Adjustments: Sometimes, the tax amounts on an invoice may need correction due to errors in tax calculation or changes in tax rates. Tax adjustments are made to rectify these discrepancies and ensure compliance with tax regulations.

 - Discount Adjustments: These adjustments account for any early payment discounts or other negotiated discounts that were not initially applied to the invoice. They help in accurately reflecting the reduced payment amount.

2. Payment Adjustments

 - Overpayment Adjustments: If a payment made to a vendor exceeds the invoiced amount, an overpayment adjustment is necessary to account for the excess payment. This adjustment ensures that the vendor's account balance is accurate and that future payments are adjusted accordingly.

  - Underpayment Adjustments: In cases where the payment made is less than the invoiced amount, an underpayment adjustment is required. This adjustment ensures that the outstanding amount is correctly recorded and that the vendor receives the full payment owed.

3. Vendor Adjustments

  - Vendor Chargebacks: These adjustments occur when the vendor issues a chargeback for returned goods or services. The chargeback amount is deducted from the vendor's outstanding balance, ensuring that the vendor account reflects the accurate amount owed.

  - Vendor Credits: Vendor credits are issued when the vendor provides a credit note for overcharged invoices or as a goodwill gesture. These credits are applied to future invoices, reducing the amount payable to the vendor.

4. Accounting Adjustments

  - Reclassification Adjustments: These adjustments are made to reclassify expenses or payments to the correct account codes or cost centers. Reclassification adjustments ensure that financial reports accurately reflect the nature and purpose of transactions.

  - Currency Adjustments: For organizations dealing with multiple currencies, currency adjustments account for exchange rate fluctuations. These adjustments ensure that the amounts recorded in the AP module align with the current exchange rates.

Types of Refunds

Refunds in the AP module are issued when the organization needs to return funds to a vendor due to various reasons. Different types of refunds include:

1. Vendor Refunds

  - Overpayment Refunds: When an overpayment is identified, the vendor may issue a refund for the excess amount paid. This ensures that the organization's funds are accurately accounted for and that the vendor's account reflects the correct balance.

  - Return Refunds: In cases where goods or services are returned to the vendor, a return refund is issued. This refund accounts for the value of the returned items and is deducted from the vendor's outstanding balance.

2. Duplicate Payment Refunds

- Accidental Duplicate Payments: If an invoice is paid more than once by mistake, the duplicate payment needs to be refunded. This type of refund ensures that the organization's funds are not unnecessarily tied up and that the vendor's account is accurate.

- Intentional Duplicate Payments: Sometimes, duplicate payments may be made intentionally as a part of a business arrangement or contract terms. In such cases, the refund process accounts for these payments and ensures proper reconciliation.

3. Contractual Refunds

- Service Level Agreement (SLA) Refunds: If the vendor fails to meet the agreed-upon service levels as per the contract, an SLA refund may be issued. This type of refund compensates the organization for the vendor's non-compliance with the contract terms.

- Rebate and Incentive Refunds: Vendors may offer rebates or incentives based on the volume of business conducted. These refunds are issued periodically as per the agreed terms and are applied to future invoices.

4. Disputed Invoice Refunds

- Quality Dispute Refunds: If there is a dispute over the quality of goods or services received, a refund may be issued after resolution. This refund accounts for any deficiencies in the delivered products or services.

- Service Dispute Refunds: Similar to quality disputes, service disputes may arise if the provided services do not meet the agreed-upon standards. Refunds for service disputes are issued to compensate for the unsatisfactory service.

Importance of Adjustments and Refunds

Adjustments and refunds play a critical role in maintaining accurate financial records and ensuring effective cash flow management. They help in correcting errors, addressing discrepancies, and ensuring that transactions are accurately recorded in the AP module. The key benefits of managing adjustments and refunds effectively include:

1. Accurate Financial Reporting: Adjustments and refunds ensure that the financial statements reflect the true financial position of the organization. This accuracy is crucial for internal decision-making and external reporting.

2. Compliance and Audit Readiness: Proper management of adjustments and refunds ensures compliance with accounting standards and regulatory requirements. It also makes the organization audit-ready, as accurate records are maintained for all transactions.

3. Enhanced Vendor Relationships: By promptly addressing discrepancies and issuing refunds, organizations can maintain positive relationships with their vendors. This fosters trust and encourages future business collaborations.

4. Efficient Cash Flow Management: Adjustments and refunds help in managing cash flow effectively by ensuring that funds are accurately accounted for and that any excess payments are recovered. This improves the organization's liquidity and financial health.

5. Operational Efficiency: Automated processes for managing adjustments and refunds reduce manual effort and minimize the risk of errors. This enhances the overall efficiency of the AP module and streamlines financial operations.

In conclusion, understanding and managing the different types of adjustments and refunds in the Oracle ERP Accounts Payable module is essential for maintaining accurate financial records and ensuring effective cash flow management. By implementing robust processes for handling adjustments and refunds, organizations can achieve greater financial accuracy, compliance, and operational efficiency.

4.4.3 Discuss the impact of adjustments and refunds on accounting records

Adjustments and refunds are critical components in the Accounts Payable (AP) module as they directly influence the accuracy and integrity of financial records. These transactions, when handled correctly, ensure that a company's financial statements accurately reflect its financial position, mitigating the risk of errors and discrepancies.

1. Impact on General Ledger (GL):

The primary impact of adjustments and refunds is on the General Ledger, which serves as the central repository of all financial transactions. Adjustments, whether they are correcting entries, reclassifications, or error rectifications, need to be accurately recorded to ensure that the ledger reflects the true financial activity of the organization.

For instance, if an invoice was recorded with an incorrect amount, an adjustment must be made to rectify this error. This adjustment will involve debiting or crediting the appropriate accounts to correct the balance. Failure to do so can lead to misstated financial statements, which can affect decision-making, financial reporting, and regulatory compliance.

Refunds also impact the GL by reversing previously recorded expenses. When a vendor issues a refund, it is crucial to record this transaction to reduce the expense or liability that was originally recorded. This ensures that the company's financial statements accurately reflect the expenses and liabilities. Refunds can also impact cash flow statements, as they represent cash inflows that were not initially anticipated.

2. Cash Flow Management:

Adjustments and refunds play a significant role in cash flow management. Properly recorded adjustments can help in maintaining an accurate picture of the company's payables, ensuring that the cash flow projections are based on actual liabilities. For example, if a prepayment adjustment is not recorded, it could overstate the company's cash outflows, leading to an inaccurate cash flow forecast.

Refunds directly affect the cash flow as they represent a return of cash previously disbursed. Accurately recording refunds ensures that the cash flow statement reflects the true cash position, helping management to make informed decisions regarding cash management and liquidity planning.

3. Financial Reporting:

Accurate financial reporting is essential for stakeholders, including management, investors, and regulatory bodies. Adjustments and refunds must be recorded promptly and accurately to ensure that financial statements reflect the true financial performance and position of the company.

For example, if a company receives a refund for overpaid services, this refund needs to be recorded in the financial statements to reduce the reported expenses. Similarly, adjustments for invoice errors need to be made to correct any discrepancies in the expense accounts. This ensures that the income statement, balance sheet, and cash flow statement are accurate and reliable.

4. Compliance and Audit Trail:

Regulatory compliance requires accurate and transparent financial records. Adjustments and refunds must be documented thoroughly to provide a clear audit trail. This documentation includes details such as the reason for the adjustment or refund, the accounts affected, and the approval from the authorized personnel.

An accurate audit trail is vital for internal and external audits. It allows auditors to verify the accuracy of financial records and ensure that the company complies with accounting standards and regulations. Inadequate documentation of adjustments and refunds can lead to audit issues and potential regulatory penalties.

5. Vendor Relationships:

Properly managing adjustments and refunds also impacts vendor relationships. Accurate records ensure that vendors are paid correctly and any discrepancies are addressed promptly. This fosters trust and reliability between the company and its vendors.

For instance, if a vendor overcharges and a refund is due, recording this refund accurately ensures that the vendor account is correctly balanced. This helps in maintaining a positive relationship with the vendor and can also improve the company's reputation for accuracy and fairness in financial dealings.

6. Internal Controls and Fraud Prevention:

Adjustments and refunds must be part of a robust internal control system to prevent fraud and errors. Implementing controls such as segregation of duties, approval hierarchies, and regular reconciliations helps in safeguarding the company's assets and ensuring the integrity of financial records.

For example, the process of issuing refunds should involve multiple steps, including verification of the refund amount, approval from authorized personnel, and recording in the financial system. These controls help prevent unauthorized refunds and detect any discrepancies promptly.

7. Impact on Budgeting and Forecasting:

Adjustments and refunds can affect the budgeting and forecasting process. Accurate recording of these transactions ensures that the financial data used for budgeting and forecasting is reliable. This helps in making informed decisions regarding future expenses, investments, and financial planning.

For example, if frequent adjustments are made due to errors in invoice processing, it indicates a need for better accuracy in the AP process. Addressing these issues can improve the reliability of financial data and enhance the accuracy of budget forecasts.

Conclusion:

In summary, adjustments and refunds have a profound impact on accounting records. They affect the General Ledger, cash flow management, financial reporting, compliance, vendor relationships, internal controls, and budgeting and forecasting. Properly managing these transactions ensures the accuracy and integrity of financial records, which is essential for the overall financial health of the organization. By emphasizing the importance of accurate recording and documentation, companies can maintain reliable financial statements, foster positive vendor relationships, and comply with regulatory requirements.

CHAPTER V
Reconciling Accounts Payable

5.1 Performing Periodic Reconciliations

5.1.1 Explain the process of performing periodic reconciliations of accounts payable balances

Performing periodic reconciliations of accounts payable (AP) balances is a crucial process in maintaining the accuracy and integrity of a company's financial records. Reconciliation ensures that the balances recorded in the accounts payable ledger match the balances in the general ledger and other relevant financial records. This process involves several key steps and requires a systematic approach to identify and resolve discrepancies.

1. Preparation and Documentation:

   - Gathering Data: Begin by collecting all necessary documentation, including supplier statements, purchase orders, invoices, and payment records. Ensure that all relevant transactions for the period under review are available and organized.

   - Reviewing Records: Review the accounts payable ledger and general ledger to identify the opening balances, transactions during the period, and closing balances. Ensure that all entries are up-to-date and reflect the actual transactions.

2. Matching Transactions:

   - Invoice Matching: Match each invoice recorded in the accounts payable ledger with the corresponding purchase order and receipt of goods or services. This three-way matching process helps verify the validity and accuracy of the transactions.

- Payment Matching: Match payments made to suppliers with the recorded invoices. Ensure that each payment is accurately recorded and linked to the corresponding invoice.

3. Identifying Discrepancies:

- Comparing Balances: Compare the accounts payable ledger balances with the supplier statements and the general ledger. Identify any discrepancies between these records. Common discrepancies include unmatched invoices, missing payments, or incorrect entries.

- Investigating Differences: Investigate the reasons for any discrepancies identified. This may involve reviewing transaction details, contacting suppliers for clarification, and verifying the accuracy of recorded amounts.

4. Adjusting Entries:

- Correcting Errors: Make necessary adjustments to correct any errors identified during the reconciliation process. This may involve adjusting invoice amounts, recording missing payments, or correcting any mispostings.

- Documenting Adjustments: Document all adjustments made during the reconciliation process. Ensure that each adjustment is properly authorized and supported by relevant documentation.

5. Final Review and Approval:

- Reviewing Adjusted Balances: Review the adjusted accounts payable ledger and general ledger balances to ensure that all discrepancies have been resolved. Verify that the reconciled balances match the supplier statements and other relevant records.

- Approval: Obtain approval from the appropriate personnel, such as the accounts payable manager or the financial controller, to finalize the reconciliation. Ensure that the approved reconciliation is documented and filed for future reference.

6. Reporting and Record-Keeping:

- Reconciliation Report: Prepare a reconciliation report that summarizes the reconciliation process, the discrepancies identified, the adjustments made, and the final reconciled balances. This report should be comprehensive and provide a clear audit trail.

- Record-Keeping: Maintain detailed records of the reconciliation process, including all supporting documentation, reconciliation reports, and approval records. Ensure that these records are securely stored and easily accessible for future reference and audits.

Importance of Performing Periodic Reconciliations

Periodic reconciliations are essential for several reasons:

1. Accuracy of Financial Records:

- Ensures that the accounts payable balances are accurate and reflect the actual amounts owed to suppliers.

- Helps prevent and detect errors, such as duplicate payments, incorrect postings, and unrecorded liabilities.

2. Financial Reporting:

- Ensures that the financial statements accurately reflect the company's liabilities.

- Provides assurance to stakeholders, including management, auditors, and investors, that the financial records are reliable and trustworthy.

3. Cash Flow Management:

- Helps manage cash flow by ensuring that payments are accurately recorded and matched with the corresponding invoices.

- Identifies any discrepancies that may impact cash flow, such as overpayments or missing payments.

4. Internal Controls:

- Enhances internal controls by providing a systematic process for verifying the accuracy of accounts payable balances.

- Helps detect and prevent fraud by ensuring that all transactions are properly authorized and recorded.

5. Compliance:

- Ensures compliance with accounting standards, regulatory requirements, and company policies.

- Provides a clear audit trail for internal and external audits, reducing the risk of audit findings and penalties.

Best Practices for Periodic Reconciliations

1. Establish a Reconciliation Schedule:

- Perform reconciliations on a regular basis, such as monthly or quarterly, depending on the volume and complexity of transactions.

- Adhere to the established schedule to ensure timely identification and resolution of discrepancies.

2. Automate the Reconciliation Process:

- Utilize accounting software and automated reconciliation tools to streamline the reconciliation process.

- Automate the matching of invoices, payments, and other transactions to reduce manual effort and improve accuracy.

3. Implement Segregation of Duties:

- Ensure that different personnel are responsible for recording transactions, reconciling accounts, and approving adjustments.

- Implementing segregation of duties helps prevent fraud and errors by providing checks and balances.

4. Conduct Regular Training:

- Provide regular training to accounts payable staff on the reconciliation process, including how to identify and resolve discrepancies.

- Keep staff updated on changes to accounting standards, regulatory requirements, and company policies.

5. Review and Update Reconciliation Procedures:

- Regularly review and update the reconciliation procedures to reflect changes in business processes, accounting standards, and regulatory requirements.

- Ensure that the procedures are comprehensive, clear, and easily accessible to all relevant personnel.

By following these best practices and maintaining a systematic approach to periodic reconciliations, companies can ensure the accuracy and reliability of their accounts payable balances, improve financial reporting, and enhance internal controls. Regular reconciliations play a vital role in maintaining the integrity of financial records and supporting effective financial management.

5.1.2 Discuss the different methods for reconciling accounts payable

Reconciling accounts payable (AP) is a critical process for ensuring the accuracy and completeness of financial records. This involves comparing the balances recorded in the AP ledger with the balances on supplier statements and other supporting documents. Various methods can be used to reconcile accounts payable, each with its advantages and potential drawbacks. Understanding these methods can help organizations choose the most appropriate approach for their specific needs.

1. Manual Reconciliation

Manual reconciliation involves physically comparing the transactions recorded in the AP ledger with supplier statements and invoices. This method is often used by smaller organizations with a limited number of transactions. The steps involved in manual reconciliation include:

- Collecting Statements and Invoices: Gather supplier statements and all relevant invoices and credit notes for the period being reconciled.

- Listing Transactions: List all transactions recorded in the AP ledger, including invoices, credit notes, and payments.

- Matching Entries: Match each entry in the AP ledger with the corresponding entry on the supplier statement.

- Identifying Discrepancies: Note any discrepancies between the AP ledger and the supplier statement, such as missing invoices, unmatched payments, or incorrect amounts.

- Investigating Differences: Investigate the cause of any discrepancies and make the necessary adjustments to the AP ledger.

Advantages:

- Provides a thorough and detailed comparison of individual transactions.

- Helps identify specific errors or discrepancies.

Drawbacks:

- Time-consuming and labor-intensive.

- Prone to human error, especially with large volumes of transactions.

2. Automated Reconciliation

Automated reconciliation uses software tools to compare the AP ledger with supplier statements and other documents. This method is suitable for organizations with a high volume of transactions and aims to reduce the manual effort involved in reconciliation. The process typically involves:

- Data Import: Importing data from the AP ledger and supplier statements into the reconciliation software.

- Automated Matching: The software automatically matches transactions based on predefined criteria, such as invoice number, date, and amount.

- Flagging Discrepancies: Any discrepancies identified by the software are flagged for further investigation.

- Generating Reports: The software generates reconciliation reports, highlighting matched transactions and discrepancies.

Advantages:

- Significantly faster than manual reconciliation.

- Reduces the risk of human error.

- Provides detailed reports and audit trails.

Drawbacks:

- Requires investment in reconciliation software.

- May require staff training to use the software effectively.

- Can be less flexible in handling unusual transactions or exceptions.

3. Two-Way Matching

Two-way matching involves comparing the purchase order (PO) with the supplier invoice to ensure that the quantities and prices match. This method helps verify that the goods or services received correspond to what was ordered and that the invoiced amounts are correct. The steps in two-way matching include:

- Reviewing Purchase Orders: Review the PO to ensure it includes all necessary details, such as item descriptions, quantities, and agreed-upon prices.

- Comparing Invoices: Compare the supplier invoice with the PO to check for consistency in quantities and prices.

- Resolving Discrepancies: Investigate and resolve any discrepancies between the PO and the invoice before making payment.

Advantages:

- Helps ensure that only authorized purchases are paid.

- Provides a straightforward comparison of quantities and prices.

Drawbacks:

- Does not account for potential discrepancies between the PO and actual goods received (e.g., damaged goods).

- May not be suitable for complex or service-based transactions without clear PO details.

4. Three-Way Matching

Three-way matching extends the two-way matching process by also comparing the receiving report with the PO and the invoice. This method is more comprehensive and helps ensure that the goods received match the quantities ordered and invoiced. The process involves:

- Reviewing Purchase Orders and Invoices: Similar to two-way matching, review the PO and invoice for consistency.

- Comparing Receiving Reports: Compare the receiving report, which details the actual quantities of goods received, with the PO and invoice.

- Resolving Discrepancies: Investigate and resolve any discrepancies among the PO, receiving report, and invoice before making payment.

Advantages:

- Provides a more comprehensive verification process, ensuring accuracy in both quantities and prices.

- Helps prevent payment for goods not received or invoiced incorrectly.

Drawbacks:

- More complex and time-consuming than two-way matching.

- Requires coordination among purchasing, receiving, and AP departments.

5. Vendor Statement Reconciliation

Vendor statement reconciliation involves comparing the vendor's statement, which summarizes all transactions with the vendor for a specific period, with the AP ledger. This method is particularly useful for identifying discrepancies in account balances. The process includes:

- Obtaining Vendor Statements: Request and obtain statements from vendors for the reconciliation period.

- Comparing Statements with AP Ledger: Compare the transactions listed on the vendor statement with those recorded in the AP ledger.

- Identifying and Investigating Discrepancies: Identify any discrepancies, such as missing invoices or payments, and investigate the causes.

- Making Adjustments: Make the necessary adjustments to the AP ledger to correct any errors or omissions.

Advantages:

- Provides a high-level overview of transactions and balances with vendors.

- Helps ensure that the AP ledger reflects the correct outstanding balances.

Drawbacks:

- May not provide detailed transaction-level matching.

- Requires accurate and timely vendor statements.

6. Bank Reconciliation

Although primarily used for reconciling bank accounts, bank reconciliation can also help ensure that payments recorded in the AP ledger match the payments cleared by the bank. The steps involved include:

- Collecting Bank Statements: Obtain bank statements for the period being reconciled.

- Comparing Bank Transactions: Compare payments recorded in the AP ledger with those on the bank statement.

- Identifying Discrepancies: Identify any discrepancies, such as unrecorded payments or bank errors.

- Resolving Differences: Investigate and resolve any differences, adjusting the AP ledger as needed.

Advantages:

- Helps ensure that recorded payments are accurate and have been processed by the bank.

- Provides an additional layer of verification for AP transactions.

Drawbacks:

- Limited to reconciling payments and not other types of AP transactions.

- Requires access to accurate and up-to-date bank statements.

7. Aging Analysis

Aging analysis involves categorizing AP balances based on the length of time they have been outstanding. This method helps identify overdue invoices and manage cash flow more effectively. The steps include:

- Categorizing Balances: Categorize AP balances into aging buckets, such as current, 30 days, 60 days, 90 days, and over 90 days.

- Reviewing Outstanding Balances: Review outstanding balances in each aging category to identify overdue invoices.

- Investigating Overdue Invoices: Investigate the reasons for overdue invoices and take appropriate actions, such as contacting suppliers or adjusting payment terms.

Advantages:

- Helps prioritize payments and manage cash flow.

- Identifies overdue invoices that may require immediate attention.

Drawbacks:

- Does not provide detailed transaction-level reconciliation.

- Requires accurate aging categorization and timely follow-up on overdue invoices.

Conclusion

Different methods for reconciling accounts payable offer various benefits and challenges. The choice of method depends on factors such as the volume of transactions, the complexity of the organization's AP processes, and available resources. By understanding and implementing the appropriate reconciliation methods, organizations can maintain accurate and reliable AP records, minimize discrepancies, and ensure efficient financial management. Regular and thorough reconciliations are essential for maintaining the integrity of the AP ledger and supporting overall financial health.

5.1.3 Emphasize the importance of regular reconciliations for maintaining accurate accounting records

Regular reconciliations in the Accounts Payable (AP) module are critical for maintaining accurate accounting records and ensuring the financial health of an organization. The process of reconciling accounts payable balances involves comparing the balances in the AP subledger to the general ledger (GL) to identify and resolve discrepancies. This practice is not only essential for accurate financial reporting but also plays a crucial role in several other aspects of financial management. Let's delve deeper into why regular reconciliations are so important.

Ensuring Accuracy in Financial Statements

One of the primary reasons for conducting regular reconciliations is to ensure the accuracy of financial statements. Discrepancies between the AP subledger and the GL can lead to inaccurate financial reporting, which can mislead stakeholders and potentially result in non-compliance with accounting standards and regulations. Regular reconciliations help identify and correct these discrepancies, ensuring that the financial statements accurately reflect the company's liabilities.

Enhancing Financial Control and Oversight

Regular reconciliations provide a mechanism for enhancing financial control and oversight within an organization. By systematically comparing AP subledger balances with the GL, companies can ensure that all transactions are accurately recorded and classified. This process helps in detecting any unauthorized or erroneous entries, thereby strengthening internal controls and reducing the risk of fraud and errors.

Facilitating Cash Flow Management

Accurate accounts payable records are vital for effective cash flow management. Regular reconciliations help ensure that the timing and amounts of payments are accurately tracked. This enables better forecasting and planning of cash outflows, which is essential for maintaining liquidity and avoiding cash flow shortages. By reconciling accounts payable regularly, companies can also identify overdue payments and take appropriate actions to manage vendor relationships and negotiate favorable payment terms.

Supporting Compliance and Audit Requirements

Maintaining accurate accounting records through regular reconciliations supports compliance with regulatory and audit requirements. Many regulatory frameworks and standards, such as the Sarbanes-Oxley Act (SOX) in the United States, mandate strict internal controls and accurate financial reporting. Regular reconciliations help ensure that these requirements are met by providing a documented process for verifying the accuracy of financial records. During audits, reconciled accounts serve as evidence of the company's commitment to financial accuracy and control.

Identifying and Resolving Discrepancies Promptly

Regular reconciliations enable the timely identification and resolution of discrepancies between the AP subledger and the GL. Discrepancies can arise from various sources, such as data entry errors, timing differences, or unrecorded transactions. By conducting reconciliations periodically, companies can detect these issues early and take corrective actions promptly, minimizing the impact on financial reporting and decision-making.

Improving Decision-Making

Accurate and reliable accounting records are essential for informed decision-making. Regular reconciliations ensure that management has access to up-to-date and accurate financial information, which is crucial for making strategic decisions. Whether it's evaluating the company's financial health, planning for future expenditures, or assessing the effectiveness of cost-saving measures, accurate accounts payable data provides the foundation for sound financial decision-making.

Enhancing Vendor Relationships

Timely and accurate payment processing is critical for maintaining good relationships with vendors. Regular reconciliations help ensure that vendor invoices are processed and paid accurately and on time. By avoiding payment delays and discrepancies, companies can build trust and maintain positive relationships with their suppliers, which can lead to more favorable terms and opportunities for collaboration.

Reducing Financial Risks

Regular reconciliations help mitigate financial risks by ensuring the integrity of accounting records. Inaccurate or incomplete accounts payable records can lead to financial misstatements, which can have serious consequences, including financial losses, regulatory penalties, and damage to the company's reputation. By maintaining accurate records through regular reconciliations, companies can reduce the risk of financial misstatements and safeguard their financial stability.

Streamlining Year-End Closing Processes

The year-end closing process can be complex and time-consuming, especially if there are unresolved discrepancies in the accounts payable records. Regular reconciliations throughout the year simplify the year-end closing process by ensuring that the accounts are accurate and up-to-date. This reduces the need for extensive adjustments and corrections at year-end, making the closing process more efficient and less stressful.

Promoting Transparency and Accountability

Regular reconciliations promote transparency and accountability within the finance and accounting functions. By maintaining a clear and documented process for verifying accounts payable balances, companies can demonstrate their commitment to financial accuracy and accountability. This transparency is important not only for internal stakeholders but also for external parties such as auditors, regulators, and investors.

Implementing Best Practices for Reconciliation

To maximize the benefits of regular reconciliations, it is important to implement best practices in the reconciliation process. Some of these best practices include:

1. Establishing a Reconciliation Schedule: Develop a regular schedule for performing reconciliations, such as monthly or quarterly, to ensure that the process is consistently followed.

2. Using Reconciliation Software: Utilize reconciliation software or tools that can automate and streamline the reconciliation process, reducing the risk of errors and improving efficiency.

3. Documenting the Process: Maintain detailed documentation of the reconciliation process, including procedures, roles, and responsibilities, to ensure consistency and accountability.

4. Reviewing and Approving Reconciliations: Implement a review and approval process for reconciliations to ensure that discrepancies are thoroughly investigated and resolved by qualified personnel.

5. Training and Educating Staff: Provide training and education to finance and accounting staff on the importance of reconciliations and the proper procedures to follow.

6. Regularly Reviewing Reconciliation Policies: Periodically review and update reconciliation policies and procedures to reflect changes in business processes, regulatory requirements, and industry best practices.

Conclusion

In conclusion, regular reconciliations of accounts payable balances are essential for maintaining accurate accounting records and ensuring the financial health of an organization. By enhancing financial control, supporting compliance, facilitating cash flow management, and improving decision-making, regular reconciliations provide numerous benefits that contribute to the overall effectiveness and efficiency of the accounts payable function. Implementing best practices and maintaining a consistent reconciliation schedule are key to achieving these benefits and promoting transparency and accountability within the organization.

5.2 Investigating and Resolving Differences

5.2.1 Describe the procedures for investigating and resolving differences identified during reconciliations

Investigating and resolving differences identified during accounts payable reconciliations is a critical task for ensuring the accuracy and integrity of financial records. Discrepancies can arise from various sources, such as data entry errors, timing differences, or unrecorded transactions. To manage this effectively, a systematic approach is essential. Below, we outline the detailed procedures for investigating and resolving these differences:

1. Identify the Discrepancy:

The first step in investigating differences is to identify the specific discrepancies. This involves comparing the accounts payable ledger to the vendor statements or other source documents. Any variances between the amounts recorded in the ERP system and the amounts on the external documents need to be flagged for further investigation.

2. Classify the Discrepancy:

Once discrepancies are identified, classify them based on their nature. Common categories include:

- Timing Differences: Transactions recorded in different periods in the ERP system and the vendor's records.

- Data Entry Errors: Mistakes in entering data, such as incorrect amounts or dates.

- Omissions: Transactions that have not been recorded in the ERP system.

- Duplicate Entries: Transactions that have been recorded more than once.

- Vendor Errors: Errors made by the vendor in their records.

3. Gather Supporting Documentation:

For each discrepancy, gather all relevant supporting documentation. This may include invoices, purchase orders, receiving reports, and payment records. Having complete and accurate documentation is essential for a thorough investigation.

4. Perform Root Cause Analysis:

Conduct a root cause analysis to determine the underlying reason for the discrepancy. This involves tracing the transaction through the accounting records and verifying the accuracy of each step. For instance, if a discrepancy is due to a timing difference, identify when the transaction was recorded in both the ERP system and the vendor's records.

5. Correct the Discrepancy:

Based on the findings of the root cause analysis, take appropriate corrective actions:

- Adjusting Entries: For timing differences, make adjusting entries to ensure the transaction is recorded in the correct period.

- Error Correction: Correct any data entry errors by updating the transaction details in the ERP system.

- Recording Omissions: If a transaction was omitted, ensure it is recorded promptly.

- Removing Duplicates: Identify and remove any duplicate entries.

6. Communicate with Vendors:

In cases where discrepancies are due to vendor errors, communicate with the vendors to resolve the issue. Provide them with the necessary documentation to support your findings and request corrections to their records if needed.

7. Update Reconciliation Records:

After resolving the discrepancies, update the reconciliation records to reflect the corrections. Ensure that the accounts payable ledger is accurate and reconciled with the vendor statements.

8. Document the Resolution Process:

Maintain detailed records of the investigation and resolution process for each discrepancy. This documentation should include the nature of the discrepancy, the steps taken to investigate and resolve it, and any communications with vendors. Proper documentation is crucial for audit purposes and future reference.

9. Review and Approve Adjustments:

Ensure that all adjustments made during the reconciliation process are reviewed and approved by the appropriate personnel. This adds a layer of oversight and ensures that the corrections are accurate and justified.

10. Continuous Improvement:

   Periodically review the reconciliation process to identify any recurring issues or areas for improvement. Implement changes to the procedures as needed to enhance the accuracy and efficiency of future reconciliations.

By following these procedures, organizations can effectively investigate and resolve discrepancies in accounts payable reconciliations. This not only ensures the accuracy of financial records but also strengthens internal controls and supports effective financial management.

5.2.2 Discuss the different types of reconciliation differences that may occur

Reconciliation is a critical process in managing accounts payable, ensuring that the recorded transactions match the actual financial activities. During this process, various types of differences or discrepancies may arise. Identifying and understanding these differences is essential for accurate financial reporting and maintaining the integrity of financial records. Here, we discuss the common types of reconciliation differences that may occur in accounts payable.

 1. Timing Differences

Definition: Timing differences occur when there is a delay between when a transaction is recorded in the accounts payable system and when it is recognized in the bank or vendor records.

Example: A company issues a check to a vendor on the last day of the accounting period, but the vendor does not deposit the check until the next accounting period. This results in a discrepancy between the company's accounts payable records and the bank statement.

Resolution: Timing differences are usually resolved by identifying the transactions that have not yet cleared the bank or vendor records. These should be noted and accounted for in the reconciliation process to ensure accurate records.

2. Data Entry Errors

Definition: Data entry errors occur when there are mistakes in entering transaction details into the accounts payable system.

Example: An invoice amount is entered as $1,000 instead of $10,000, or the vendor name is incorrectly recorded.

Resolution: To resolve data entry errors, cross-referencing the accounts payable records with original documents such as invoices, receipts, and bank statements is necessary. Correcting these errors promptly ensures that the financial records reflect the true nature of the transactions.

3. Unrecorded Transactions

Definition: Unrecorded transactions are those that have occurred but have not been entered into the accounts payable system.

Example: A vendor has provided services and issued an invoice, but the invoice has not yet been recorded in the accounts payable system.

Resolution: Regularly reviewing outstanding invoices and purchase orders helps identify unrecorded transactions. Once identified, these transactions should be promptly entered into the system to maintain accurate records.

4. Duplicate Transactions

Definition: Duplicate transactions occur when the same transaction is recorded more than once in the accounts payable system.

Example: An invoice is entered into the system twice, resulting in an overstated accounts payable balance.

Resolution: Identifying duplicate transactions requires careful review of the accounts payable records and comparison with original documents. Once detected, duplicate entries should be corrected by removing or adjusting the duplicate records.

5. Incorrect Account Coding

Definition: Incorrect account coding happens when transactions are recorded under the wrong account codes, leading to misclassification of expenses.

Example: An office supply purchase is incorrectly coded as a capital expenditure.

Resolution: Reviewing account codes and ensuring proper classification during data entry can prevent this type of discrepancy. If incorrect coding is identified during reconciliation, reclassifying the transactions to the correct accounts is necessary.

6. Unauthorized Transactions

Definition: Unauthorized transactions are those that have been entered into the accounts payable system without proper approval or authorization.

Example: A purchase order is created and recorded without the necessary managerial approval.

Resolution: Implementing strong internal controls and approval processes can minimize the occurrence of unauthorized transactions. During reconciliation, any unauthorized transactions should be flagged, investigated, and addressed appropriately.

7. Bank Errors

Definition: Bank errors occur when the bank records transactions incorrectly, leading to discrepancies between the bank statement and the company's accounts payable records.

Example: The bank mistakenly debits an incorrect amount from the company's account.

Resolution: To resolve bank errors, it is necessary to contact the bank, provide evidence of the discrepancy, and request a correction. Updating the accounts payable records accordingly will ensure alignment with the corrected bank statement.

8. Vendor Errors

Definition: Vendor errors occur when the vendor's records do not match the company's accounts payable records due to mistakes on the vendor's part.

Example: A vendor sends an invoice for $1,200, but the correct amount should be $1,000.

Resolution: Communicating with vendors to verify and correct any discrepancies in their invoices or statements is essential. Once corrected, adjusting the accounts payable records to reflect the accurate amounts will resolve the differences.

9. Adjustments and Write-offs

Definition: Adjustments and write-offs are changes made to accounts payable balances to correct errors or account for uncollectible amounts.

Example: Writing off a portion of an overdue invoice that is deemed uncollectible.

Resolution: Proper documentation and authorization for adjustments and write-offs are necessary. These transactions should be accurately recorded in the accounts payable system to ensure that the financial statements reflect the true financial position.

10. Exchange Rate Variances

Definition: Exchange rate variances occur when there are differences between the recorded exchange rate and the actual exchange rate at the time of transaction settlement.

Example: An invoice recorded in a foreign currency is settled at a different exchange rate than initially recorded, leading to a discrepancy.

Resolution: Regularly updating exchange rates and revaluing foreign currency transactions can help manage exchange rate variances. Adjustments should be made to accounts payable records to reflect the actual exchange rates at the time of settlement.

Conclusion

Understanding the different types of reconciliation differences that may occur in accounts payable is crucial for maintaining accurate financial records. By identifying and addressing these discrepancies promptly, companies can ensure the integrity of their accounts payable system, support accurate financial reporting, and maintain strong vendor relationships. Regular reconciliations, combined with robust internal controls and effective communication with banks and vendors, are key to achieving these goals..

5.2.3 Explain the methods for analyzing and correcting reconciliation differences

Reconciling accounts payable is a critical function within an organization's financial management process. The purpose of reconciliation is to ensure that the accounts payable ledger matches the actual amounts owed to vendors, as recorded in the financial statements. Differences can arise due to various reasons, including timing discrepancies, data entry errors, or issues with vendor invoices. Analyzing and correcting these differences promptly is essential to maintain the accuracy of the financial records and to ensure the integrity of the accounting system. This section will delve into the methods for analyzing and correcting reconciliation differences in detail.

Methods for Analyzing Reconciliation Differences

1. Identifying the Source of Differences

  - Comparison with Vendor Statements: One of the first steps in analyzing reconciliation differences is to compare the accounts payable ledger with the vendor statements. This comparison helps identify discrepancies such as unrecorded invoices, payments not yet reflected by the vendor, or duplicate entries.

  - Reviewing Aging Reports: Aging reports categorize outstanding invoices by their due dates. By reviewing these reports, you can identify overdue invoices or payments that may not have been matched correctly in the system.

  - Cross-Checking Purchase Orders and Receipts: Cross-checking the purchase orders and receipts with the accounts payable entries can help identify if goods or services have been received but not invoiced, or if there are discrepancies in the quantities or prices.

2. Investigating Timing Differences

  - Cutoff Issues: Timing differences often occur at the period-end cutoff. Ensure that all invoices and payments pertaining to the period have been recorded in the correct accounting period.

- Accruals and Prepayments: Verify if accruals and prepayments have been appropriately recorded. Accrued expenses should reflect the cost of goods or services received but not yet invoiced, while prepayments should match advance payments made to vendors.

3. Data Entry and System Errors

- Manual Entry Errors: Manual data entry errors are common sources of discrepancies. Review entries for typographical errors, incorrect amounts, or misposted transactions.

- System Integration Issues: If your accounts payable system is integrated with other systems such as inventory management or procurement, ensure that data flows correctly between systems. Integration issues can lead to incomplete or duplicate entries.

4. Vendor Discrepancies

- Vendor Invoicing Errors: Sometimes, the discrepancies arise from the vendor's side. Common issues include incorrect pricing, duplicate invoices, or missed discounts. Communicate with vendors to resolve these issues.

- Disputed Invoices: If there are disputed invoices, ensure that they are documented and follow up with the vendor to resolve the disputes promptly.

Methods for Correcting Reconciliation Differences

1. Adjusting Entries

- Journal Entries: Once the source of the discrepancy is identified, make the necessary journal entries to correct the accounts payable ledger. Ensure that these entries are approved and documented according to the organization's policies.

- Reversals and Reclassifications: If errors were found in the initial recording of transactions, reverse the incorrect entries and reclassify them to the correct accounts.

2. Updating Vendor Records

- Vendor Communication: Communicate with vendors to correct errors in their invoices. Request corrected invoices or credit notes as needed.

- Payment Adjustments: If overpayments or underpayments have been identified, adjust future payments to the vendor accordingly. Ensure that these adjustments are clearly documented.

3. System Updates and Corrections

- Data Corrections: If the discrepancies were due to system errors or integration issues, update the system data to reflect the correct information. This may involve working with IT support to resolve any underlying issues.

- Process Improvements: Implement process improvements to prevent future discrepancies. This could include additional training for staff, updating procedures, or enhancing system integrations.

4. Documentation and Follow-Up

- Detailed Documentation: Document all reconciliation differences and the steps taken to resolve them. This documentation is important for audit trails and future reference.

- Regular Follow-Up: Establish a regular follow-up process to ensure that all identified discrepancies are resolved in a timely manner. This includes setting deadlines for resolving issues and monitoring progress.

5. Use of Reconciliation Tools and Software

- Automated Reconciliation Tools: Utilize automated reconciliation tools that can match invoices and payments, highlight discrepancies, and suggest corrections. These tools can significantly reduce manual effort and improve accuracy.

- Analytics and Reporting: Use analytics and reporting tools to generate detailed reports on reconciliation differences. These reports can help identify patterns and recurring issues, allowing for more targeted corrective actions.

6. Internal Controls and Audits

- Strengthening Internal Controls: Implement and strengthen internal controls around the accounts payable process. This includes segregation of duties, approval workflows, and regular reviews.

- Internal Audits: Conduct regular internal audits to review the reconciliation process and identify any areas of improvement. Audits can help ensure compliance with policies and detect issues early.

Importance of Accurate Reconciliation

Accurate reconciliation of accounts payable is vital for several reasons:

- Financial Accuracy: Ensures that the financial statements reflect the true financial position of the company.

- Vendor Relationships: Maintains good relationships with vendors by ensuring timely and accurate payments.

- Compliance: Helps in meeting regulatory compliance requirements by ensuring accurate and complete records.

- Cash Flow Management: Improves cash flow management by ensuring that liabilities are accurately recorded and managed.

- Fraud Prevention: Detects and prevents fraudulent activities by ensuring that all transactions are properly recorded and reconciled.

In conclusion, the process of analyzing and correcting reconciliation differences in accounts payable involves a systematic approach to identifying discrepancies, investigating their causes, and implementing corrective actions. By maintaining rigorous reconciliation processes and utilizing appropriate tools and controls, organizations can ensure the accuracy and integrity of their accounts payable records, ultimately supporting sound financial management and decision-making.

5.3 Maintaining Account Balances

5.3.1 Explain the process of adjusting and updating account balances based on reconciliation results

Maintaining accurate account balances in the Accounts Payable (AP) module is crucial for ensuring the integrity of financial records and supporting effective financial decision-making. The process of adjusting and updating account balances based on reconciliation results involves several steps, each designed to identify discrepancies, determine their causes, and make necessary adjustments to ensure the accuracy of financial statements. This section provides a detailed explanation of these steps.

Step 1: Review Reconciliation Reports

The first step in adjusting and updating account balances is to review the reconciliation reports generated during the reconciliation process. These reports provide a detailed comparison of the accounts payable balances as recorded in the general ledger with the corresponding balances in the subsidiary ledger. The reports highlight any discrepancies between the two sets of records, which need to be investigated and resolved.

Step 2: Identify Discrepancies

After reviewing the reconciliation reports, the next step is to identify the specific discrepancies between the general ledger and subsidiary ledger. Common types of discrepancies include unmatched invoices, duplicate entries, missing transactions, and incorrect amounts. Identifying these discrepancies accurately is crucial for determining the appropriate adjustments.

Step 3: Investigate the Causes of Discrepancies

Once the discrepancies have been identified, the next step is to investigate their causes. This involves tracing the transactions back to their source documents, such as invoices, purchase orders, and payment records. The goal is to determine whether the discrepancies are due to data entry errors, timing differences, or other issues. This investigation may require collaboration with other departments, such as procurement and receiving, to gather the necessary information.

Step 4: Determine the Appropriate Adjustments

Based on the results of the investigation, the appropriate adjustments to the account balances can be determined. These adjustments may include correcting data entry errors, recording missing transactions, reversing duplicate entries, and making adjustments for timing differences. It is important to document the rationale for each adjustment and obtain any necessary approvals before making the changes.

Step 5: Make the Adjustments in the AP Module

Once the appropriate adjustments have been determined and approved, they can be made in the AP module. This involves updating the account balances in the subsidiary ledger to reflect the correct amounts. The adjustments should be entered as journal entries or other appropriate transaction types, depending on the nature of the discrepancies. It is important to ensure that the adjustments are accurately recorded and properly categorized.

Step 6: Update the General Ledger

After making the adjustments in the AP module, the corresponding updates need to be made in the general ledger. This ensures that the general ledger reflects the corrected account balances and is in sync with the subsidiary ledger. The updates should be entered as journal entries, and the adjustments should be properly documented and categorized to ensure accurate financial reporting.

Step 7: Reconcile the Updated Balances

After making the adjustments in both the AP module and the general ledger, the updated balances need to be reconciled again to ensure that the discrepancies have been resolved. This involves generating new reconciliation reports and comparing the updated balances. If any discrepancies remain, they need to be investigated and resolved following the same process as before.

Step 8: Review and Approve the Adjustments

The final step in the process is to review and approve the adjustments. This involves reviewing the updated reconciliation reports, verifying the accuracy of the adjustments, and ensuring that all necessary documentation is in place. The adjustments should be approved by the appropriate personnel, such as the AP manager or the finance director, to ensure that they are properly authorized.

Importance of Accurate Account Balances

Maintaining accurate account balances is essential for several reasons. First, it ensures the integrity of financial records and supports accurate financial reporting. Second, it helps to identify and resolve discrepancies promptly, reducing the risk of errors and fraud. Third, it supports effective cash flow management by ensuring that the correct amounts are recorded and paid to vendors. Finally, it helps to maintain good relationships with vendors by ensuring that payments are made accurately and on time.

Challenges in Maintaining Account Balances

Maintaining accurate account balances can be challenging due to several factors. First, the volume of transactions in the AP module can be high, making it difficult to identify and resolve discrepancies promptly. Second, the complexity of the transactions, such as multiple line items on invoices and different payment terms, can complicate the reconciliation process. Third, the involvement of multiple departments and systems can make it difficult to gather the necessary information for investigating discrepancies.

Best Practices for Maintaining Account Balances

To overcome these challenges and ensure the accuracy of account balances, it is important to follow best practices. These include:

1. Regular Reconciliations: Perform regular reconciliations of the AP balances, such as monthly or quarterly, to identify and resolve discrepancies promptly.

2. Automated Reconciliation Tools: Use automated reconciliation tools to streamline the reconciliation process and reduce the risk of errors.

3. Clear Documentation: Maintain clear and detailed documentation of the reconciliation process, including the causes of discrepancies and the adjustments made.

4. Cross-Department Collaboration: Collaborate with other departments, such as procurement and receiving, to gather the necessary information for investigating discrepancies.

5. Training and Support: Provide training and support to the AP staff to ensure that they are knowledgeable about the reconciliation process and the importance of maintaining accurate account balances.

6. Regular Audits: Conduct regular audits of the AP balances to ensure that the reconciliations are performed accurately and that the adjustments are properly documented and approved.

By following these best practices, organizations can ensure the accuracy of their AP balances and support effective financial management.

Conclusion

Maintaining accurate account balances based on reconciliation results is a critical aspect of the accounts payable process. It involves reviewing reconciliation reports, identifying discrepancies, investigating their causes, determining the appropriate adjustments, making the adjustments in the AP module and the general ledger, and reconciling the updated balances. By following best practices and addressing the challenges in maintaining account balances, organizations can ensure the integrity of their financial records and support effective financial decision-making.

5.3.2 Discuss the impact of reconciliation adjustments on financial statements

Reconciliation adjustments play a critical role in ensuring the accuracy and reliability of financial statements. These adjustments are essential for identifying discrepancies and ensuring that all financial data is correctly recorded and reported. The process of making reconciliation adjustments involves examining the differences between the company's internal records and the external statements received from vendors, banks, or other entities. This examination helps in pinpointing errors, omissions, or fraudulent activities that could otherwise go unnoticed. The impact of these adjustments on financial statements is profound and multifaceted.

Ensuring Accuracy and Completeness

The primary impact of reconciliation adjustments is the enhancement of the accuracy and completeness of financial statements. By identifying and correcting discrepancies, businesses can ensure that their financial records reflect the true state of their financial position. This accuracy is crucial for stakeholders who rely on financial statements for decision-making purposes. Accurate financial statements provide a reliable basis for assessing the company's performance, making investment decisions, and evaluating the effectiveness of management strategies.

Enhancing Financial Integrity

Reconciliation adjustments help maintain the integrity of financial statements by ensuring that all transactions are properly recorded and classified. This process involves verifying that all accounts payable transactions are accurately captured, including invoices, payments, and credits. Any discrepancies identified during reconciliations are investigated and resolved, which helps prevent the misstatement of financial information. By maintaining high standards of financial integrity, companies can build trust with investors, creditors, and other stakeholders.

Compliance with Accounting Standards

Another significant impact of reconciliation adjustments is ensuring compliance with accounting standards and regulatory requirements. Financial statements must adhere to generally accepted accounting principles (GAAP) or international financial reporting standards (IFRS), depending on the jurisdiction. Reconciliation adjustments help ensure that financial records are prepared in accordance with these standards, thereby avoiding potential legal and regulatory issues. Accurate and compliant financial statements are essential for external audits and for meeting the reporting requirements of regulatory bodies.

Improving Financial Reporting Quality

Reconciliation adjustments contribute to the overall quality of financial reporting by providing a clear and accurate picture of the company's financial health. High-quality financial statements are essential for effective communication with stakeholders. They help convey a true and fair view of the company's financial performance and position, which is critical for gaining the confidence of investors, creditors, and other interested parties. Improved financial reporting quality can lead to better decision-making and enhanced credibility in the financial markets.

Identifying and Mitigating Risks

The reconciliation process involves a thorough review of accounts payable records, which can help identify potential risks and areas of concern. For instance, discrepancies may indicate issues such as duplicate payments, unrecorded liabilities, or fraudulent activities. By making reconciliation adjustments, companies can address these risks promptly and implement measures to mitigate them in the future. This proactive approach to risk management helps protect the company's financial resources and ensures the sustainability of its operations.

Impact on Financial Ratios and Metrics

Reconciliation adjustments can also affect key financial ratios and metrics used to evaluate the company's performance. For example, adjustments to accounts payable balances can impact the current ratio, quick ratio, and days payable outstanding (DPO). Accurate and timely reconciliations ensure that these ratios reflect the true financial condition of the company, providing valuable insights for management and external stakeholders. Changes in financial ratios can influence investor perceptions and affect the company's ability to secure financing.

Effect on Cash Flow Management

Adjustments resulting from reconciliations can have a direct impact on cash flow management. Accurate accounts payable records ensure that cash disbursements are properly tracked and managed. Discrepancies identified during reconciliations, such as unpaid invoices or duplicate payments, can be corrected, leading to more efficient cash flow management. Effective cash flow management is crucial for meeting short-term obligations, funding operations, and supporting strategic initiatives.

Enhancing Decision-Making

The reliability of financial statements, enhanced by reconciliation adjustments, supports better decision-making by management. Accurate financial data is essential for budgeting, forecasting, and strategic planning. Management relies on financial statements to make informed decisions about resource allocation, cost control, and investment opportunities. By ensuring the accuracy of accounts payable balances, reconciliation adjustments provide a solid foundation for these decisions, ultimately contributing to the company's growth and profitability.

Building Stakeholder Confidence

Finally, the impact of reconciliation adjustments on financial statements extends to building confidence among stakeholders. Transparent and accurate financial reporting demonstrates the company's commitment to sound financial management and ethical practices. This transparency is vital for maintaining positive relationships with investors, creditors, customers, and employees. Confidence in the company's financial health can lead to increased investment, favorable credit terms, and enhanced reputation in the marketplace.

Conclusion

In conclusion, reconciliation adjustments are a critical component of maintaining accurate account balances and ensuring the reliability of financial statements. These adjustments enhance the accuracy and completeness of financial records, ensure compliance with accounting standards, improve financial reporting quality, identify and mitigate risks, affect key financial ratios and metrics, impact cash flow management, support better decision-making, and build stakeholder confidence. By performing regular reconciliations and making necessary adjustments, companies can achieve a high level of financial integrity and transparency, which is essential for long-term success and sustainability. The importance of maintaining accurate account balances cannot be overstated, as it underpins the overall financial health and stability of the organization.

5.3.3 Emphasize the importance of maintaining accurate account balances for financial reporting

Accurate account balances are the foundation of reliable financial reporting. They provide a true and fair view of the financial health of an organization, which is essential for a variety of reasons:

1. Stakeholder Confidence:

  - Investors and Shareholders: Accurate financial statements are vital for maintaining investor and shareholder confidence. Investors rely on these statements to make informed decisions about buying, holding, or selling shares. Any discrepancies in account balances can lead to a loss of trust and a decline in share prices.

  - Creditors and Lenders: Banks and other financial institutions use financial statements to assess the creditworthiness of a business. Accurate account balances indicate financial stability and the ability to meet debt obligations, which can impact the terms and availability of credit.

2. Regulatory Compliance:

  - Adherence to Standards: Companies must comply with accounting standards such as Generally Accepted Accounting Principles (GAAP) or International Financial Reporting Standards (IFRS). Accurate account balances ensure that financial statements are prepared in accordance with these standards, avoiding potential legal issues and penalties.

  - Tax Compliance: Accurate account balances are necessary for correct tax calculations and reporting. Errors in account balances can lead to incorrect tax filings, resulting in fines, penalties, and damage to the company's reputation.

3. Internal Decision-Making:

  - Management Decisions: Accurate financial data is critical for management to make strategic decisions. Whether it's budgeting, forecasting, or investment planning, reliable account balances provide the necessary insights for effective decision-making.

- Operational Efficiency: Correct account balances help in monitoring the financial performance of various departments, enabling managers to identify and address inefficiencies promptly.

4. Financial Health and Sustainability:

- Profitability Analysis: Accurate account balances allow for a precise calculation of profits and losses. This analysis helps in understanding the company's financial health and making informed decisions about future operations and investments.

- Cash Flow Management: Maintaining accurate balances is essential for effective cash flow management. It ensures that there are sufficient funds to meet obligations, avoid overdrafts, and optimize the use of cash reserves.

5. Audit Readiness:

- External Audits: Accurate account balances simplify the audit process, reducing the risk of audit adjustments and the associated costs. They demonstrate the company's commitment to transparency and good governance, which can enhance its reputation and stakeholder trust.

- Internal Audits: Regular internal audits are essential for identifying and correcting discrepancies before they escalate. Accurate balances facilitate thorough and effective internal audits, contributing to overall financial control.

6. Impact on Financial Statements:

- Balance Sheet: Accurate account balances ensure that the balance sheet reflects the true financial position of the company. This includes correct reporting of assets, liabilities, and equity, which are critical for assessing the company's solvency and liquidity.

- Income Statement: The income statement relies on accurate account balances to correctly report revenues and expenses. This affects the calculation of net income, which is a key indicator of the company's profitability.

- Cash Flow Statement: Maintaining accurate balances is crucial for the cash flow statement, which tracks the flow of cash in and out of the business. This statement is essential for understanding the company's liquidity and financial flexibility.

Practical Steps to Maintain Accurate Account Balances

To maintain accurate account balances, organizations should implement the following best practices:

1. Regular Reconciliation:

  - Frequent Reviews: Periodic reconciliations, such as monthly or quarterly, help in identifying and correcting discrepancies promptly. This practice ensures that the account balances are always up-to-date and accurate.

  - Detailed Documentation: Keeping detailed records of reconciliation processes and adjustments made helps in tracking changes and understanding the reasons behind discrepancies.

2. Robust Internal Controls:

  - Segregation of Duties: Implementing internal controls, such as the segregation of duties, reduces the risk of errors and fraud. Different individuals should be responsible for recording transactions, authorizing transactions, and reconciling accounts.

  - Automated Systems: Utilizing accounting software and automated systems can minimize human error and enhance the accuracy of account balances. These systems can also provide real-time updates and alerts for discrepancies.

3. Continuous Training:

  - Employee Training: Regular training programs for accounting staff ensure that they are up-to-date with the latest accounting standards and best practices. Well-trained employees are better equipped to maintain accurate account balances.

  - Cross-Functional Training: Training employees from other departments on the importance of accurate financial data can foster a culture of accountability and accuracy throughout the organization.

4. Regular Audits:

  - Internal Audits: Conducting regular internal audits helps in proactively identifying and addressing discrepancies. Internal auditors should review account balances, reconciliation processes, and internal controls to ensure accuracy and compliance.

  - External Audits: Periodic external audits provide an independent assessment of the company's financial statements and account balances. External auditors can offer valuable insights and recommendations for improving accuracy and compliance.

5. Clear Policies and Procedures:

- Documented Procedures: Establishing clear policies and procedures for recording transactions, reconciling accounts, and making adjustments ensures consistency and accuracy. These procedures should be documented and accessible to all relevant employees.

- Policy Adherence: Regularly reviewing and updating policies to reflect changes in accounting standards and business operations helps in maintaining accurate account balances.

6. Use of Technology:

- Accounting Software: Leveraging advanced accounting software can streamline the process of maintaining accurate account balances. Features such as automated reconciliations, real-time data updates, and error detection can significantly enhance accuracy.

- Data Analytics: Utilizing data analytics tools can help in identifying patterns and trends in financial data, making it easier to spot discrepancies and address them promptly.

Conclusion

Maintaining accurate account balances is critical for the integrity of financial reporting and the overall financial health of an organization. It ensures stakeholder confidence, regulatory compliance, effective internal decision-making, and audit readiness. By implementing best practices such as regular reconciliation, robust internal controls, continuous training, regular audits, clear policies and procedures, and leveraging technology, organizations can maintain accurate account balances and support the reliability of their financial statements. Accurate financial reporting not only reflects the true financial position of the company but also contributes to its long-term sustainability and success.

CHAPTER VI
Advanced Accounts Payable Functions

6.1 Managing Foreign Currency Transactions

Handling foreign currency transactions in the Accounts Payable (AP) module is crucial for businesses that operate internationally or engage with suppliers and vendors in different countries. The process involves various steps, from setting up the necessary configurations to managing exchange rates and ensuring accurate financial reporting. In this section, we will delve into the detailed process of managing foreign currency transactions within the Oracle ERP Accounts Payable module.

6.1.1 Explain the process of handling foreign currency transactions in the Accounts Payable module

Managing foreign currency transactions in the Accounts Payable module involves several key steps:

1. Setting Up Foreign Currency Vendors:

   - When dealing with international suppliers, it is essential to set up vendor profiles with the appropriate currency details. This includes specifying the currency in which the vendor operates and expects payments.

   - Navigate to the vendor setup screen in the Accounts Payable module, and enter the necessary details, including the vendor's currency.

2. Configuring Exchange Rates:

- Exchange rates are critical in converting foreign currency transactions to the functional currency of the company. The Accounts Payable module allows for the configuration of exchange rates through the Currency Exchange Rate Maintenance screen.

- Exchange rates can be set up as daily, periodical, or specific to transaction dates. This flexibility ensures that the most accurate and up-to-date rates are applied to transactions.

- It is important to regularly update exchange rates to reflect market changes, ensuring the accuracy of financial records.

3. Entering Invoices in Foreign Currency:

- When an invoice is received from a foreign currency vendor, it is entered into the Accounts Payable system in the vendor's currency. The system will automatically apply the relevant exchange rate to convert the transaction amount into the functional currency.

- The invoice entry screen will have fields for the foreign currency amount, and the system will calculate the equivalent amount in the company's base currency.

4. Handling Payment Processing:

- Payments to foreign vendors can be processed in their respective currencies. The Accounts Payable module supports the issuance of payments in foreign currencies, which involves generating payment batches that include foreign currency transactions.

- The system ensures that the correct exchange rates are applied at the time of payment, and the payment amount in the foreign currency is recorded accurately.

5. Managing Exchange Rate Variances:

- Due to fluctuations in exchange rates, there can be variances between the invoice date and the payment date. These variances need to be accounted for to maintain accurate financial records.

- The Accounts Payable module has functionalities to handle exchange rate variances automatically. When the payment is made, the system calculates any gain or loss due to the difference in exchange rates and posts the adjustment to the appropriate accounts.

6. Reconciling Foreign Currency Transactions:

- Regular reconciliation of foreign currency transactions is necessary to ensure accuracy. This involves comparing the recorded amounts in the Accounts Payable system with the actual payments made and the exchange rates applied.

- Discrepancies should be investigated and resolved promptly to maintain the integrity of financial data.

7. Reporting on Foreign Currency Transactions:

- Accurate and detailed reporting is essential for managing foreign currency transactions. The Accounts Payable module provides various reports that help in monitoring and analyzing foreign currency activities.

- Key reports include the Foreign Currency Invoice Register, Payment Register, and Exchange Rate Variance Report. These reports provide insights into the volume of foreign currency transactions, the impact of exchange rate fluctuations, and overall financial performance.

Detailed Steps for Handling Foreign Currency Transactions

To elaborate on the steps mentioned above, let's break down each process in more detail:

1. Setting Up Foreign Currency Vendors

Setting up foreign currency vendors involves navigating to the vendor management screen and entering the necessary details. Here's how you can do it:

- Navigate to Vendor Setup:

  - In the Oracle ERP Accounts Payable module, go to the Vendor Management section.

  - Select 'Create New Vendor' or 'Edit Vendor' if you are updating an existing vendor profile.

- Enter Vendor Details:

  - Fill in the basic information such as vendor name, address, contact details, and tax information.

  - In the currency field, select the appropriate foreign currency in which the vendor transacts. This ensures that all invoices and payments are recorded in the vendor's currency.

- Save Vendor Profile:

- Once all details are entered, save the vendor profile. This setup ensures that any transaction with this vendor will be processed in the specified foreign currency.

2. Configuring Exchange Rates

Configuring exchange rates accurately is essential for converting foreign currency transactions to the company's base currency. Here's how to configure exchange rates:

- Access Exchange Rate Maintenance:

  - In the Accounts Payable module, go to the Currency Management section.

  - Select 'Exchange Rate Maintenance.'

- Enter Exchange Rate Details:

  - Enter the exchange rate details, including the currency pair (e.g., USD/EUR), the rate, and the effective date.

  - Choose the type of rate (daily, periodical, or transaction-specific) based on your business needs.

- Update Regularly:

  - Ensure that exchange rates are updated regularly to reflect current market rates. This can be done manually or through automated updates if the system supports integration with exchange rate providers.

3. Entering Invoices in Foreign Currency

When entering invoices received from foreign currency vendors, follow these steps:

- Invoice Entry Screen:

  - Navigate to the Invoice Entry screen in the Accounts Payable module.

  - Select the vendor from whom the invoice was received. The system will automatically recognize the vendor's currency.

- Enter Invoice Details:

  - Enter the invoice number, date, and other relevant details.

- In the amount field, enter the invoice amount in the foreign currency. The system will display the equivalent amount in the base currency using the applicable exchange rate.

- Save Invoice:

- Save the invoice entry. The system will record the transaction in both the foreign currency and the base currency, ensuring accurate financial records.

4. Handling Payment Processing

Processing payments to foreign currency vendors involves generating payment batches that include foreign currency transactions:

- Create Payment Batch:

  - In the Accounts Payable module, go to the Payment Processing section.

  - Create a new payment batch and select the invoices to be paid. Ensure that the selected invoices include those in foreign currencies.

- Generate Payments:

  - The system will generate payments in the respective foreign currencies. It will apply the current exchange rates and record the payment amounts in both the foreign currency and the base currency.

  - Print or transmit the payment instructions to the bank as required.

5. Managing Exchange Rate Variances

To manage exchange rate variances, the system will automatically calculate any gain or loss at the time of payment:

- Automatic Variance Calculation:

  - When a payment is made, the system compares the exchange rate at the invoice date with the rate at the payment date.

  - It calculates the variance and posts the gain or loss to the appropriate accounts. This ensures that financial records reflect the true impact of exchange rate fluctuations.

- Review Variance Reports:

- Regularly review exchange rate variance reports to monitor the impact of currency fluctuations on your financial performance.

6. Reconciling Foreign Currency Transactions

Regular reconciliation ensures that foreign currency transactions are accurately recorded:

- Reconciliation Process:

 - Compare the recorded transaction amounts in the Accounts Payable system with the actual payment amounts.

 - Verify that the correct exchange rates have been applied and that any variances are accounted for.

- Resolve Discrepancies:

 - Investigate and resolve any discrepancies promptly to maintain accurate financial records.

7. Reporting on Foreign Currency Transactions

Generating and analyzing reports on foreign currency transactions provides valuable insights:

- Key Reports:

 - Foreign Currency Invoice Register: Lists all invoices received in foreign currencies.

 - Payment Register: Details payments made in foreign currencies.

 - Exchange Rate Variance Report: Highlights the impact of exchange rate fluctuations on transactions.

- Analyze Data:

 - Use these reports to analyze the volume and impact of foreign currency transactions on your business. This helps in making informed financial decisions and managing currency risks effectively.

Conclusion

Managing foreign currency transactions in the Oracle ERP Accounts Payable module involves a series of detailed steps, from setting up vendors and configuring exchange rates to processing payments and managing variances. By following these steps and utilizing the available features, businesses can ensure accurate and efficient handling of foreign currency transactions, thereby maintaining robust financial records and compliance with reporting requirements. Regular reconciliation and detailed reporting further enhance the management of foreign currency activities, providing valuable insights for informed decision-making.

6.1.2 Discuss the setup and configuration required for foreign currency transactions

Managing foreign currency transactions effectively in Oracle ERP's Accounts Payable (AP) module requires meticulous setup and configuration. This process ensures accurate financial reporting and seamless transaction processing across multiple currencies. The following steps outline the key areas of configuration needed to handle foreign currency transactions within the AP module.

1. Enabling Multi-Currency Functionality

The first step in managing foreign currency transactions is enabling the multi-currency functionality in Oracle ERP. This involves configuring the system to support transactions in different currencies. To enable multi-currency functionality, follow these steps:

1. System Options Configuration:

   - Navigate to the Financial Options or System Options setup within Oracle ERP.

   - Enable the multi-currency option by setting the appropriate flags.

   - Define the primary currency for your organization, which will be used as the base currency for reporting and consolidation purposes.

2. Currency Setup:

- Define all the currencies that your organization will transact in. This includes specifying the currency codes, symbols, and precision (number of decimal places).

- Set up currency conversion rates and rate types (e.g., spot rates, corporate rates, and average rates) to ensure accurate conversion between different currencies.

2. Defining Currency Conversion Rates

Currency conversion rates are critical for translating foreign currency transactions into the base currency. Oracle ERP allows you to define multiple rate types and maintain historical rates for accurate financial reporting. To set up currency conversion rates:

1. Conversion Rate Types:

- Define the different types of conversion rates your organization will use (e.g., daily rates, monthly average rates).

- Specify the default rate type for transactions if applicable.

2. Entering Conversion Rates:

- Navigate to the Currency Rates Manager or similar function in Oracle ERP.

- Enter the conversion rates for each currency pair and rate type.

- Ensure that rates are updated regularly to reflect market changes.

3. Automating Rate Updates:

- Configure the system to automatically update conversion rates by integrating with external data providers or financial institutions.

- Set up schedules for automatic rate imports to keep the rates current.

3. Configuring Payment Currencies

For organizations that make payments in multiple currencies, it's essential to configure payment currencies in the AP module. This involves defining which currencies are allowed for payments and setting up the necessary banking information.

1. Allowed Payment Currencies:

- Define the list of currencies in which your organization can make payments.

- Specify default payment currencies for vendors based on their preferred currencies.

2. Bank Accounts Configuration:

  - Set up bank accounts for each currency your organization uses for payments.

  - Ensure that each bank account is linked to the appropriate currency and has the correct account details, including bank codes, account numbers, and SWIFT codes.

4. Setting Up Exchange Rate Tolerances

Exchange rate tolerances help manage fluctuations in currency rates between the time of invoice entry and payment. Configuring exchange rate tolerances ensures that minor discrepancies do not cause transaction rejections.

1. Defining Tolerance Limits:

  - Set up exchange rate tolerance limits for each currency pair.

  - Specify the acceptable range for rate fluctuations (e.g., ±2%).

2. Automating Tolerance Checks:

  - Configure the system to automatically check exchange rates against tolerance limits during transaction processing.

  - Set up notifications or alerts for transactions that fall outside the defined tolerance range.

5. Configuring Foreign Currency Revaluation

Foreign currency revaluation is a process that adjusts the value of open transactions and balances to reflect current exchange rates. This is crucial for accurate financial reporting, especially at period-end.

1. Revaluation Accounts:

  - Define the accounts to be used for revaluation gains and losses.

  - Ensure that these accounts are properly mapped in the chart of accounts.

2. Revaluation Schedules:

  - Set up regular revaluation schedules (e.g., monthly, quarterly) to update the value of foreign currency transactions.

  - Configure the system to automatically post revaluation adjustments to the general ledger.

6. Vendor and Invoice Configuration

Properly configuring vendor and invoice settings ensures that foreign currency transactions are processed correctly.

1. Vendor Currency Setup:

  - Define the default currency for each vendor in the vendor master record.

  - Allow for exceptions where vendors may invoice in multiple currencies.

2. Invoice Entry:

  - Configure the AP module to allow invoice entry in different currencies.

  - Ensure that the system automatically calculates and records the base currency equivalent using the appropriate conversion rates.

7. Reporting and Analytics

Effective management of foreign currency transactions also requires robust reporting and analytics capabilities.

1. Multi-Currency Reports:

  - Configure reports to display transactions and balances in both the transaction currency and the base currency.

  - Set up consolidation reports to aggregate data across multiple currencies.

2. Currency Exposure Analysis:

  - Implement tools to analyze currency exposure and identify potential risks.

- Use dashboards and analytics to monitor exchange rate fluctuations and their impact on financial performance.

8. Compliance and Regulatory Considerations

Finally, it's important to ensure that all foreign currency transactions comply with relevant regulations and standards.

1. Regulatory Reporting:

 - Configure the system to generate reports required by regulatory authorities, such as those for foreign currency transactions and exchange rate gains/losses.

 - Ensure compliance with international financial reporting standards (IFRS) and local regulations.

2. Audit Trails:

 - Set up audit trails to track changes in exchange rates, revaluations, and foreign currency transactions.

 - Ensure that all adjustments and conversions are properly documented and traceable.

Conclusion

Setting up and configuring foreign currency transactions in Oracle ERP's Accounts Payable module involves a comprehensive approach that covers system options, currency rates, payment configurations, exchange rate tolerances, revaluation processes, vendor and invoice settings, reporting, and compliance considerations. By following these steps, organizations can manage foreign currency transactions efficiently, minimize risks associated with currency fluctuations, and ensure accurate financial reporting. Proper configuration not only streamlines the AP processes but also enhances the overall financial management capabilities of the organization.

6.1.3 Emphasize the importance of exchange rate management and reporting for foreign currency transactions

Managing foreign currency transactions within the Oracle ERP Accounts Payable module is not just about processing invoices in different currencies; it requires meticulous management of exchange rates and comprehensive reporting to ensure financial accuracy and compliance. Exchange rate management and reporting are critical components for organizations that deal with multiple currencies, and their significance extends beyond simple transactional accuracy.

1. Financial Accuracy and Integrity

The primary importance of exchange rate management lies in maintaining financial accuracy and integrity. When transactions are conducted in foreign currencies, fluctuations in exchange rates can lead to discrepancies in financial records if not managed correctly. Accurate exchange rate management ensures that the values recorded in the system reflect the true cost or value of transactions at the time they occurred. This prevents misstatements in financial statements and ensures that the organization's financial position is accurately represented.

2. Real-Time Exchange Rate Updates

Oracle ERP allows for the integration of real-time exchange rate updates, which is crucial for businesses operating in volatile currency markets. By leveraging real-time data feeds from financial institutions or other reliable sources, organizations can ensure that the exchange rates applied to transactions are current. This minimizes the risk of exchange rate discrepancies and ensures that the organization is using the most accurate data available.

3. Exchange Rate Types and Usage

Within Oracle ERP, multiple exchange rate types can be configured, such as spot rates, corporate rates, and average rates. Each type serves a specific purpose and can be applied to different types of transactions. For example, spot rates may be used for immediate transactions, while average rates could be used for budgeting purposes. Understanding and appropriately applying these exchange rate types is crucial for accurate financial reporting and compliance.

4. Consistency and Compliance

Consistency in exchange rate application is essential for compliance with accounting standards and regulatory requirements. Organizations must adhere to Generally Accepted Accounting Principles (GAAP) or International Financial Reporting Standards (IFRS), which dictate how foreign currency transactions should be recorded and reported. Consistent use of exchange rates ensures that the organization remains compliant with these standards and can withstand audits and regulatory scrutiny.

5. Impact on Profit and Loss

Exchange rate fluctuations can significantly impact an organization's profit and loss (P&L) statements. Unrealized gains and losses from foreign currency transactions need to be accounted for accurately to reflect the true financial performance of the organization. Proper exchange rate management allows for the timely recognition of these gains and losses, thereby providing a clear picture of the organization's profitability and financial health.

6. Cash Flow Management

Effective exchange rate management is also vital for cash flow management. Organizations need to manage their cash flows in different currencies to ensure they have sufficient liquidity to meet their obligations. Exchange rate fluctuations can affect the timing and amount of cash inflows and outflows. By accurately managing exchange rates, organizations can better forecast their cash needs and make informed decisions about currency conversions, hedging strategies, and investment opportunities.

7. Multi-Currency Reporting and Consolidation

For organizations with subsidiaries or operations in multiple countries, multi-currency reporting and consolidation are critical. Oracle ERP's robust reporting capabilities allow organizations to generate financial reports that consolidate transactions from different currencies into a single reporting currency. This provides a comprehensive view of the organization's financial performance and position across all its operations. Accurate exchange rate management ensures that these consolidated reports are reliable and reflect the true economic reality of the organization.

8. Strategic Decision-Making

Exchange rate management and reporting provide valuable insights for strategic decision-making. By analyzing trends in exchange rates and their impact on financial performance, organizations can make informed decisions about market entry, pricing strategies, and financial risk management. For instance, if a particular currency is consistently volatile, the organization might decide to hedge its exposure or negotiate contracts in a more stable currency.

9. Automation and Efficiency

Oracle ERP offers automation tools for managing exchange rates, which enhances efficiency and reduces the risk of manual errors. Automated exchange rate updates, integration with financial institutions, and predefined exchange rate types streamline the process of handling foreign currency transactions. This not only saves time but also ensures that exchange rate management is consistent and accurate across the organization.

10. Reporting and Analysis

Accurate and detailed reporting on foreign currency transactions is essential for financial analysis and decision-making. Oracle ERP provides comprehensive reporting tools that allow organizations to generate detailed reports on exchange rate variances, realized and unrealized gains and losses, and the impact of exchange rate fluctuations on financial performance. These reports are invaluable for internal stakeholders, auditors, and regulatory authorities.

11. Training and Best Practices

To ensure effective exchange rate management, organizations should invest in training and development for their finance and accounting teams. Understanding the complexities of foreign currency transactions and the features of the Oracle ERP Accounts Payable module is crucial for accurate exchange rate management. Implementing best practices, such as regular reconciliation of exchange rates and continuous monitoring of currency markets, can further enhance the organization's ability to manage foreign currency transactions effectively.

12. Risk Management

Exchange rate risk, also known as currency risk, is a significant concern for organizations dealing with multiple currencies. Proper exchange rate management and reporting help mitigate this risk by providing accurate data for hedging decisions and financial planning. Organizations can use derivative instruments such as forward contracts, options, and swaps to hedge against adverse currency movements. Accurate exchange rate data is essential for evaluating the effectiveness of these hedging strategies and for making informed decisions about risk management.

13. Global Competitiveness

In today's globalized economy, effective exchange rate management enhances an organization's competitiveness. By accurately managing and reporting on foreign currency transactions, organizations can better navigate international markets, price their products and services competitively, and optimize their financial operations. This capability is particularly important for multinational corporations and businesses with significant international trade activities.

14. Technology Integration

Oracle ERP's integration capabilities with other financial systems and tools further enhance exchange rate management. By integrating with treasury management systems, banks, and financial data providers, organizations can ensure seamless and accurate exchange rate updates. This integration also supports comprehensive financial planning and analysis, enabling organizations to make data-driven decisions based on real-time exchange rate information.

15. Future-Proofing Financial Operations

As global markets continue to evolve, the ability to manage foreign currency transactions effectively will remain a critical competency for organizations. By leveraging Oracle ERP's advanced features for exchange rate management and reporting, organizations can future-proof their financial operations against currency volatility and ensure long-term financial stability.

In conclusion, the importance of exchange rate management and reporting in Oracle ERP's Accounts Payable module cannot be overstated. Accurate exchange rate management ensures financial accuracy, compliance, and strategic decision-making. It enhances cash flow management, supports multi-currency reporting and consolidation, and provides valuable insights for risk management and global competitiveness. By leveraging Oracle ERP's robust tools and features, organizations can navigate the complexities of foreign currency transactions and maintain financial integrity in a dynamic global environment.

6.2 Processing Accruals and Deferred Payments

6.2.1 Describe the process of creating and managing accruals and deferred payments in the Accounts Payable module

Accruals and deferred payments are critical components of financial management in any organization. They allow for the accurate representation of expenses and liabilities, ensuring that financial statements reflect the true financial position of the company. In Oracle ERP's Accounts Payable module, the processes for creating and managing accruals and deferred payments are designed to be comprehensive, efficient, and compliant with accounting standards.

Understanding Accruals and Deferred Payments

Accruals are expenses that have been incurred but not yet paid. These expenses are recorded in the accounting period in which they are incurred, regardless of when the actual payment is made. This practice aligns with the accrual basis of accounting, which aims to match expenses with the revenues they help to generate.

Deferred Payments, on the other hand, refer to payments that have been postponed to a future date. These payments are typically associated with expenses or liabilities that have been recognized but will be settled later. Deferred payments ensure that expenses are recorded in the correct period, even if the cash outflow occurs at a different time.

Step-by-Step Process for Creating Accruals

1. Identifying Accruals: The first step in creating accruals is identifying expenses that have been incurred but not yet paid. This could include items such as utility bills, salaries, and services received but not yet invoiced.

2. Recording Accruals: In Oracle ERP, accruals are recorded using journal entries. Navigate to the 'Accruals' section within the Accounts Payable module and select 'Create New

Accrual'. Enter the details of the expense, including the account code, description, amount, and the accounting period to which the expense relates.

3. Approving Accruals: Once recorded, accrual entries need to be approved. This step ensures that all accruals are reviewed and validated before being posted to the general ledger. Approval workflows can be customized to fit the organization's internal control requirements.

4. Posting Accruals: After approval, the accruals are posted to the general ledger. This step ensures that the expenses are recognized in the financial statements of the appropriate accounting period.

5. Reversing Accruals: At the beginning of the next accounting period, accruals need to be reversed. This reversal ensures that expenses are not double-counted when the actual invoice is received and processed. Oracle ERP automates the reversal process, reducing the risk of errors and ensuring accuracy.

Step-by-Step Process for Managing Deferred Payments

1. Setting Up Deferred Payments: Deferred payments are set up by creating a liability for the amount to be paid in the future. Navigate to the 'Deferred Payments' section within the Accounts Payable module and select 'Create New Deferred Payment'. Enter the details of the liability, including the account code, description, amount, and the due date for the payment.

2. Scheduling Payments: Define the payment schedule for the deferred payment. This schedule outlines when the payment will be made and can include multiple installments if necessary. Oracle ERP allows for flexible payment scheduling to accommodate various business needs.

3. Monitoring Deferred Payments: Once set up, deferred payments need to be monitored to ensure timely settlement. The Accounts Payable module provides tools for tracking upcoming payments, generating reminders, and flagging overdue payments.

4. Processing Deferred Payments: When the payment due date arrives, the deferred payment is processed like any other payment in the Accounts Payable module. Generate the payment batch, approve the payments, and issue the payment to the vendor.

5. Adjusting Deferred Payments: If necessary, deferred payments can be adjusted to reflect changes in the payment schedule or amount. This flexibility ensures that deferred payments remain accurate and up-to-date.

Key Considerations for Accruals and Deferred Payments

1. Accuracy: Accurate recording of accruals and deferred payments is essential for reliable financial reporting. Ensure that all expenses and liabilities are properly documented and recorded in the correct accounting period.

2. Compliance: Adherence to accounting standards and internal policies is crucial. Ensure that all accruals and deferred payments comply with relevant regulations and organizational guidelines.

3. Review and Approval: Implement robust review and approval processes to validate all accruals and deferred payments. This step reduces the risk of errors and ensures that all entries are legitimate and accurate.

4. Automation: Leverage the automation capabilities of Oracle ERP to streamline the creation, management, and reversal of accruals and deferred payments. Automation reduces manual effort, minimizes errors, and enhances efficiency.

5. Reporting: Utilize the reporting tools in Oracle ERP to generate detailed reports on accruals and deferred payments. These reports provide insights into outstanding liabilities, upcoming payments, and the financial impact of accruals.

Benefits of Managing Accruals and Deferred Payments

1. Improved Financial Accuracy: Proper management of accruals and deferred payments ensures that financial statements reflect the true financial position of the organization. This accuracy is critical for informed decision-making and stakeholder trust.

2. Enhanced Cash Flow Management: By accurately recording expenses and liabilities, organizations can better manage their cash flow. This capability allows for more effective budgeting and financial planning.

3. Compliance and Audit Readiness: Robust processes for managing accruals and deferred payments ensure compliance with accounting standards and regulatory requirements. This readiness simplifies audits and enhances transparency.

4. Operational Efficiency: Automation and streamlined workflows in Oracle ERP reduce manual effort and administrative overhead. This efficiency allows finance teams to focus on higher-value activities and strategic initiatives.

In conclusion, the process of creating and managing accruals and deferred payments in Oracle ERP's Accounts Payable module is essential for accurate financial reporting and effective financial management. By following best practices and leveraging the capabilities of Oracle ERP, organizations can ensure that their accruals and deferred payments are handled efficiently, accurately, and in compliance with accounting standards. This management not only enhances the accuracy of financial statements but also improves overall financial health and operational efficiency.

6.2.2 Explain the different types of accruals and deferred payments

In the context of accounts payable, accruals and deferred payments are essential for accurate financial reporting and effective cash flow management. Understanding the different types of accruals and deferred payments is crucial for businesses to manage their expenses and liabilities efficiently.

Types of Accruals

1. Expense Accruals:

  - Definition: Expense accruals are liabilities recognized when goods or services are received but not yet paid for. These accruals ensure that expenses are recorded in the period they are incurred, matching the revenue they help generate.

- Examples: Common examples include utilities, salaries, and rent. For instance, a company may accrue expenses for electricity consumed in a month but billed in the next month.

2. Revenue Accruals:

- Definition: Though not typically part of accounts payable, it's essential to understand that revenue accruals record revenue earned but not yet received. This ensures the matching principle of accounting, where revenue is matched with the expenses incurred to generate it.

- Examples: Interest earned but not yet received or services provided but not yet billed.

3. Interest Accruals:

- Definition: Interest accruals are incurred on borrowed funds over a period. These accruals ensure that interest expenses are recorded in the period they are incurred, even if the payment is due in a later period.

- Examples: Accrued interest on loans, bonds, or credit lines. For instance, if a company has a loan with monthly interest payments, the interest expense is accrued each month.

4. Payroll Accruals:

- Definition: Payroll accruals include salaries, wages, bonuses, and benefits earned by employees but not yet paid. These accruals ensure that labor costs are matched with the revenue of the period.

- Examples: Salaries for the last week of the month paid in the next month, accrued bonuses, and vacation pay.

5. Tax Accruals:

- Definition: Tax accruals are liabilities for taxes incurred but not yet paid. These accruals ensure that tax expenses are recorded in the appropriate period.

- Examples: Income taxes, property taxes, and sales taxes accrued but not yet paid.

Types of Deferred Payments

1. Deferred Expenses:

- Definition: Deferred expenses, also known as prepaid expenses, are payments made for goods or services to be received in the future. These payments are initially recorded as assets and expensed over time as the benefits are realized.

- Examples: Insurance premiums, rent, and subscription services. For example, a company might pay an annual insurance premium upfront, which is then expensed monthly over the policy period.

2. Deferred Revenue:

- Definition: Deferred revenue, or unearned revenue, is money received by a company for goods or services to be delivered in the future. This is recorded as a liability until the revenue is earned.

- Examples: Advance payments for products, subscription services, or memberships. For instance, a software company receiving an annual subscription fee upfront will recognize the revenue monthly as the service is provided.

3. Deferred Tax Liabilities:

- Definition: Deferred tax liabilities arise when there are temporary differences between the tax base and the carrying amount of assets or liabilities. These differences result in taxable amounts in future periods.

- Examples: Depreciation methods and differences in recognizing revenue for tax and accounting purposes. For example, a company might use an accelerated depreciation method for tax purposes, resulting in deferred tax liabilities.

4. Deferred Compensation:

- Definition: Deferred compensation refers to an arrangement where a portion of an employee's income is paid out at a later date, typically to take advantage of tax benefits or retirement planning.

- Examples: Pension plans, stock options, and retirement savings plans. For instance, a company might offer a deferred compensation plan where part of an executive's salary is set aside for future payment upon retirement.

The Importance of Accruals and Deferred Payments

Accruals and deferred payments are vital for ensuring that financial statements accurately reflect a company's financial position and performance. Here are some key reasons why these concepts are important:

1. Accurate Financial Reporting:

- Accruals ensure that expenses and revenues are recorded in the periods they are incurred, providing a more accurate picture of financial performance. Deferred payments ensure that prepayments are expensed over the periods they benefit, aligning expenses with revenue.

2. Compliance with Accounting Standards:

- Both accruals and deferred payments are fundamental principles of accrual accounting, required by Generally Accepted Accounting Principles (GAAP) and International Financial Reporting Standards (IFRS). Compliance with these standards is essential for transparent and comparable financial reporting.

3. Enhanced Decision-Making:

- Accurate financial statements enable better decision-making by management. Understanding accruals and deferred payments helps in forecasting cash flows, budgeting, and assessing financial health.

4. Improved Cash Flow Management:

- Managing accruals and deferred payments helps in planning for future cash needs. Knowing when expenses will be incurred and when payments will be made allows for more effective cash flow management.

Setting Up and Managing Accruals and Deferred Payments in Oracle ERP

Oracle ERP provides robust functionality for setting up and managing accruals and deferred payments. Here's a step-by-step overview of the process:

1. Configuring Accruals:

- Define Accrual Accounts: Set up specific general ledger accounts for various types of accruals (e.g., expense accruals, interest accruals).

- Create Accrual Rules: Establish rules for accruing expenses, such as when to recognize expenses and the duration of the accrual period.

- Automate Accrual Entries: Use Oracle ERP's automation features to generate accrual entries at the end of each period, ensuring timely and accurate recording.

2. Managing Deferred Payments:

- Set Up Deferred Expense Accounts: Create accounts for recording deferred expenses and configure the system to amortize these expenses over the appropriate periods.

- Define Deferred Revenue Accounts: Establish accounts for deferred revenue and set up rules for recognizing revenue as the related goods or services are delivered.

- Automate Deferred Entries: Utilize Oracle ERP's automation capabilities to handle deferred expense and revenue entries, ensuring accurate and consistent recognition.

3. Monitoring and Reporting:

- Regular Reconciliation: Perform regular reconciliations to ensure that accrued expenses and deferred payments are accurately recorded and reported.

- Generate Reports: Use Oracle ERP's reporting tools to generate detailed reports on accruals and deferred payments, providing insights into financial performance and obligations.

4. Ensuring Compliance:

- Adhere to Accounting Standards: Ensure that all accruals and deferred payments are in compliance with relevant accounting standards (GAAP, IFRS).

- Stay Updated with Regulations: Regularly review and update accrual and deferred payment processes to comply with changing regulations and accounting standards.

Challenges and Best Practices

Managing accruals and deferred payments can be complex, but adopting best practices can help mitigate challenges:

1. Challenges:

   - Complexity: Accurately recording and managing multiple types of accruals and deferred payments requires a thorough understanding of accounting principles and Oracle ERP functionality.

   - Manual Errors: Manual processes can lead to errors and inconsistencies in recording accruals and deferred payments.

   - Compliance: Ensuring compliance with accounting standards and regulations requires continuous monitoring and updates.

2. Best Practices:

   - Automation: Utilize Oracle ERP's automation features to reduce manual errors and improve efficiency.

   - Training: Provide regular training for finance and accounting staff to ensure they understand the principles and processes related to accruals and deferred payments.

   - Documentation: Maintain detailed documentation of accrual and deferred payment processes, including rules, procedures, and compliance requirements.

   - Regular Reviews: Conduct regular reviews and audits of accrual and deferred payment entries to ensure accuracy and compliance.

Conclusion

Understanding and managing accruals and deferred payments are critical for accurate financial reporting and effective financial management. By leveraging Oracle ERP's capabilities and adopting best practices, businesses can ensure that their financial statements reflect true financial performance and position. Proper setup, regular monitoring, and continuous improvement in processes will help in achieving compliance and optimizing cash flow management.

6.2.3 Discuss the impact of accruals and deferred payments on financial reporting

Accruals and deferred payments play a significant role in financial reporting, particularly in the context of accounts payable within an organization. Their correct handling ensures the accuracy of financial statements and reflects the true financial health of a business. Here, we explore the various ways in which accruals and deferred payments impact financial reporting, focusing on their implications for financial accuracy, compliance, and overall financial management.

Financial Accuracy and Completeness

One of the primary impacts of accruals and deferred payments on financial reporting is ensuring the accuracy and completeness of financial statements. Accrual accounting requires that expenses and revenues are recognized when they are incurred, not necessarily when cash is exchanged. This principle ensures that all financial activities are recorded in the period they occur, providing a more accurate picture of the organization's financial performance.

Accruals are expenses that have been incurred but not yet paid by the end of an accounting period. Recording these accruals ensures that the expenses are matched with the revenues they help generate, adhering to the matching principle of accounting. This matching provides a more accurate representation of profitability for a specific period.

Deferred payments, on the other hand, are payments for expenses that will be recognized in future periods. These may include prepaid expenses such as insurance or rent, where the benefit of the payment extends beyond the current accounting period. By deferring these payments, the organization can match the expense to the period in which the related benefit is received, ensuring that financial statements accurately reflect the timing of these costs.

By correctly accounting for both accruals and deferred payments, organizations ensure that their financial statements reflect all relevant expenses, thereby avoiding understatements or overstatements of income. This accuracy is crucial for stakeholders, including investors, creditors, and management, who rely on financial statements for decision-making.

Impact on Key Financial Statements

The handling of accruals and deferred payments directly impacts key financial statements, including the balance sheet, income statement, and cash flow statement. Each of these statements is affected in specific ways:

Balance Sheet:

Accruals and deferred payments influence the liabilities and assets sections of the balance sheet. Accrued expenses are recorded as current liabilities, reflecting amounts owed but not yet paid. Deferred payments, such as prepaid expenses, are recorded as current assets, representing payments made for services or goods to be received in the future. Accurate recording of these items ensures that the balance sheet provides a truthful representation of the company's financial position at a specific point in time.

Income Statement:

The income statement is affected through the recognition of expenses. Accrued expenses are included in the period they are incurred, ensuring that the expenses match the revenues they help generate. Deferred payments are expensed over the periods in which the benefits are received. This treatment aligns expenses with the corresponding revenue periods, providing a clearer picture of operational performance and profitability.

Cash Flow Statement:

While accruals and deferred payments impact the balance sheet and income statement, they also affect the cash flow statement. Accruals do not involve cash transactions at the time they are recorded, hence they are adjusted in the operating activities section to reconcile net income to net cash provided by operating activities. Deferred payments are recorded as cash outflows when the payment is made, but the expense recognition is spread over multiple periods.

Enhanced Financial Planning and Analysis

Proper management of accruals and deferred payments enhances an organization's financial planning and analysis capabilities. By recognizing expenses when they are incurred, businesses can better anticipate future cash outflows, leading to more accurate budgeting and forecasting. This foresight is essential for maintaining adequate liquidity and ensuring that the company can meet its financial obligations as they come due.

Accruals and deferred payments also provide valuable insights into the timing and nature of expenses, enabling more detailed variance analysis. By comparing actual expenses to budgeted amounts, organizations can identify discrepancies and investigate their causes. This analysis helps management make informed decisions about cost control and resource allocation, ultimately improving financial performance.

Compliance with Accounting Standards

Adhering to generally accepted accounting principles (GAAP) or International Financial Reporting Standards (IFRS) is crucial for compliance and maintaining the integrity of financial reporting. Both GAAP and IFRS require the use of accrual accounting, which mandates the recognition of expenses and revenues in the period they occur, regardless of cash flow.

Accurate accounting for accruals and deferred payments ensures compliance with these standards, thereby avoiding regulatory issues and potential penalties. It also enhances the credibility of financial statements, making them more reliable for investors, auditors, and other stakeholders.

Impact on Financial Ratios

Financial ratios are key indicators of an organization's performance and financial health. Accruals and deferred payments can significantly impact these ratios, affecting how the company is perceived by external parties.

Liquidity Ratios:

Accrued expenses increase current liabilities, which can impact liquidity ratios such as the current ratio and quick ratio. Higher accrued liabilities may indicate a need for improved cash management practices to ensure that the company can meet its short-term obligations.

Profitability Ratios:

Deferred payments impact profitability ratios by spreading expenses over multiple periods. This treatment can smooth out fluctuations in profitability, providing a more stable view of the company's performance. Properly matching expenses to revenues ensures that profitability ratios accurately reflect the company's ability to generate profit from its operations.

Solvency Ratios:

Accrued expenses and deferred payments also affect solvency ratios, which measure the company's ability to meet long-term obligations. Accrued liabilities increase total liabilities, impacting the debt-to-equity ratio and other solvency measures. Accurate recording of these items ensures that solvency ratios provide a true reflection of the company's financial leverage and risk.

Strategic Decision-Making

Effective management of accruals and deferred payments supports strategic decision-making by providing a clear and accurate financial picture. Understanding the timing and nature of expenses allows management to make informed decisions about investments, resource allocation, and cost control.

For example, if accruals indicate a pattern of increasing expenses, management may decide to implement cost-saving measures or renegotiate vendor contracts. Deferred payments, such as prepaid expenses, can highlight opportunities for optimizing cash flow by spreading large payments over multiple periods.

Accurate financial reporting through proper handling of accruals and deferred payments also supports strategic initiatives such as mergers and acquisitions. Potential investors and acquirers rely on financial statements to assess the value and financial health of a target company. Transparent and accurate reporting enhances the credibility of the financial information, facilitating successful transactions.

Risk Management

Accruals and deferred payments are integral to an organization's risk management strategy. By accurately recording and reporting these items, businesses can identify potential financial risks and take proactive measures to mitigate them.

For instance, large accruals may indicate a risk of future cash outflows that could strain liquidity. Recognizing these risks early allows management to plan for adequate cash reserves or financing options. Deferred payments, particularly those related to long-term contracts, can highlight potential risks associated with future obligations. By spreading these payments over multiple periods, companies can manage their financial commitments more effectively.

Conclusion

In conclusion, the impact of accruals and deferred payments on financial reporting is multifaceted, affecting financial accuracy, compliance, financial planning, and strategic decision-making. Proper management of these items ensures that financial statements provide a true and fair view of the organization's financial performance and position. This accuracy is crucial for stakeholders, including investors, creditors, and management, who rely on financial information for decision-making and assessing the company's financial health. By adhering to accounting standards and accurately recording accruals and deferred payments, organizations can enhance the credibility and reliability of their financial reporting, supporting long-term financial success and stability.

6.3 Utilizing Tax Withholding and Remittance Features

6.3.1 Explain the process of setting up and using tax withholding and remittance features in the Accounts Payable module

Tax withholding and remittance are critical features in the Accounts Payable (AP) module of Oracle ERP, designed to ensure compliance with various tax regulations. These features facilitate the automatic calculation, deduction, and remittance of taxes from vendor payments, streamlining the tax management process. Here, we will outline the step-by-step process of setting up and using these features in Oracle ERP.

1. Understanding Tax Withholding and Remittance

Before delving into the setup process, it's essential to understand what tax withholding and remittance entail. Tax withholding refers to the practice of deducting a specific amount from a vendor's payment as mandated by tax authorities. This withheld amount is then remitted to the tax authority on behalf of the vendor. The remittance process involves reporting and paying the collected tax to the appropriate government agency within a specified period.

2. Prerequisites for Setting Up Tax Withholding

To set up tax withholding and remittance in the Accounts Payable module, ensure that the following prerequisites are met:

- Tax Authority Configuration: The relevant tax authorities must be defined in the system. This includes details such as tax rates, tax codes, and reporting requirements.

- Vendor Tax Information: Vendors should have accurate tax information, including tax identification numbers and applicable tax rates.

- Legal Entity and Ledger Configuration: Ensure that the legal entities and ledgers in the system are configured correctly, as these will be used for tax calculations and reporting.

3. Setting Up Tax Withholding

The setup process for tax withholding involves several key steps:

Step 1: Define Tax Withholding Authorities

1. Navigate to the Tax Manager Responsibility:

   - Access the Tax Manager responsibility within Oracle ERP.

2. Define Tax Authorities:

   - Go to the 'Tax Authorities' window and define the tax authorities to which the withheld taxes will be remitted. Provide details such as the tax authority name, address, and contact information.

Step 2: Configure Tax Codes

1. Create Tax Codes:

   - Define the tax codes that will be used for withholding. Each tax code should include the tax rate, type (e.g., federal, state), and the associated tax authority.

2. Assign Tax Codes to Tax Authorities:

   - Link the defined tax codes to the appropriate tax authorities to ensure that the correct rates and reporting structures are applied.

Step 3: Set Up Withholding Tax Groups

1. Define Withholding Tax Groups:

   - Create withholding tax groups that can be applied to vendors. Each group can include multiple tax codes, allowing for complex tax scenarios.

2. Assign Tax Codes to Withholding Tax Groups:

   - Assign the relevant tax codes to the withholding tax groups, specifying the sequence in which they should be applied.

Step 4: Configure Vendor Tax Information

1. Update Vendor Records:

 - Access the vendor records and input the necessary tax information, including tax identification numbers and applicable withholding tax groups.

2. Assign Withholding Tax Groups to Vendors:

 - Link the withholding tax groups to the respective vendors. This ensures that the correct tax rates and rules are applied when processing payments.

 4. Using Tax Withholding in Accounts Payable

Once the setup is complete, you can start using the tax withholding features in the Accounts Payable module. The following steps outline the process:

 Step 1: Invoice Entry

1. Create an Invoice:

 - Enter the invoice details in the AP module. Ensure that the vendor information is accurate and that the withholding tax group is assigned.

2. Calculate Withholding Tax:

 - The system will automatically calculate the withholding tax based on the configured tax codes and rates. The calculated tax amount will be displayed on the invoice.

 Step 2: Invoice Approval and Payment

1. Approve the Invoice:

 - Follow the standard invoice approval process. The withholding tax amount will be included in the total amount payable to the vendor.

2. Process the Payment:

 - When processing the payment, the system will deduct the withholding tax amount from the total payable amount. The deducted tax amount will be recorded separately for remittance purposes.

Step 3: Tax Remittance

1. Generate Remittance Report:

- At the end of the reporting period, generate the tax remittance report. This report will include details of all withheld taxes, the respective vendors, and the total amount to be remitted.

2. Remit Withheld Taxes:

- Use the generated report to remit the withheld taxes to the relevant tax authorities. Ensure that the remittance is done within the specified timeline to avoid penalties.

5. Monitoring and Compliance

Regular monitoring and compliance checks are essential to ensure the accuracy and timeliness of tax withholding and remittance. The following best practices can help maintain compliance:

- Periodic Audits:

- Conduct periodic audits of vendor records and tax withholding transactions to ensure accuracy and completeness.

- Timely Remittance:

- Ensure that withheld taxes are remitted to the tax authorities within the stipulated timeframe to avoid interest and penalties.

- Accurate Reporting:

- Generate and review tax withholding and remittance reports regularly to ensure accurate reporting to tax authorities.

- Vendor Communication:

- Maintain clear communication with vendors regarding withheld taxes and provide them with necessary documentation for their tax reporting purposes.

6. Conclusion

Setting up and using tax withholding and remittance features in the Accounts Payable module of Oracle ERP is crucial for maintaining tax compliance and streamlining financial processes. By following the detailed steps outlined above, organizations can effectively manage tax withholding, ensure timely remittance, and maintain accurate financial records. Proper configuration and diligent monitoring of these features will not only enhance compliance but also improve the overall efficiency of the accounts payable process.

6.3.2 Discuss the different types of taxes that can be withheld and remitted

In the realm of accounts payable, effective tax management is crucial for compliance and financial integrity. The Oracle ERP Accounts Payable module provides robust features to manage tax withholding and remittance, ensuring businesses adhere to various tax regulations. Understanding the different types of taxes that can be withheld and remitted is essential for optimizing these processes.

Income Taxes

Income taxes are perhaps the most common form of tax withholding that organizations encounter. These taxes are usually mandated by federal, state, or local governments and are applied to payments made to vendors or contractors. The withheld amount is typically a percentage of the payment, which the paying organization must remit to the appropriate tax authority. In Oracle ERP, users can set up withholding tax codes and rates specific to different jurisdictions, ensuring accurate calculation and remittance of income taxes.

Value Added Tax (VAT) and Goods and Services Tax (GST)

VAT and GST are consumption taxes levied on the sale of goods and services. While the end consumer ultimately bears the tax burden, businesses are responsible for collecting and remitting these taxes to the government. In some cases, VAT or GST can be withheld at the source, especially in transactions involving cross-border trade or certain services. Oracle ERP facilitates the setup of VAT/GST withholding rules, allowing users to configure tax codes, define tax rates, and manage the remittance process seamlessly.

Withholding Tax on Professional Services

Certain jurisdictions impose withholding taxes on payments made for professional services. These taxes apply to fees paid to consultants, lawyers, accountants, and other professionals. The withholding rate may vary based on the type of service, the jurisdiction, and specific tax treaties in place. Oracle ERP allows organizations to set up and apply these withholding taxes, ensuring compliance with local tax laws and treaties. Users can configure specific tax codes for professional services, define withholding rates, and automate the calculation and remittance process.

Dividend and Interest Withholding Tax

Payments made to shareholders or creditors, such as dividends and interest, may be subject to withholding tax. These taxes are often required by tax authorities to ensure that individuals or entities receiving such payments fulfill their tax obligations. Oracle ERP supports the setup of withholding tax codes for dividends and interest, enabling businesses to accurately calculate and withhold the required amounts before remitting them to the relevant tax authorities.

Royalty Withholding Tax

Royalty payments, often made for the use of intellectual property, trademarks, or patents, can also be subject to withholding tax. The rate and rules for royalty withholding vary by jurisdiction and the terms of any applicable tax treaties. Oracle ERP's flexible configuration options allow users to define withholding tax rates and rules for royalties, ensuring compliance with local regulations and international agreements.

Construction and Contractor Withholding Tax

In the construction industry, payments to contractors and subcontractors are frequently subject to withholding tax. This is designed to ensure that contractors comply with their tax obligations. The withheld amount is usually a percentage of the payment made for labor or services. Oracle ERP provides tools to manage construction and contractor withholding tax, including setting up specific tax codes, defining withholding rates, and automating the calculation and remittance processes.

Social Security and Payroll Taxes

While primarily associated with payroll processing, social security and payroll taxes may also be relevant in the accounts payable context, especially for payments to individual contractors or temporary workers. These taxes fund social security programs and other government benefits. Oracle ERP can be configured to withhold and remit social security and payroll taxes from applicable payments, ensuring compliance with employment tax regulations.

Excise Taxes

Excise taxes are typically levied on specific goods, such as alcohol, tobacco, and fuel. While these taxes are generally collected at the point of sale, certain business-to-business transactions may also involve excise tax withholding. Oracle ERP supports the configuration of excise tax codes and rates, enabling businesses to withhold and remit these taxes as required.

Non-resident Withholding Tax

Payments to non-residents, such as foreign vendors or contractors, often attract withholding tax to ensure that the non-resident fulfills their tax obligations in the country where the payment is sourced. The withholding rate and rules may vary based on local tax laws and international tax treaties. Oracle ERP's robust tax configuration capabilities allow users to set up non-resident withholding tax codes, define rates, and manage the remittance process efficiently.

Environmental and Carbon Taxes

Environmental and carbon taxes are becoming increasingly common as governments seek to reduce carbon emissions and promote sustainable practices. These taxes may be applied to payments for certain goods or services with environmental implications. Oracle ERP enables the setup and management of environmental and carbon tax withholding, allowing businesses to comply with relevant regulations and contribute to environmental sustainability efforts.

Property Taxes

While typically associated with property ownership, certain jurisdictions may require withholding of property-related taxes in specific scenarios, such as the sale of real estate or rental income payments. Oracle ERP can be configured to manage property tax withholding, ensuring accurate calculation and timely remittance to the appropriate tax authorities.

Configuration and Reporting in Oracle ERP

Oracle ERP's Accounts Payable module provides comprehensive tools for managing the various types of withholding taxes. Users can configure tax codes, define withholding rates, and set up remittance schedules for different jurisdictions and tax types. The system also supports detailed reporting, enabling organizations to track withheld amounts, generate remittance reports, and ensure compliance with tax regulations.

Compliance and Best Practices

Accurate and timely tax withholding and remittance are crucial for compliance with tax regulations. Businesses must stay informed about the tax laws in the jurisdictions where they operate and ensure that their Oracle ERP system is configured correctly. Regular audits and reviews of withholding tax processes can help identify any discrepancies and ensure that the organization remains compliant.

In conclusion, understanding the different types of taxes that can be withheld and remitted is essential for effective tax management in the Oracle ERP Accounts Payable module. By leveraging Oracle ERP's robust features and adhering to best practices, organizations can ensure compliance, reduce the risk of penalties, and maintain financial integrity.

6.3.3 Emphasize the importance of tax compliance for withholding and remittance obligations

Tax compliance is a critical component of managing any business, and it becomes especially crucial when dealing with tax withholding and remittance obligations in the Accounts Payable (AP) module of Oracle ERP. Proper tax compliance ensures that an organization adheres to all relevant tax laws and regulations, avoiding penalties and maintaining a good standing with tax authorities. In this section, we will delve into the importance of tax compliance for withholding and remittance, the consequences of non-compliance, and best practices to ensure compliance.

1. The Role of Tax Compliance in Business Operations

Tax compliance involves adhering to the tax laws and regulations set by local, state, and federal authorities. In the context of Accounts Payable, this includes accurately calculating, withholding, and remitting taxes to the appropriate authorities. Tax compliance is not just about avoiding penalties; it is also about maintaining the integrity and reputation of the business.

2. Consequences of Non-Compliance

Non-compliance with tax withholding and remittance obligations can lead to severe consequences, including:

- Financial Penalties: Failure to comply with tax regulations can result in substantial fines and interest on unpaid taxes. These financial penalties can significantly impact the organization's profitability.

- Legal Repercussions: Non-compliance can lead to legal actions against the organization, including audits, legal disputes, and in severe cases, criminal charges against responsible individuals.

- Reputational Damage: Non-compliance can damage the organization's reputation with stakeholders, including customers, suppliers, investors, and regulatory bodies. This loss of trust can have long-term negative effects on the business.

- Operational Disruptions: Tax audits and investigations can disrupt normal business operations, diverting resources and focus away from core activities.

3. Importance of Accurate Tax Withholding

Accurate tax withholding is essential to ensure that the correct amount of tax is deducted from vendor payments and remitted to the tax authorities. This involves:

- Understanding Tax Regulations: Businesses must stay informed about the tax regulations that apply to their operations. This includes knowing the tax rates, thresholds, and exemptions applicable to different types of transactions and vendors.

- Proper Classification of Transactions: Different types of transactions may be subject to different tax treatments. Accurate classification ensures that the correct tax amount is withheld.

- Timely Updates: Tax laws and rates can change frequently. It is crucial to update the tax settings in the AP module promptly to reflect these changes and ensure ongoing compliance.

4. Ensuring Proper Remittance of Withheld Taxes

Once taxes are withheld, they must be remitted to the appropriate tax authorities within the stipulated timelines. Proper remittance involves:

- Timely Payments: Ensuring that withheld taxes are remitted on or before the due dates to avoid late payment penalties.

- Accurate Reporting: Submitting accurate tax returns and reports to the tax authorities, detailing the amounts withheld and remitted.

- Record-Keeping: Maintaining detailed records of all tax transactions, including supporting documentation, to provide evidence of compliance during audits or reviews.

5. Best Practices for Tax Compliance in Accounts Payable

To ensure tax compliance for withholding and remittance obligations, businesses can adopt the following best practices:

- Automate Tax Calculations: Use the automation features of the Oracle ERP AP module to calculate and withhold taxes accurately. Automation reduces the risk of human error and ensures consistency.

- Regular Audits and Reviews: Conduct regular internal audits and reviews of tax transactions to identify and correct any discrepancies or non-compliance issues.

- Training and Education: Provide ongoing training to AP staff on tax regulations and compliance requirements. This ensures that the team stays updated on the latest tax laws and procedures.

- Use of Tax Experts: Engage tax professionals or consultants to provide expert guidance on complex tax matters and ensure compliance with all applicable regulations.

- Implement Robust Controls: Establish robust internal controls and procedures for tax withholding and remittance processes. This includes segregation of duties, approval workflows, and regular monitoring of tax activities.

6. Leveraging Oracle ERP Features for Tax Compliance

Oracle ERP offers several features that can help businesses manage tax compliance effectively:

- Tax Configuration: The AP module allows for detailed tax configuration, including setting up tax codes, rates, and jurisdictions. This ensures that the correct tax is applied to each transaction.

- Withholding Tax Reports: Oracle ERP provides comprehensive withholding tax reports that detail the taxes withheld and remitted. These reports can be used for compliance reporting and audits.

- Integration with Tax Authorities: The AP module can integrate with external tax authorities' systems, enabling electronic filing and remittance of taxes. This streamlines the compliance process and reduces the risk of errors.

- Audit Trails: Oracle ERP maintains detailed audit trails of all tax-related transactions, providing a clear record of compliance activities.

7. Adapting to Global Tax Requirements

For businesses operating in multiple countries, tax compliance becomes even more complex due to varying tax regulations across different jurisdictions. Oracle ERP's AP module supports global tax compliance by allowing businesses to:

- Configure Multi-Jurisdiction Tax Rules: Set up tax rules for different countries and regions within the AP module, ensuring compliance with local tax laws.

- Manage Currency Conversions: Handle currency conversions accurately for cross-border transactions, ensuring correct tax calculations and remittances.

- Generate Country-Specific Reports: Produce country-specific tax reports that comply with local reporting requirements.

8. Conclusion

Tax compliance for withholding and remittance obligations is a crucial aspect of managing the Accounts Payable function in Oracle ERP. By understanding the importance of compliance, adopting best practices, and leveraging the features of Oracle ERP, businesses can ensure that they meet their tax obligations accurately and on time. This not only helps avoid penalties and legal issues but also contributes to the overall financial health and reputation of the organization. Ensuring tax compliance requires a proactive approach, continuous monitoring, and a commitment to adhering to the highest standards of accuracy and integrity in financial reporting.

6.4 Implementing Invoice Hold and Release Functionality

6.4.1 Describe the process of implementing and using invoice hold and release functionality in the Accounts Payable module

Implementing and using invoice hold and release functionality in the Oracle ERP Accounts Payable module is a critical process that ensures proper control and validation of invoices before payment is made. This functionality allows organizations to manage cash flow effectively, prevent unauthorized payments, and ensure compliance with internal and external policies.

Overview of Invoice Hold and Release

The invoice hold and release functionality enables users to temporarily halt the processing of invoices under certain conditions. These conditions might include discrepancies in the invoice, missing documentation, pending approvals, or other issues that need resolution. Once the issues are resolved, the invoices can be released for further processing and payment.

Steps for Implementing Invoice Hold Functionality

1. Configuration of Hold Reasons:

   - Define the various reasons for placing invoices on hold. This could include reasons like "Pending Approval," "Discrepancy in Invoice," "Missing Documentation," "Vendor Dispute," or "Audit Requirement."

   - Ensure that these hold reasons are well-documented and communicated to all relevant personnel to maintain consistency in the use of holds.

2. Setting Up Hold Codes:

- Create hold codes that correspond to each hold reason. These codes simplify the process of applying and managing holds within the system.

- Assign descriptive names and detailed explanations to each hold code to avoid any ambiguity.

3. User Permissions and Roles:

- Assign appropriate permissions to users who will have the authority to place invoices on hold. This typically includes roles like Accounts Payable Clerks, Supervisors, and Managers.

- Ensure that users are trained on the importance of using holds correctly and the potential impacts of incorrect usage.

4. Applying Holds to Invoices:

- Users can apply holds to invoices during the invoice entry or validation process. This can be done manually by selecting the appropriate hold code from a predefined list.

- In some cases, holds can be applied automatically based on predefined business rules. For example, if an invoice exceeds a certain amount and lacks a required approval, the system can automatically place it on hold.

5. Notifications and Alerts:

- Configure the system to send notifications and alerts to relevant stakeholders when an invoice is placed on hold. This ensures that the necessary actions can be taken promptly to resolve the issue.

- These notifications can be sent via email or through the ERP system's internal messaging functionality.

6. Monitoring and Reporting:

- Implement monitoring and reporting mechanisms to track all invoices currently on hold. This includes generating reports that detail the hold reasons, the duration of the hold, and the actions taken to resolve the issues.

- Regularly review these reports to identify any recurring issues or bottlenecks in the process.

Steps for Releasing Invoice Holds

1. Resolution of Hold Reasons:

- Work collaboratively with relevant departments (e.g., procurement, finance, legal) to resolve the issues that led to the hold. This might involve obtaining missing documentation, correcting discrepancies, or completing required approvals.

- Ensure that all necessary information is documented and attached to the invoice record for future reference.

2. Approval Process for Release:

- Establish an approval process for releasing holds. This typically involves obtaining authorization from a supervisor or manager who verifies that the hold reason has been resolved satisfactorily.

- Document the approval process clearly to ensure that all stakeholders understand their roles and responsibilities.

3. Releasing the Hold:

- Once the hold reason has been resolved and the necessary approvals obtained, the hold can be released. This is typically done by selecting the invoice in the ERP system and changing its status from "On Hold" to "Released."

- The system should automatically update the invoice status and notify relevant stakeholders of the release.

4. Post-Release Validation:

- Conduct a post-release validation to ensure that the invoice meets all required criteria for further processing and payment. This includes verifying that all discrepancies have been corrected and all necessary documentation is attached.

- If any issues remain unresolved, consider placing the invoice back on hold until all criteria are met.

5. Payment Processing:

   - Once the invoice is released and validated, it can proceed to the payment processing stage. Ensure that the invoice is included in the appropriate payment run and that all necessary approvals for payment are in place.

   - Monitor the payment process to ensure that the invoice is paid on time and that no further issues arise.

 Best Practices for Using Invoice Hold and Release Functionality

1. Clear Communication and Documentation:

   - Ensure that all stakeholders are aware of the hold and release procedures, including the reasons for holds and the steps required to release them.

   - Maintain detailed documentation for each invoice on hold, including the hold reason, the actions taken to resolve the issue, and the approval for release.

2. Regular Training and Updates:

   - Provide regular training to accounts payable personnel on the correct use of hold and release functionality. This includes understanding the business rules and criteria for placing and releasing holds.

   - Keep users updated on any changes to the hold and release procedures or system configurations.

3. Audit and Compliance:

   - Implement regular audits of the hold and release process to ensure compliance with internal policies and external regulations. This includes reviewing the reasons for holds, the duration of holds, and the actions taken to resolve issues.

   - Use audit findings to identify areas for improvement and implement corrective actions as needed.

4. Efficiency and Effectiveness:

- Monitor the efficiency and effectiveness of the hold and release process. This includes tracking the time taken to resolve issues and release holds, as well as the impact on overall invoice processing times.

- Use metrics and key performance indicators (KPIs) to identify bottlenecks and areas for improvement.

5. Continuous Improvement:

- Foster a culture of continuous improvement by encouraging feedback from accounts payable personnel and other stakeholders. Use this feedback to refine the hold and release procedures and address any challenges or inefficiencies.

- Stay informed about best practices in accounts payable management and incorporate new strategies and technologies as appropriate.

By implementing and using invoice hold and release functionality effectively, organizations can enhance control over their accounts payable processes, prevent unauthorized payments, and ensure compliance with policies and regulations. This functionality not only supports accurate financial reporting but also contributes to overall operational efficiency and effectiveness.

6.4.2 Explain the different reasons for placing invoices on hold

In the management of accounts payable, placing an invoice on hold is a critical control function. This action can prevent the premature or inappropriate disbursement of funds, ensure compliance with internal policies, and address discrepancies before they escalate. Below, we delve into the various reasons for placing invoices on hold within the Accounts Payable module in Oracle ERP.

1. Discrepancies in Invoice Details

One of the most common reasons for placing an invoice on hold is the presence of discrepancies between the invoice details and the associated purchase order or receipt. These discrepancies can include differences in:

- Quantity: The quantity of goods or services billed does not match the quantity received or ordered.

- Price: The unit price on the invoice is different from the agreed-upon price in the purchase order.

- Terms: Payment terms on the invoice differ from those agreed upon in the contract or purchase order.

When these discrepancies occur, the invoice is flagged and placed on hold until the issue is resolved. This helps prevent overpayments or underpayments and ensures that the organization only pays for what it has received and agreed upon.

2. Missing or Incomplete Documentation

Invoices may also be placed on hold if they lack the necessary supporting documentation. Essential documents that might be missing include:

- Purchase Orders: The invoice is not accompanied by a corresponding purchase order.

- Receipts: There is no proof of receipt of goods or services.

- Approval Forms: Missing authorization or approval forms required by the organization's internal controls.

The hold remains until the required documentation is provided and verified, ensuring compliance with procurement policies and audit requirements.

3. Approval Delays

In many organizations, invoices must be approved by designated personnel before payment can be processed. Approval delays can occur due to:

- Absence of Approvers: Key approvers are unavailable due to leave, travel, or other reasons.

- Workload: Approvers are overloaded with other tasks, causing delays in the approval process.

- Hierarchy and Escalation: The need for multiple levels of approval or escalation to higher authorities for large or unusual transactions.

In such cases, the invoice is placed on hold until all necessary approvals are obtained. This ensures that only authorized payments are made, reducing the risk of fraud and errors.

4. Vendor Disputes

Disputes with vendors can also lead to invoices being placed on hold. Common issues that might lead to such disputes include:

- Incorrect or Damaged Goods: The goods received are incorrect or damaged, leading to a dispute over the invoice.

- Service Quality: The services rendered do not meet the agreed-upon quality standards or specifications.

- Contract Terms: Disagreements over the interpretation of contract terms, such as delivery timelines or warranty conditions.

During the dispute resolution process, the invoice is held until an agreement is reached with the vendor, ensuring that the organization does not pay for goods or services that do not meet its standards.

5. Duplicate Invoices

Duplicate invoices are a common issue in accounts payable and can lead to double payments if not caught. Duplicate invoices may arise from:

- Vendor Errors: Vendors mistakenly sending the same invoice multiple times.

- Internal Errors: Mistakes within the organization, such as entering the same invoice twice into the system.

When duplicates are detected, the invoice is placed on hold until it is confirmed whether it is indeed a duplicate or if there are any justifiable reasons for the apparent duplication. This helps prevent financial losses due to duplicate payments.

6. Policy Compliance

Organizations often have internal policies governing the processing of invoices. An invoice might be placed on hold if it violates these policies. Examples include:

- Invoice Amount: Invoices exceeding a certain threshold may require additional scrutiny or approval.

- Vendor Compliance: Invoices from vendors who are not compliant with contractual terms or regulatory requirements.

- Budgetary Constraints: Invoices that cause spending to exceed budgeted amounts or require reallocation of funds.

Placing these invoices on hold ensures adherence to internal controls and financial policies, maintaining fiscal discipline and governance.

7. Fraud Prevention

Invoices may be placed on hold if there are suspicions of fraudulent activity. Indicators of potential fraud include:

- Unusual Patterns: Invoices showing unusual patterns, such as multiple invoices just under the approval threshold.

- Vendor Anomalies: New or infrequent vendors with invoices for substantial amounts or unusual services.

- Employee Collusion: Suspicion of collusion between employees and vendors.

In such cases, the invoice is held while an investigation is conducted. This helps protect the organization from fraudulent activities and financial losses.

8. Compliance with Regulatory Requirements

Regulatory compliance is another crucial reason for placing invoices on hold. Invoices might be held to ensure compliance with:

- Tax Regulations: Ensuring that the invoice complies with applicable tax laws and includes the correct tax information.

- Environmental Regulations: Verifying that the goods or services comply with environmental regulations.

- Trade Compliance: Ensuring that the transaction complies with trade regulations, such as import/export controls.

Holds for regulatory compliance ensure that the organization avoids legal penalties and maintains its reputation.

9. Payment Scheduling

Sometimes, invoices are placed on hold to align with the organization's payment schedule or cash flow management strategies. Reasons include:

- Cash Flow Management: Holding invoices until funds are available to optimize cash flow.

- Early Payment Discounts: Strategically scheduling payments to take advantage of early payment discounts.

- Payment Terms Negotiation: Holding invoices while negotiating more favorable payment terms with the vendor.

This strategic management of payments helps improve the organization's liquidity and financial health.

Conclusion

Placing invoices on hold is an essential function in the Accounts Payable module of Oracle ERP. It ensures accuracy, compliance, and financial control within the organization. By understanding the various reasons for placing invoices on hold, organizations can better manage their accounts payable processes, mitigate risks, and maintain strong vendor relationships. The implementation of robust hold and release procedures contributes significantly to the overall effectiveness and efficiency of financial operations.

6.4.3 Discuss the controls and procedures for releasing invoices from hold

In Oracle ERP's Accounts Payable module, releasing invoices from hold is a critical process that ensures accuracy and compliance in financial transactions. The release of held invoices involves several controls and procedures to maintain the integrity of the accounting system. These controls and procedures are designed to ensure that invoices are released only when all issues have been resolved and all necessary approvals have been obtained. Here, we will delve into the various aspects of these controls and procedures.

Controls for Releasing Invoices

1. Approval Workflow:

One of the primary controls for releasing invoices from hold is the implementation of an approval workflow. This workflow ensures that only authorized personnel can release an invoice. The approval process typically involves multiple levels, depending on the organization's structure and the amount of the invoice.

 Multi-Level Approval: For larger invoices, multiple approvers might be required to ensure that the release is thoroughly reviewed. This prevents unauthorized or erroneous releases.

Segregation of Duties: To minimize the risk of fraud, the tasks of holding and releasing invoices are often segregated. For instance, the person who places the invoice on hold should not be the same person who releases it.

2. Reason Codes and Documentation:

Whenever an invoice is placed on hold or released, reason codes and detailed documentation are used to track the reasons behind these actions. This documentation serves as an audit trail and helps in future reference and compliance audits.

Reason Codes: Predefined reason codes are used to categorize the reasons for holding invoices. These codes standardize the process and make it easier to analyze trends or recurring issues.

Documentation: Detailed notes and supporting documents (such as emails, memos, or dispute resolutions) are attached to the invoice record. This provides context and justification for the hold and release actions.

3. Automated Notifications:

Automated notifications play a crucial role in the control process by ensuring that relevant stakeholders are informed about the status of held invoices.

Notification Alerts: Stakeholders, such as the finance team, department heads, or approvers, receive alerts when an invoice is placed on hold or is ready for release. This ensures timely action and reduces delays in processing.

Escalation Procedures: If an invoice remains on hold beyond a certain period, escalation procedures are triggered to notify higher-level management. This helps in resolving issues promptly.

4. Compliance and Audit Checks:

Regular compliance and audit checks are performed to ensure that the invoice hold and release process adheres to the organization's policies and regulatory requirements.

Internal Audits: Periodic internal audits review the held and released invoices to ensure compliance with the established procedures. This helps in identifying any discrepancies or areas for improvement.

External Audits: External auditors may also review the invoice hold and release process as part of their financial audits. Maintaining accurate and complete documentation is crucial for these audits.

Procedures for Releasing Invoices

1. Review and Resolution of Hold Reasons:

Before an invoice can be released from hold, the reasons for the hold must be thoroughly reviewed and resolved.

Issue Identification: The finance team identifies the issues that caused the invoice to be placed on hold. This could be due to discrepancies in the invoice, missing documentation, or pending approvals.

Issue Resolution: The team works to resolve the identified issues. This might involve reconciling discrepancies, obtaining missing documents, or securing the necessary approvals.

2. Approval for Release:

Once the issues have been resolved, the next step is to obtain approval for the release of the invoice.

Request for Approval: A request for approval is submitted through the ERP system, detailing the resolution of the issues and providing supporting documentation.

Approval Process: The approvers review the request and supporting documents. If satisfied, they approve the release of the invoice. This approval is documented in the ERP system for audit purposes.

3. Updating the ERP System:

After approval, the ERP system is updated to reflect the release of the invoice from hold.

Status Change: The status of the invoice is changed from "On Hold" to "Released." This update is logged in the system, along with the date and time of the release and the identity of the person who performed the release.

Notification: Automated notifications are sent to relevant stakeholders to inform them that the invoice has been released and is ready for further processing.

4. Final Review and Processing:

The final step involves a review to ensure that the release was processed correctly and that the invoice can proceed to the next stage of the Accounts Payable workflow.

Quality Check: A quality check is performed to verify that all necessary steps were followed and that the invoice is accurate and complete.

Further Processing: The released invoice proceeds to the payment processing stage, where it is scheduled for payment according to the terms agreed upon with the vendor.

Best Practices for Effective Control and Procedure Implementation

1. Comprehensive Training:

Ensure that all employees involved in the invoice hold and release process are adequately trained. This includes understanding the reasons for holds, the approval workflow, and the documentation requirements.

2. Clear Policies and Procedures:

Develop and document clear policies and procedures for placing invoices on hold and releasing them. Ensure that these documents are easily accessible and regularly updated.

3. Regular Audits and Reviews:

Conduct regular internal audits and reviews to ensure compliance with the established controls and procedures. Use audit findings to improve the process and address any identified issues.

4. Utilize Technology:

Leverage the capabilities of the ERP system to automate and streamline the invoice hold and release process. This includes using automated workflows, notifications, and audit trails to enhance control and efficiency.

5. Maintain Open Communication:

Foster open communication between the finance team, department heads, and vendors. This helps in quickly resolving issues that cause invoices to be placed on hold and ensures timely release and payment.

By implementing these controls and procedures, organizations can effectively manage the invoice hold and release process in the Accounts Payable module of Oracle ERP. This not only ensures accuracy and compliance but also enhances the efficiency of financial operations and strengthens vendor relationships.

CHAPTER VII
Reporting and Analysis with Oracle ERP

7.1 Generating Standard Accounts Payable Reports

7.1.1 Explain the process of generating standard accounts payable reports using Oracle ERP's reporting tools

Generating standard accounts payable (AP) reports in Oracle ERP involves a series of steps to ensure accurate and comprehensive financial reporting. These reports are crucial for tracking and analyzing the AP activity, aiding in financial decision-making, and ensuring compliance with internal and external regulations. Here, we will detail the process of generating these reports using Oracle ERP's reporting tools.

Step 1: Accessing the Reporting Tools

Oracle ERP provides various reporting tools, including Oracle Financials, Oracle Reports, and Oracle Business Intelligence (OBI). To begin generating standard AP reports, users must first access the reporting tools available within the Oracle ERP interface. This typically involves logging into the Oracle ERP system and navigating to the appropriate module where the reporting tools are housed.

Step 2: Selecting the Accounts Payable Module

Once logged in, users should navigate to the Accounts Payable module. This module contains specific reporting functionalities tailored to AP operations. Within the AP module, users will find a range of standard reports that can be generated to review different aspects of AP activities.

Step 3: Choosing the Desired Report

Oracle ERP offers a variety of standard AP reports, including:

- AP Trial Balance Report: Provides a summary of outstanding payables and their respective balances.

- Invoice Aging Report: Shows the age of unpaid invoices, helping in assessing overdue payments.

- Payment History Report: Details the history of payments made to vendors.

- Vendor Activity Report: Summarizes transactions and activities associated with specific vendors.

- Invoice Register: Lists all invoices processed within a specified period.

- AP Liability Report: Displays the total liabilities due for payment.

Users should select the report that best meets their informational needs. Each report serves a specific purpose and provides insights into different facets of the AP process.

Step 4: Setting Report Parameters

After selecting the desired report, users must set the report parameters. These parameters allow for customization of the report output and include:

- Date Range: Defines the period for which the report will generate data (e.g., monthly, quarterly, yearly).

- Vendor Selection: Filters the report to include data for specific vendors or vendor groups.

- Invoice Status: Specifies whether to include all invoices, only unpaid invoices, or only paid invoices.

- Currency: Chooses the currency in which the report will display financial data.

- Business Unit: Selects the specific business unit or department for which the report is being generated.

Accurate parameter settings are crucial for generating a report that meets the user's requirements and provides relevant information.

Step 5: Running the Report

Once the parameters are set, the user can run the report. Oracle ERP's reporting tools often provide options for generating the report immediately or scheduling it to run at a later time. The system will process the report based on the selected parameters and compile the data into the desired format.

Step 6: Reviewing and Exporting the Report

After the report is generated, users can review it within the Oracle ERP interface. Oracle ERP typically provides options to view the report in different formats, such as PDF, Excel, or HTML. Reviewing the report allows users to ensure the accuracy and completeness of the data presented.

If necessary, users can export the report for further analysis or distribution. Exporting the report to Excel, for instance, allows for additional data manipulation and integration with other financial data. Exported reports can also be shared with stakeholders who may not have direct access to Oracle ERP.

Step 7: Analyzing Report Data

The final step involves analyzing the data presented in the report. This analysis helps in identifying trends, assessing performance, and making informed financial decisions. Users should focus on key metrics such as outstanding liabilities, payment due dates, and vendor performance.

Common Standard Accounts Payable Reports in Oracle ERP

To provide a comprehensive understanding, let's delve into some of the commonly used standard accounts payable reports available in Oracle ERP:

1. AP Trial Balance Report

The AP Trial Balance Report provides a snapshot of the organization's outstanding payables. It includes details such as vendor names, invoice numbers, and the amounts due. This report is essential for reconciling accounts payable balances with the general ledger and ensuring that all liabilities are accurately recorded.

2. Invoice Aging Report

The Invoice Aging Report categorizes unpaid invoices based on their age. The report typically divides invoices into aging buckets (e.g., 0-30 days, 31-60 days, 61-90 days, and over 90 days). This helps in identifying overdue payments and managing cash flow more effectively.

3. Payment History Report

The Payment History Report provides a detailed history of payments made to vendors. It includes information such as payment dates, amounts, and payment methods. This report is useful for tracking past transactions and ensuring that all payments are accounted for.

4. Vendor Activity Report

The Vendor Activity Report summarizes the transactions and activities associated with specific vendors. It includes details such as purchase orders, invoices, and payments. This report helps in evaluating vendor performance and managing vendor relationships.

5. Invoice Register

The Invoice Register lists all invoices processed within a specified period. It includes details such as invoice numbers, dates, amounts, and payment status. This report is essential for maintaining a comprehensive record of all invoices and ensuring that all transactions are documented.

6. AP Liability Report

The AP Liability Report displays the total liabilities due for payment. It includes details such as vendor names, invoice numbers, and amounts due. This report helps in managing outstanding payables and planning for upcoming payments.

Benefits of Generating Standard Accounts Payable Reports

Generating standard accounts payable reports in Oracle ERP offers several benefits:

1. Improved Financial Visibility

Standard AP reports provide a clear view of the organization's financial obligations. They help in tracking outstanding liabilities, monitoring payment due dates, and managing cash flow. Improved financial visibility enables better financial planning and decision-making.

2. Enhanced Compliance

Standard AP reports ensure that all financial transactions are accurately recorded and documented. This enhances compliance with internal policies and external regulations. Accurate reporting also helps in auditing and financial reporting processes.

3. Efficient Vendor Management

Standard AP reports provide insights into vendor activities and performance. They help in evaluating vendor relationships, identifying issues, and negotiating better terms. Efficient vendor management contributes to improved procurement processes and cost savings.

4. Timely Payment Processing

Standard AP reports help in tracking payment due dates and ensuring timely payment processing. This helps in avoiding late payment penalties, maintaining good vendor relationships, and taking advantage of early payment discounts.

5. Data-Driven Decision Making

Standard AP reports provide valuable data for analyzing financial performance and making informed decisions. They help in identifying trends, assessing performance, and implementing improvements in accounts payable processes.

Conclusion

Generating standard accounts payable reports using Oracle ERP's reporting tools is a crucial process for managing and analyzing AP activities. By following the steps outlined above, users can generate accurate and comprehensive reports that provide valuable insights into the organization's financial performance. These reports help in improving financial visibility, enhancing compliance, managing vendors efficiently, processing payments timely, and making data-driven decisions.

7.1.2 Discuss the different types of standard accounts payable reports available

Oracle ERP provides a comprehensive suite of standard reports within the Accounts Payable (AP) module, enabling organizations to monitor and manage their payable activities effectively. These reports are critical for maintaining financial health, ensuring compliance, and optimizing the AP process. The following sections will discuss various types of standard AP reports available in Oracle ERP, their purposes, and how they contribute to efficient AP management.

1. Aged Payables Report

The Aged Payables Report is a crucial tool for tracking outstanding invoices and managing cash flow. It categorizes payables by age, typically into aging buckets such as 30, 60, 90, and 120+ days. This report helps identify overdue payments, prioritize vendor invoices for payment, and avoid late fees.

Key Components:

- Invoice Date: The date the invoice was issued.

- Due Date: The date by which the invoice should be paid.

- Aging Buckets: Groupings of invoices based on their age.

- Vendor Name: The supplier who issued the invoice.

Benefits:

- Cash Flow Management: Helps in planning cash outflows by identifying which invoices are due and overdue.

- Vendor Relationship Management: Avoids late payments, thereby maintaining good relationships with suppliers.

- Financial Planning: Provides insights into the company's short-term liabilities.

2. Invoice Aging Report

The Invoice Aging Report offers a detailed view of unpaid invoices by aging period, allowing AP departments to monitor and address overdue invoices proactively. It is similar to the Aged Payables Report but may include more granular details specific to invoices.

Key Components:

- Invoice Number: The unique identifier for each invoice.

- Vendor Information: Details of the vendor, including contact information.

- Amount Due: The outstanding amount for each invoice.

- Aging Categories: Breakdown of invoices into various aging periods.

Benefits:

- Improved Collections: Identifies overdue invoices that need immediate attention.

- Risk Management: Assesses the risk of overdue payments affecting cash flow.

- Efficiency: Enhances the efficiency of the AP team by focusing on critical invoices.

3. Vendor Payment History Report

This report provides a historical overview of payments made to vendors over a specified period. It is essential for analyzing vendor performance, understanding spending patterns, and negotiating better terms.

Key Components:

- Vendor Name: The supplier's name.

- Payment Dates: Dates on which payments were made.

- Payment Amounts: Amounts paid to each vendor.

- Invoice References: Invoices associated with each payment.

Benefits:

- Spend Analysis: Helps in analyzing total spend with each vendor.

- Vendor Performance: Assists in assessing vendor reliability based on payment history.

- Negotiation: Provides data to support negotiations for better payment terms.

4. Cash Requirements Report

The Cash Requirements Report is instrumental for cash flow planning. It outlines the total cash required to pay upcoming invoices within a specific period. This report helps in ensuring that sufficient funds are available to meet payment obligations.

Key Components:

- Due Dates: Dates by which payments are due.

- Total Amounts Due: Aggregate amount required for upcoming payments.

- Priority Payments: Identifies high-priority payments.

Benefits:

- Cash Flow Forecasting: Assists in forecasting cash requirements for future periods.

- Payment Planning: Ensures timely payments by planning cash reserves.

- Financial Stability: Helps maintain financial stability by avoiding cash shortfalls.

5. Supplier Balance Report

This report provides a summary of outstanding balances with each supplier. It helps in managing payables by supplier, ensuring that the company is aware of its total liabilities towards each vendor.

Key Components:

- Supplier Name: The name of the supplier.

- Outstanding Amount: The total amount owed to each supplier.

- Invoice Details: Summary of outstanding invoices.

Benefits:

- Liability Management: Keeps track of total liabilities towards suppliers.

- Payment Scheduling: Aids in scheduling payments based on outstanding balances.

- Supplier Negotiations: Useful for negotiating payment terms and resolving disputes.

6. Payment Register Report

The Payment Register Report records all payments made during a specific period. It includes details such as payment dates, amounts, and methods, providing a comprehensive view of the company's disbursement activities.

Key Components:

- Payment Date: The date on which each payment was made.

- Payment Method: The method used for each payment (e.g., check, wire transfer).

- Payment Amount: The amount of each payment.

- Vendor Information: Details of the vendors who received payments.

Benefits:

- Audit Trail: Provides an audit trail of payments for compliance purposes.

- Expense Tracking: Helps in tracking and analyzing company expenses.

- Transparency: Ensures transparency in financial transactions.

7. Expense Report

The Expense Report aggregates data on various expenses incurred by the organization, categorized by type, department, or project. It helps in monitoring and controlling costs, ensuring that spending aligns with the budget.

Key Components:

- Expense Categories: Different categories of expenses (e.g., travel, office supplies).

- Department/Project: The department or project to which expenses are attributed.

- Expense Amounts: Total amounts spent in each category.

Benefits:

- Cost Control: Identifies areas where expenses can be reduced.

- Budget Compliance: Ensures spending stays within budget limits.

- Financial Planning: Assists in future financial planning and budgeting.

8. 1099 Report

The 1099 Report is crucial for tax compliance in the United States. It details payments made to vendors who are classified as independent contractors, ensuring that the organization meets IRS reporting requirements.

Key Components:

- Vendor Information: Details of the vendors who require 1099 reporting.

- Payment Amounts: Total amounts paid to each vendor during the year.

- 1099 Categories: Different categories of 1099 payments.

Benefits:

- Tax Compliance: Ensures compliance with IRS 1099 reporting requirements.

- Accurate Reporting: Provides accurate data for year-end tax reporting.

- Audit Preparedness: Helps in preparing for potential audits by tax authorities.

9. Payment Aging Report

The Payment Aging Report provides insights into the aging of payments made, helping organizations track their payment patterns and improve their payment processes.

Key Components:

- Payment Dates: Dates on which payments were made.

- Aging Categories: Grouping of payments based on the time taken to make them.

- Vendor Information: Details of vendors who received payments.

Benefits:

- Payment Efficiency: Helps in identifying delays in the payment process.

- Cash Flow Optimization: Aids in optimizing cash outflows.

- Vendor Relations: Improves relationships with vendors by ensuring timely payments.

10. Liability Report

The Liability Report provides a snapshot of the organization's total liabilities, including outstanding invoices and other payables. It is essential for understanding the company's financial position and managing liabilities effectively.

Key Components:

- Outstanding Invoices: Summary of unpaid invoices.

- Total Liabilities: Aggregate amount of all liabilities.

- Due Dates: Dates by which liabilities should be settled.

Benefits:

- Financial Health: Provides insights into the company's financial health.

- Risk Management: Helps in managing financial risks associated with liabilities.

- Strategic Planning: Assists in strategic financial planning and decision-making.

These standard reports in Oracle ERP's Accounts Payable module offer a wealth of information that is crucial for effective financial management. By leveraging these reports, organizations can gain a better understanding of their payables, improve cash flow management, ensure compliance, and enhance overall financial performance.

7.1.3 Emphasize the use of reports for monitoring accounts payable activity and performance

The importance of using reports to monitor accounts payable (AP) activity and performance cannot be overstated. In the realm of financial management, reports serve as vital tools that provide insights into various aspects of AP operations, enabling organizations to maintain control, ensure compliance, and enhance efficiency. Let's delve into the specific ways in which standard accounts payable reports can be utilized to achieve these objectives.

1. Tracking Invoice Processing Efficiency

One of the primary functions of AP reports is to track the efficiency of invoice processing. By generating reports that highlight the time taken to process invoices from receipt to payment, organizations can identify bottlenecks in their processes. For instance, an AP Aging Report can reveal the average number of days invoices remain unpaid, providing a clear picture of the organization's payment cycle.

Regular analysis of these reports helps in pinpointing delays and inefficiencies, whether they are due to manual errors, approval delays, or system issues. Armed with this information, AP managers can implement targeted improvements, such as streamlining approval workflows, enhancing data accuracy, or investing in automation technologies to expedite invoice processing.

2. Ensuring Compliance with Payment Terms

Reports play a crucial role in ensuring compliance with payment terms agreed upon with vendors. The Payment Terms Analysis Report, for instance, can provide insights into how well the organization adheres to agreed payment schedules. By analyzing this report, AP managers can identify instances of early or late payments, assess the impact on cash flow, and take corrective actions to align with the terms.

Compliance with payment terms is not only essential for maintaining good vendor relationships but also for optimizing working capital. Reports that track payment terms compliance enable organizations to leverage early payment discounts and avoid late payment penalties, thereby improving financial health.

3. Monitoring Vendor Performance

Vendor performance is a critical aspect of AP management that can be effectively monitored through reports. The Vendor Performance Report provides a comprehensive overview of vendor reliability, delivery timelines, and invoice accuracy. By analyzing this report, organizations can assess the performance of their suppliers and make informed decisions about future engagements.

Consistent monitoring of vendor performance through reports allows organizations to foster strong vendor relationships, negotiate better terms, and ensure a reliable supply chain. It also helps in identifying underperforming vendors, providing an opportunity to address issues or seek alternative suppliers.

4. Managing Cash Flow

Effective cash flow management is paramount for any organization, and AP reports are instrumental in achieving this objective. The Cash Requirements Report offers a detailed view of upcoming payment obligations, enabling organizations to plan their cash disbursements strategically. By forecasting cash outflows, businesses can ensure they have sufficient liquidity to meet their financial commitments.

Additionally, reports that track discount opportunities, such as the Discount Analysis Report, help organizations identify potential savings from early payments. By taking advantage of these discounts, businesses can improve their cash flow position while reducing overall expenses.

5. Identifying Fraud and Errors

Reports are essential tools for detecting fraud and errors within the AP process. The Duplicate Invoice Report, for example, helps identify instances where the same invoice may have been entered and paid multiple times. By regularly reviewing this report, organizations can mitigate the risk of financial losses due to duplicate payments.

Similarly, the Exception Report highlights anomalies in the AP process, such as unusual payment patterns or discrepancies between invoice amounts and purchase orders. By scrutinizing these exceptions, AP managers can investigate and resolve issues promptly, safeguarding the organization's financial integrity.

6. Enhancing Strategic Decision-Making

Strategic decision-making in AP is greatly enhanced through the use of comprehensive reports. The Spend Analysis Report provides detailed insights into spending patterns, categorizing expenses by vendor, department, or expense type. This information is invaluable for budgeting, forecasting, and identifying opportunities for cost reduction.

Moreover, reports that track key performance indicators (KPIs) such as invoice processing time, payment accuracy, and discount capture rates enable AP managers to set benchmarks and measure progress. By aligning these KPIs with organizational goals, businesses can drive continuous improvement and achieve better financial outcomes.

7. Supporting Audit and Compliance Requirements

AP reports are indispensable during audits and compliance reviews. The Audit Trail Report offers a detailed record of all transactions, including invoice approvals, modifications, and payments. This report provides transparency and accountability, ensuring that all AP activities are well-documented and traceable.

Compliance with regulatory requirements is also facilitated through reports that track tax obligations, such as the Tax Report. By maintaining accurate records of tax payments and withholdings, organizations can ensure compliance with local and international tax laws, avoiding potential legal issues and penalties.

8. Improving Vendor Relationships

Strong vendor relationships are built on trust and transparency, which can be reinforced through regular reporting. The Vendor Statement Report provides a summary of all transactions with a specific vendor, including invoices, payments, and credit memos. Sharing this report with vendors fosters transparency and helps resolve any discrepancies or disputes promptly.

By consistently providing vendors with accurate and timely reports, organizations demonstrate their commitment to maintaining open and collaborative relationships. This approach not only enhances vendor satisfaction but also strengthens the overall supply chain.

Conclusion

In conclusion, the use of standard accounts payable reports is essential for monitoring AP activity and performance. These reports provide valuable insights into various aspects of AP operations, enabling organizations to track efficiency, ensure compliance, manage cash flow, detect fraud, enhance decision-making, support audits, and improve vendor relationships. By leveraging the power of reports, businesses can achieve greater control, transparency, and efficiency in their AP processes, ultimately contributing to their overall financial health and success.

To maximize the benefits of reporting, organizations should establish a regular reporting schedule, ensure data accuracy, and continuously analyze and act upon the insights gained from these reports. By doing so, they can drive continuous improvement and maintain a competitive edge in today's dynamic business environment.

7.2 Creating Custom Reports with Oracle Business Intelligence

Oracle Business Intelligence (OBI) is a powerful tool that enables organizations to create custom reports tailored to their unique needs. Creating custom reports involves several key steps: understanding the requirements, designing the report, developing the report, testing and validating the report, and finally deploying it for end-users. Each step is critical to ensure the report meets the business needs and provides accurate, actionable insights.

7.2.1 Describe the process of creating custom reports using Oracle Business Intelligence (OBI) tools

Step 1: Understanding the Requirements

The first step in creating custom reports with OBI is to gather and understand the requirements. This involves engaging with stakeholders to determine what information they need, how they plan to use it, and what format would be most useful. Requirements gathering often includes:

- Identifying key metrics and data points.

- Understanding the business processes the report will support.

- Defining the scope and objectives of the report.

- Clarifying the level of detail required.

- Establishing timelines and frequency of report generation.

Effective communication with stakeholders during this phase is crucial. It ensures that the final report will meet their needs and expectations.

Step 2: Designing the Report

Once the requirements are clear, the next step is designing the report. This involves creating a blueprint that outlines the structure, layout, and format of the report. Key aspects of the design phase include:

- Data Sources: Identifying and connecting to the necessary data sources. This may involve integrating multiple data sources to provide a comprehensive view.

- Data Model: Designing a data model that organizes and structures the data in a logical and efficient manner.

- Report Layout: Planning the layout of the report, including sections, headings, charts, and tables. This should be user-friendly and visually appealing.

- Filters and Parameters: Defining filters and parameters that allow users to customize the report view based on their needs.

- Visualization Tools: Selecting appropriate visualization tools such as graphs, pie charts, and bar charts to represent the data effectively.

During the design phase, it's beneficial to create a mock-up or prototype of the report. This allows stakeholders to provide feedback before the actual development begins.

Step 3: Developing the Report

With the design in place, the development phase involves building the report using OBI tools. This includes:

- Data Extraction: Writing queries to extract data from the identified sources. This often involves SQL queries to retrieve specific data points.

- Data Transformation: Transforming and cleaning the data to ensure accuracy and consistency. This may involve calculations, aggregations, and data formatting.

- Report Creation: Using OBI's report builder to create the report layout, insert data fields, and apply formatting. This is where the visual elements and data are brought together.

- Interactive Elements: Adding interactive elements such as drill-down capabilities, hyperlinks, and dynamic filters to enhance user experience.

OBI provides a range of tools and functionalities to facilitate report development. These tools help ensure that the report is both functional and visually appealing.

Step 4: Testing and Validation

Before deploying the report, it's essential to test and validate it to ensure accuracy and reliability. This involves:

- Data Accuracy: Verifying that the data in the report matches the source data and is accurate.

- Functionality: Ensuring all interactive elements, filters, and parameters work as intended.

- Performance: Testing the report for performance issues, such as load times and responsiveness.

- User Feedback: Conducting a review with stakeholders to ensure the report meets their requirements and expectations.

During this phase, any issues or discrepancies should be identified and corrected. Thorough testing helps prevent errors and ensures a smooth deployment.

Step 5: Deploying the Report

The final step is deploying the report for end-users. This involves:

- Publishing: Publishing the report to a shared location where users can access it. This may involve setting up access permissions and security settings.

- Training: Providing training to users on how to access and use the report. This ensures they can fully utilize its features and functionalities.

- Maintenance: Establishing a maintenance plan to update the report as needed. This includes periodic reviews to ensure the report remains relevant and accurate.

Deployment is not the end of the process. Continuous feedback and maintenance are crucial to keep the report useful and up-to-date.

Benefits of Using OBI for Custom Reports

Using OBI for custom reports offers several benefits:

- Flexibility: OBI provides the flexibility to create reports tailored to specific business needs, offering a range of customization options.

- Advanced Analytics: OBI's advanced analytics capabilities enable in-depth analysis and insights, helping organizations make data-driven decisions.

- User-Friendly: The intuitive interface and interactive elements make it easy for users to navigate and utilize the reports.

- Integration: OBI can integrate with various data sources, providing a comprehensive view of the business.

In conclusion, creating custom reports with Oracle Business Intelligence involves a systematic process of understanding requirements, designing, developing, testing, and deploying the report. Each step is essential to ensure the report meets business needs and provides valuable insights. The flexibility and advanced capabilities of OBI make it a powerful tool for creating custom reports that drive business success.

7.2.2 Explain the benefits of using OBI for advanced reporting and analysis

Oracle Business Intelligence (OBI) is a powerful suite of tools that enables organizations to make informed decisions by providing comprehensive and advanced reporting and analysis capabilities. The use of OBI for advanced reporting and analysis within the Accounts Payable module offers a multitude of benefits that can significantly enhance an organization's financial management processes. Below are the key benefits of using OBI for advanced reporting and analysis:

1. Enhanced Data Integration and Accessibility:

Oracle Business Intelligence integrates seamlessly with Oracle ERP, allowing users to access and consolidate data from multiple sources within the organization. This integration ensures that the reports generated are comprehensive and reflect the most accurate and up-to-date information. Users can easily access data related to accounts payable, including vendor transactions, payment histories, and invoice details, all within a single platform.

2. Customizable Reporting:

One of the most significant advantages of OBI is its ability to create highly customizable reports tailored to the specific needs of the organization. Users can design reports that focus on various aspects of accounts payable, such as aging reports, payment term compliance, and vendor performance. The customization options ensure that the reports generated provide relevant insights that align with the organization's strategic objectives.

3. Advanced Analytical Capabilities:

OBI offers advanced analytical tools that go beyond standard reporting. These tools enable users to perform complex analyses, such as trend analysis, variance analysis, and predictive modeling. By leveraging these capabilities, organizations can gain deeper insights into their accounts payable processes, identify patterns, and make data-driven decisions to improve efficiency and effectiveness.

4. Interactive Dashboards:

Oracle Business Intelligence provides interactive dashboards that allow users to visualize data in a user-friendly manner. These dashboards can display key performance indicators (KPIs), metrics, and other important data points related to accounts payable. Users can drill down into the data to explore underlying details, facilitating a more in-depth understanding of the financial information presented.

5. Real-Time Reporting:

The ability to generate real-time reports is a critical benefit of using OBI. Real-time reporting ensures that decision-makers have access to the most current data, enabling them to respond quickly to changing business conditions. In the context of accounts payable, real-time reports can help identify overdue invoices, track payment statuses, and monitor cash flow, thereby improving the overall financial health of the organization.

6. Improved Decision-Making:

With OBI's advanced reporting and analytical capabilities, organizations can make more informed decisions. The insights gained from OBI reports enable finance managers to identify inefficiencies, optimize payment schedules, and negotiate better terms with vendors. This improved decision-making process can lead to cost savings, enhanced vendor relationships, and better cash flow management.

7. Enhanced Data Visualization:

Data visualization is a powerful feature of OBI that transforms raw data into graphical representations, such as charts, graphs, and maps. These visualizations make it easier for users to interpret complex data and identify trends or anomalies. Enhanced data visualization helps stakeholders quickly grasp the financial health of the accounts payable department and communicate insights effectively across the organization.

8. Automated Reporting:

OBI allows for the automation of report generation and distribution. Users can schedule reports to be generated and delivered at specific intervals, ensuring that stakeholders receive timely and consistent information. Automated reporting reduces the manual effort required to produce reports and minimizes the risk of errors, leading to more reliable and efficient reporting processes.

9. Scalability and Flexibility:

Oracle Business Intelligence is highly scalable and can accommodate the reporting needs of organizations of all sizes. Whether a small business or a large enterprise, OBI provides the flexibility to create reports that match the organization's complexity and scale. As the organization grows, OBI can scale with it, ensuring that the reporting infrastructure remains robust and effective.

10. Compliance and Auditability:

Compliance with regulatory requirements is crucial for any organization. OBI helps ensure that the accounts payable processes adhere to relevant regulations by providing detailed audit trails and comprehensive reports. The ability to generate audit-ready reports on demand facilitates compliance and makes it easier to respond to audit inquiries.

11. User-Friendly Interface:

OBI is designed with a user-friendly interface that simplifies the reporting and analysis process. Users with varying levels of technical expertise can easily navigate the platform, create reports, and perform analyses. The intuitive design reduces the learning curve and empowers users to leverage the full potential of OBI's capabilities.

12. Collaboration and Sharing:

OBI supports collaboration and information sharing across the organization. Users can share reports and dashboards with colleagues, enabling collaborative decision-making. The ability to share insights and findings promotes a more cohesive and informed approach to managing accounts payable processes.

13. Performance Management:

By utilizing OBI, organizations can establish a robust performance management framework. The insights gained from OBI reports help set benchmarks, track performance against goals, and identify areas for improvement. This continuous monitoring and evaluation process drives the organization towards achieving its strategic objectives.

14. Cost Savings:

The analytical insights provided by OBI can lead to significant cost savings. By identifying inefficiencies, optimizing payment processes, and improving vendor negotiations, organizations can reduce unnecessary expenses and enhance their bottom line. The cost savings realized through improved accounts payable management contribute to the organization's overall financial health.

15. Future-Proofing:

Oracle Business Intelligence is continuously updated with new features and enhancements, ensuring that organizations have access to the latest tools and technologies for advanced reporting and analysis. By investing in OBI, organizations future-proof their reporting infrastructure, staying ahead of industry trends and maintaining a competitive edge.

In conclusion, Oracle Business Intelligence offers a comprehensive suite of tools that provide numerous benefits for advanced reporting and analysis within the Accounts Payable module. From enhanced data integration and customizable reporting to advanced analytical capabilities and real-time insights, OBI empowers organizations to make data-driven decisions that improve financial processes and drive overall business success. By leveraging the full potential of OBI, organizations can achieve greater efficiency, cost savings, and strategic advantage in their accounts payable operations.

7.2.3 Discuss the steps involved in designing, developing, and deploying custom accounts payable reports

Creating custom accounts payable (AP) reports using Oracle Business Intelligence (OBI) involves a comprehensive process that includes several critical steps. These steps ensure that the reports are tailored to meet specific business requirements and provide valuable insights into the AP operations. Here's a detailed breakdown of each step:

1. Identifying Reporting Requirements

The first step in designing custom AP reports is to identify the specific reporting requirements. This involves:

- Stakeholder Consultation: Engaging with stakeholders such as finance managers, AP clerks, and executives to understand their reporting needs. This could involve meetings, surveys, or interviews to gather detailed requirements.

- Defining Objectives: Clearly outlining the objectives of the custom reports. For instance, the reports might aim to provide insights into vendor payment cycles, invoice aging, or discount utilization.

- Data Requirements: Determining what data is needed to fulfill these objectives. This includes identifying the relevant data sources, such as AP transactions, vendor records, and payment history.

2. Designing the Report

Once the requirements are clear, the next step is to design the report:

- Report Layout: Planning the layout of the report. This includes deciding on the structure, such as tables, charts, and graphs, to present the data effectively.

- Data Fields: Selecting the specific data fields that will be included in the report. For example, an invoice aging report might include fields such as invoice number, invoice date, due date, and days past due.

- Filters and Parameters: Adding filters and parameters to allow users to customize the report view. This could include date ranges, vendor names, or invoice status filters.

- Visualization: Deciding on the type of visualizations to be used, such as bar charts for payment trends, pie charts for vendor spend distribution, or line graphs for tracking invoice processing times.

3. Developing the Report

With the design finalized, the report development process begins:

- Data Modeling: Creating the necessary data models within OBI. This involves defining how the data is structured and related. For instance, linking invoice data with vendor information and payment records.

- Query Building: Writing SQL queries or using the OBI's query-building tools to extract the required data. The queries should be optimized for performance to ensure the reports run efficiently.

- Report Creation: Using the OBI report designer to create the report based on the layout and data fields defined earlier. This involves placing data elements on the report canvas and configuring visualizations.

4. Testing the Report

Before deploying the report, thorough testing is essential:

- Data Validation: Ensuring that the data presented in the report is accurate and matches the source data. This may involve cross-referencing with existing reports or performing manual checks.

- Performance Testing: Checking the performance of the report, particularly with large datasets, to ensure it runs efficiently without long load times.

- User Acceptance Testing (UAT): Conducting UAT with a group of end-users to ensure the report meets their needs and functions as expected. Collecting feedback and making necessary adjustments based on user input.

5. Deploying the Report

Once testing is complete, the report is ready for deployment:

- Report Publishing: Publishing the report to the OBI server and making it accessible to authorized users. This involves setting up permissions and access controls to ensure only relevant personnel can view or modify the report.

- User Training: Providing training sessions or documentation to end-users to help them understand how to use the report. This may include guides on navigating the report, using filters, and interpreting the data.

- Feedback Loop: Establishing a feedback loop to gather ongoing input from users. This allows for continuous improvement and ensures the report remains relevant and useful over time.

6. Maintaining and Updating the Report

After deployment, ongoing maintenance and updates are necessary:

- Regular Updates: Periodically reviewing and updating the report to reflect any changes in business requirements or data structures. This ensures the report continues to meet the evolving needs of the organization.

- Issue Resolution: Monitoring the report for any issues or errors and resolving them promptly. This may involve addressing data discrepancies, performance issues, or user access problems.

- Enhancements: Based on user feedback and changing business needs, adding new features or enhancements to the report. This could include additional data fields, new visualizations, or improved filtering options.

Conclusion

Creating custom accounts payable reports with Oracle Business Intelligence is a multi-step process that requires careful planning, development, and maintenance. By following these steps, organizations can develop robust, tailored reports that provide valuable insights into their AP operations, enabling better decision-making and improved financial management. The key to successful report creation lies in thorough requirement analysis, meticulous design, rigorous testing, and ongoing maintenance to ensure the reports continue to deliver actionable insights.

7.3 Analyzing Accounts Payable Data for Insights

7.3.1 Explain techniques for analyzing accounts payable data to gain insights into spending patterns, vendor relationships, and payment trends

Analyzing accounts payable (AP) data is crucial for understanding and optimizing the financial health of an organization. The techniques used for analyzing AP data help uncover patterns and trends that can lead to more informed decision-making, improved vendor relationships, and enhanced cash flow management. This section delves into various techniques that can be employed to analyze AP data effectively.

1. Data Collection and Preparation

Before any analysis can be performed, it is essential to ensure that the data collected is accurate, complete, and in a format suitable for analysis. This involves:

- Data Cleansing: Removing duplicates, correcting errors, and standardizing data formats.

- Data Integration: Combining data from various sources such as invoices, purchase orders, and payment records into a cohesive dataset.

- Data Classification: Categorizing expenses and payments by type, department, vendor, and other relevant classifications.

2. Descriptive Analytics

Descriptive analytics involves summarizing historical AP data to understand what has happened over a specific period. Key techniques include:

- Trend Analysis: Identifying trends in spending patterns over time, such as increases in expenditure, seasonal fluctuations, or changes in payment behaviors.

- Vendor Spend Analysis: Analyzing the total spend per vendor to identify key suppliers and monitor dependency on particular vendors.

- Payment Analysis: Examining payment data to understand the distribution of payments, identify late payments, and track early payment discounts.

3. Exploratory Data Analysis (EDA)

EDA is an approach to analyzing data sets to summarize their main characteristics, often with visual methods. Techniques include:

- Data Visualization: Using graphs, charts, and dashboards to visualize spending patterns, payment trends, and vendor performance. Common tools include bar charts, line graphs, and heatmaps.

- Outlier Detection: Identifying unusual data points that may indicate errors, fraud, or significant changes in spending behavior.

- Correlation Analysis: Examining relationships between different variables, such as the correlation between payment terms and payment delays.

4. Predictive Analytics

Predictive analytics uses historical data to make predictions about future AP behavior. Techniques include:

- Regression Analysis: Modeling the relationship between variables to predict future spending patterns based on historical data.

- Time Series Analysis: Analyzing time-ordered data points to forecast future trends in accounts payable, such as seasonal spending patterns or cyclical vendor payment cycles.

- Machine Learning Models: Employing algorithms to predict future payment behaviors, identify potential risks, and optimize payment schedules.

5. Prescriptive Analytics

Prescriptive analytics provides recommendations on actions to take based on predictive insights. Techniques include:

- Optimization Models: Developing models to optimize payment schedules, manage cash flow, and maximize early payment discounts.

- Scenario Analysis: Simulating different scenarios to understand the impact of various decisions, such as changes in payment terms or vendor negotiations.

- Decision Trees: Using decision trees to map out possible outcomes and make informed decisions based on the likelihood of various events.

6. Data Mining

Data mining involves discovering patterns and relationships in large data sets. Techniques include:

- Association Rule Learning: Identifying relationships between different variables, such as which vendors are most often associated with delayed payments.

- Clustering: Grouping similar data points together to identify patterns, such as grouping vendors by payment behavior or categorizing expenses by type.

- Classification: Assigning data points to predefined categories, such as classifying payments as on-time, early, or late.

7. Vendor Analysis

Analyzing vendor performance is critical for maintaining healthy vendor relationships and ensuring efficient AP processes. Techniques include:

- Vendor Scorecards: Creating scorecards to evaluate vendor performance based on criteria such as delivery times, invoice accuracy, and payment terms compliance.

- Spend Analysis by Vendor: Analyzing spending per vendor to identify opportunities for consolidation, negotiation of better terms, or diversification of the supplier base.

- Vendor Risk Assessment: Evaluating the financial health and reliability of vendors to mitigate risks associated with vendor dependency or potential supply chain disruptions.

8. Payment Trend Analysis

Understanding payment trends helps organizations manage cash flow and optimize working capital. Techniques include:

- Aging Analysis: Analyzing the age of unpaid invoices to identify overdue payments and manage accounts payable aging.

- Payment Cycle Analysis: Examining the time taken to process payments from invoice receipt to payment completion to identify inefficiencies and opportunities for improvement.

- Discount Analysis: Tracking the utilization of early payment discounts to maximize savings and improve cash flow management.

9. Benchmarking

Benchmarking involves comparing AP performance against industry standards or best practices. Techniques include:

- Performance Metrics: Tracking key performance indicators (KPIs) such as days payable outstanding (DPO), invoice processing time, and payment accuracy.

- Industry Comparisons: Comparing AP performance with industry peers to identify areas for improvement and adopt best practices.

- Internal Benchmarking: Comparing AP performance across different departments or business units to identify internal best practices and standardize processes.

10. Financial Impact Analysis

Analyzing the financial impact of AP activities helps organizations understand the broader implications of their AP processes. Techniques include:

- Cost-Benefit Analysis: Evaluating the costs and benefits of different AP strategies, such as early payment discounts versus extending payment terms.

- ROI Analysis: Measuring the return on investment for AP initiatives, such as implementing automated invoicing systems or renegotiating vendor contracts.

- Cash Flow Analysis: Analyzing the impact of AP activities on cash flow to ensure sufficient liquidity and optimize working capital.

11. Continuous Improvement

Continuous improvement involves using insights from AP data analysis to drive ongoing improvements in AP processes. Techniques include:

- Root Cause Analysis: Identifying the root causes of issues such as late payments or invoice discrepancies to implement corrective actions.

- Process Mapping: Mapping out AP processes to identify bottlenecks, redundancies, and areas for improvement.

- Feedback Loops: Establishing feedback loops with stakeholders such as vendors, finance teams, and procurement teams to continuously refine and improve AP processes.

12. Advanced Analytics and Artificial Intelligence (AI)

Leveraging advanced analytics and AI can significantly enhance AP data analysis capabilities. Techniques include:

- Natural Language Processing (NLP): Using NLP to analyze unstructured data such as vendor communications or invoice notes to gain additional insights.

- Robotic Process Automation (RPA): Automating repetitive AP tasks to improve efficiency and reduce errors.

- AI-Driven Insights: Employing AI algorithms to uncover hidden patterns, predict future behaviors, and recommend actions for optimizing AP processes.

Conclusion

Analyzing accounts payable data is a powerful way to gain insights into spending patterns, vendor relationships, and payment trends. By employing a combination of descriptive, exploratory, predictive, and prescriptive analytics, organizations can make data-driven decisions that enhance financial performance, improve vendor relationships, and optimize cash flow management. Continuous improvement, driven by insights from advanced analytics and AI, ensures that AP processes remain efficient, effective, and aligned with the organization's strategic objectives.

7.3.2 Discuss the use of data visualization tools for effective analysis of accounts payable data

In the modern business environment, the ability to analyze and interpret vast amounts of data efficiently is crucial. This is especially true for the accounts payable (AP) function, where timely and accurate insights can drive significant improvements in cash flow management, vendor relationships, and overall financial performance. Data visualization tools play a pivotal role in making sense of AP data, transforming complex datasets into intuitive visual representations that facilitate better decision-making.

Introduction to Data Visualization Tools

Data visualization tools, such as Oracle Business Intelligence (OBI), Tableau, Power BI, and others, are designed to convert raw data into graphical formats like charts, graphs, dashboards, and heat maps. These visual representations make it easier to spot trends, patterns, and anomalies that might not be immediately apparent in spreadsheets or raw data tables.

Benefits of Data Visualization in Accounts Payable

1. Enhanced Data Comprehension:

   Visual tools simplify complex data, making it more accessible to users at all levels of the organization. By presenting data visually, these tools help users quickly grasp key metrics, such as outstanding invoices, payment timelines, and vendor performance.

2. Improved Decision-Making:

Visualization facilitates quicker and more informed decision-making. For instance, a dashboard showing real-time AP metrics can help managers identify overdue invoices, monitor cash flow, and prioritize payments based on strategic importance.

3. Trend Identification:

Visual tools can highlight trends over time, such as changes in spending patterns or payment behaviors. This can help businesses anticipate future cash needs, negotiate better terms with vendors, or identify opportunities for cost savings.

4. Anomaly Detection:

Visualization can make outliers and anomalies stand out, such as unusually large invoices or unexpected payment delays. Identifying these anomalies early can prevent potential issues and ensure that the AP process runs smoothly.

5. Effective Communication:

Data visualizations are not only useful for analysis but also for communicating insights to stakeholders. A well-designed chart or dashboard can convey complex information succinctly and persuasively, making it easier to gain buy-in for process improvements or strategic initiatives.

Key Data Visualization Tools and Their Features

1. Oracle Business Intelligence (OBI):

Oracle's suite of BI tools offers robust capabilities for data analysis and visualization. OBI allows users to create interactive dashboards, ad-hoc queries, and detailed reports. It integrates seamlessly with Oracle ERP, providing real-time insights into AP data.

2. Tableau:

Known for its user-friendly interface, Tableau enables users to create a wide range of visualizations, from simple bar charts to complex multi-dimensional analyses. Its drag-and-drop functionality makes it accessible to non-technical users while offering advanced features for data analysts.

3. Power BI:

Developed by Microsoft, Power BI is a powerful tool for creating interactive visualizations and business intelligence reports. It integrates well with other Microsoft products and services, making it a popular choice for organizations already using the Microsoft ecosystem.

4. QlikView:

QlikView offers a unique associative data model that allows users to explore data freely, without the constraints of predefined drill paths. This makes it easier to discover hidden relationships within AP data and gain deeper insights.

5. Domo:

Domo provides cloud-based business intelligence solutions, enabling users to create custom dashboards and visualizations. Its platform supports collaboration and sharing, making it easier for teams to work together on data analysis.

Steps to Implement Data Visualization for AP Analysis

1. Identify Key Metrics:

Start by identifying the key metrics that are most relevant to your AP function. These might include total outstanding payables, average payment processing time, vendor performance ratings, and discount capture rates.

2. Gather and Prepare Data:

Ensure that your data is accurate, complete, and up-to-date. This may involve extracting data from multiple sources, such as your ERP system, financial software, and vendor management tools. Clean and normalize the data to ensure consistency.

3. Choose the Right Visualization Tool:

Select a data visualization tool that fits your organization's needs and capabilities. Consider factors such as ease of use, integration with existing systems, and the level of support available.

4. Design Visualizations:

Design your visualizations with clarity and usability in mind. Choose the appropriate chart types for your data and ensure that your dashboards are easy to navigate. Use colors and labels effectively to highlight important information.

5. Create Dashboards:

Build interactive dashboards that provide a comprehensive view of your AP metrics. Ensure that the dashboards can be customized and filtered to meet the specific needs of different users, such as AP managers, financial analysts, and executives.

6. Test and Refine:

Test your visualizations with real users and gather feedback. Make adjustments as needed to improve usability and ensure that the visualizations effectively communicate the desired insights.

7. Train Users:

Provide training and resources to help users get the most out of the visualization tools. Ensure that they understand how to interact with the dashboards, interpret the data, and use the insights to make informed decisions.

8. Monitor and Update:

Regularly review and update your visualizations to ensure that they remain relevant and accurate. As your business needs evolve, adjust the metrics and visualizations to reflect new priorities and goals.

Practical Applications of Data Visualization in AP

1. Cash Flow Management:

Dashboards showing the status of outstanding invoices and payment schedules can help manage cash flow more effectively. Visualizing the timing and amounts of upcoming payments allows businesses to plan for cash needs and avoid liquidity issues.

2. Vendor Performance Analysis:

Visualizations can help track vendor performance metrics such as on-time delivery rates, invoice accuracy, and compliance with payment terms. This information can be used to negotiate better terms, select preferred vendors, and improve supplier relationships.

3. Expense Tracking:

By visualizing expense data, businesses can identify spending patterns and areas where costs can be reduced. For example, a heat map showing the distribution of expenses across different categories can highlight opportunities for cost savings.

4. Payment Trends:

Analyzing payment trends over time can reveal patterns such as seasonal fluctuations in spending or changes in payment behavior. This information can be used to optimize payment strategies and improve cash flow management.

5. Compliance Monitoring:

Visualization tools can help monitor compliance with internal policies and external regulations. Dashboards showing compliance metrics, such as adherence to payment terms and tax codes, can help ensure that the AP function operates within legal and organizational guidelines.

Conclusion

Data visualization is an essential tool for modern accounts payable management. By transforming raw data into intuitive visual formats, businesses can gain valuable insights into their AP processes, identify areas for improvement, and make more informed decisions. The use of visualization tools not only enhances data comprehension and decision-making but also facilitates effective communication of insights to stakeholders. As technology continues to evolve, the capabilities of data visualization tools will only improve, offering even greater potential for optimizing accounts payable operations and driving financial success.

7.3.3 Emphasize the importance of data-driven insights for improving accounts payable processes

In the realm of accounts payable (AP), data-driven insights play a pivotal role in optimizing processes, enhancing efficiency, and driving strategic decision-making. Leveraging data effectively can transform AP from a reactive, transactional function into a proactive, strategic asset. This section explores the importance of data-driven insights for improving accounts payable processes and the various ways organizations can harness these insights for tangible benefits.

1. Enhancing Operational Efficiency

Operational efficiency in accounts payable is crucial for maintaining a smooth and effective financial workflow. Data-driven insights can identify bottlenecks and inefficiencies in the AP process. For example, by analyzing the time taken to process invoices, organizations can pinpoint stages where delays frequently occur and implement targeted improvements. This might involve automating certain steps, reassigning tasks to balance workloads, or providing additional training to staff.

Additionally, insights into the frequency and reasons for invoice discrepancies can lead to the development of more robust validation and matching procedures. By minimizing errors and rework, organizations can streamline their AP processes, reducing the overall time and cost involved in handling payables.

2. Optimizing Cash Flow Management

Effective cash flow management is essential for the financial health of any organization. Data-driven insights provide a clear picture of payment patterns, allowing businesses to optimize their cash flow. For instance, analyzing payment trends can help identify opportunities to take advantage of early payment discounts offered by vendors. Conversely, understanding the timing of outgoing payments can aid in planning and maintaining sufficient liquidity to meet obligations without incurring unnecessary financing costs.

Moreover, predictive analytics can forecast future cash flow needs based on historical data and upcoming obligations. This proactive approach enables organizations to make informed decisions about managing working capital, such as scheduling payments strategically to maintain optimal cash balances.

3. Strengthening Vendor Relationships

Vendor relationships are a critical component of the accounts payable function. Data-driven insights can help organizations evaluate vendor performance and strengthen these relationships. By analyzing data on payment histories, organizations can assess their compliance with agreed-upon payment terms, identifying instances of late payments that might negatively impact vendor relationships.

Furthermore, insights into the frequency and nature of vendor disputes can highlight areas where communication or contract terms might need improvement. By addressing these issues proactively, organizations can foster stronger, more collaborative relationships with their vendors, leading to better terms, improved service levels, and potential cost savings.

4. Improving Compliance and Risk Management

Compliance with regulatory requirements and internal policies is a key concern for accounts payable departments. Data-driven insights can enhance compliance efforts by providing visibility into adherence to payment terms, tax regulations, and other relevant standards. For example, regular analysis of payment data can ensure that transactions are correctly classified and reported for tax purposes, reducing the risk of penalties and audits.

Additionally, data-driven insights can identify patterns indicative of potential fraud or errors. By continuously monitoring AP transactions for unusual activity, organizations can implement controls and corrective actions to mitigate risks, ensuring the integrity of their financial processes.

5. Supporting Strategic Decision-Making

Beyond operational improvements, data-driven insights enable strategic decision-making within the accounts payable function. For instance, insights into spending patterns can inform budgeting and forecasting efforts, helping organizations allocate resources more effectively. By understanding the impact of payment terms and vendor negotiations on overall costs, organizations can make more informed decisions about their procurement strategies.

Moreover, data-driven insights can support broader financial planning and analysis (FP&A) activities. By integrating AP data with other financial data, organizations can gain a comprehensive view of their financial health and make strategic decisions that align with their long-term objectives.

6. Enabling Continuous Improvement

The concept of continuous improvement is fundamental to modern business practices, and data-driven insights are a cornerstone of this approach. By regularly analyzing AP data, organizations can identify trends and areas for improvement, setting the stage for ongoing enhancements to processes and performance.

For example, insights into invoice processing times and error rates can guide the implementation of process improvements, such as adopting new technologies or revising workflows. By continuously monitoring the impact of these changes, organizations can ensure that improvements are sustained and further refined over time.

7. Leveraging Technology for Data-Driven Insights

To fully realize the benefits of data-driven insights, organizations must leverage the right technologies. Advanced analytics tools, such as Oracle Business Intelligence (OBI), provide powerful capabilities for analyzing and visualizing AP data. These tools enable organizations to create custom reports and dashboards that deliver real-time insights into AP performance.

Moreover, integrating AP systems with other enterprise resource planning (ERP) modules ensures that data flows seamlessly across the organization, providing a holistic view of financial processes. This integration facilitates more comprehensive analysis and supports informed decision-making at all levels of the organization.

8. Case Studies and Best Practices

Examining case studies and best practices from leading organizations can provide valuable insights into how data-driven approaches can transform accounts payable processes. For instance, companies that have successfully implemented data-driven AP strategies often report significant improvements in efficiency, cost savings, and vendor satisfaction.

Best practices for leveraging data-driven insights in accounts payable include:

- Regularly Reviewing AP Metrics: Establishing a routine for reviewing key performance indicators (KPIs) such as invoice processing time, payment accuracy, and discount capture rates helps maintain focus on continuous improvement.

- Investing in Training: Ensuring that AP staff are proficient in using analytics tools and interpreting data is crucial for maximizing the value of data-driven insights.

- Collaborating with Stakeholders: Engaging with stakeholders across the organization, including procurement, finance, and IT, helps ensure that AP data is used effectively to support broader business objectives.

- Adopting Agile Practices: Embracing agile methodologies in the AP function allows organizations to quickly adapt to changes and continuously refine processes based on data-driven feedback.

Conclusion

In conclusion, data-driven insights are essential for optimizing accounts payable processes and achieving broader organizational goals. By leveraging data effectively, organizations can enhance operational efficiency, optimize cash flow management, strengthen vendor relationships, improve compliance, and support strategic decision-making. As technology continues to evolve, the ability to harness data-driven insights will become increasingly important for organizations seeking to stay competitive in a rapidly changing business environment. Embracing these insights and integrating them into everyday AP practices is key to unlocking the full potential of the accounts payable function.

7.4 Using Reports to Improve Financial Processes

7.4.1 Describe how to use accounts payable reports to identify areas for improvement in financial processes

In the realm of financial management, accounts payable (AP) reports play a crucial role in providing detailed insights into an organization's expenditure patterns, vendor performance, and overall efficiency of the payment processes. Utilizing these reports effectively can help organizations identify areas for improvement, streamline operations, and enhance their financial health. Here, we will delve into how accounts payable reports can be leveraged to pinpoint specific areas that require enhancement in financial processes.

Understanding Accounts Payable Reports

Accounts payable reports come in various formats and serve different purposes, but they all share the common goal of presenting actionable data. These reports can be broadly categorized into standard reports and custom reports.

Standard Accounts Payable Reports:

- Aging Reports: These reports provide a snapshot of outstanding payables, categorized by the length of time they have been due. They help in identifying overdue payments and assessing the effectiveness of payment strategies.

- Vendor Activity Reports: These detail transactions with each vendor, highlighting spending patterns and vendor reliability.

- Payment Analysis Reports: These show payment trends, including methods of payment and timing, helping to optimize cash flow management.

Custom Accounts Payable Reports:

- Spend Analysis Reports: Customized to focus on specific categories of spend, these reports help in understanding where most of the company's money is going.

- Exception Reports: These highlight discrepancies and anomalies in the accounts payable process, such as duplicate payments or payments made without proper authorization.

- Performance Metrics Reports: Focused on key performance indicators (KPIs) like payment cycle time and discount utilization, these reports help measure the efficiency of the accounts payable department.

Identifying Improvement Areas

To use accounts payable reports effectively, it is essential to establish a structured approach to analyzing the data. Here are some key steps and strategies:

1. Benchmarking Performance:

   - Compare current performance metrics against historical data and industry standards. This helps in identifying deviations and potential areas of improvement.

   - Use reports like the Vendor Activity Report and Performance Metrics Report to evaluate whether the accounts payable processes are in line with best practices.

2. Analyzing Payment Cycles:

   - Use Aging Reports to examine the payment cycle and identify delays in processing invoices. Late payments can lead to strained vendor relationships and lost early payment discounts.

   - Analyze Payment Analysis Reports to assess whether payments are being made promptly and efficiently. Identify any bottlenecks in the approval or payment process.

3. Monitoring Vendor Performance:

   - Evaluate Vendor Activity Reports to identify vendors with frequent discrepancies or late deliveries. This can help in renegotiating terms or finding more reliable suppliers.

   - Use Spend Analysis Reports to determine if there are opportunities to consolidate vendors and negotiate better terms.

4. Assessing Compliance and Risk:

- Generate Exception Reports to identify any unauthorized payments or deviations from established protocols. This helps in mitigating fraud risks and ensuring compliance.

- Regularly review Tax Reports to ensure compliance with local and international tax regulations. Mismanagement in this area can lead to significant financial penalties.

5. Evaluating Process Efficiency:

- Utilize Performance Metrics Reports to measure the efficiency of the accounts payable process. Metrics such as the average time to process an invoice, the rate of on-time payments, and the percentage of invoices processed without exceptions are critical indicators of process health.

- Implement Workflow Analysis Reports to understand how invoices move through the system and where delays or redundancies occur. This can highlight areas for process automation or re-engineering.

Practical Applications and Case Studies

Case Study 1: Reducing Payment Cycle Time

- Company Profile: A mid-sized manufacturing firm.

- Challenge: The company faced significant delays in processing invoices, resulting in late payments and strained vendor relationships.

- Solution: By analyzing Aging Reports and Performance Metrics Reports, the firm identified bottlenecks in the approval process. Implementing an automated workflow reduced the average invoice processing time from 30 days to 15 days.

- Outcome: Improved vendor relationships and captured more early payment discounts, leading to a 5% reduction in overall costs.

Case Study 2: Enhancing Vendor Management

- Company Profile: A large retail chain.

- Challenge: The retail chain had a fragmented vendor base with varied performance levels.

- Solution: Using Vendor Activity Reports and Spend Analysis Reports, the company consolidated its vendor base, selecting the most reliable and cost-effective suppliers.

- Outcome: Improved vendor performance, reduced discrepancies, and negotiated better payment terms, resulting in significant cost savings.

Case Study 3: Ensuring Compliance and Mitigating Fraud

- Company Profile: A global technology company.

- Challenge: The company faced challenges in ensuring compliance with various tax jurisdictions and detecting unauthorized payments.

- Solution: By leveraging Exception Reports and Tax Compliance Reports, the company identified and corrected unauthorized transactions and improved its tax compliance process.

- Outcome: Reduced risk of financial penalties and improved internal controls, enhancing overall financial governance.

Leveraging Technology for Improved Reporting

Modern accounts payable systems, like Oracle ERP, offer advanced reporting and analytics tools that can transform raw data into meaningful insights. Key technological enablers include:

1. Oracle Business Intelligence (OBI):

  - Customization: OBI allows for the creation of tailored reports that address specific business needs, providing deeper insights into accounts payable processes.

  - Visualization: Advanced data visualization tools help in presenting complex data in an easily understandable format, facilitating better decision-making.

2. Automation:

  - Workflow Automation: Automating routine tasks like invoice matching and approval reduces manual errors and speeds up the process.

- Automated Alerts: Setting up alerts for exceptions and anomalies ensures timely action on potential issues, maintaining process integrity.

3. Integration with Other Modules:

- Seamless Integration: Integrating accounts payable with other ERP modules like procurement and inventory ensures a holistic view of the financial processes, enabling more comprehensive reporting and analysis.

Conclusion

Effective use of accounts payable reports is essential for identifying areas for improvement in financial processes. By leveraging standard and custom reports, organizations can gain valuable insights into their payment cycles, vendor performance, compliance, and overall process efficiency. Utilizing advanced reporting tools like Oracle Business Intelligence, companies can transform data into actionable insights, driving continuous improvement and achieving financial excellence. By adopting a structured approach to analyzing accounts payable data, organizations can optimize their financial processes, reduce costs, and enhance their overall financial health.

7.4.2 Discuss the use of reports to track metrics such as payment terms compliance, invoice processing time, and discounts captured

In the world of accounts payable, the ability to track and analyze key performance metrics is essential for optimizing financial processes and ensuring the organization's financial health. Oracle ERP's robust reporting capabilities provide invaluable insights into these metrics, allowing organizations to identify areas for improvement and implement data-driven strategies. This section delves into the specifics of using reports to track critical accounts payable metrics, including payment terms compliance, invoice processing time, and discounts captured.

Payment Terms Compliance

Understanding Payment Terms Compliance

Payment terms compliance refers to the degree to which an organization adheres to the agreed-upon terms with its vendors. These terms dictate the time frame within which payments should be made, which can have significant implications for cash flow management and vendor relationships. Ensuring compliance with payment terms is crucial for maintaining supplier trust and taking advantage of early payment discounts.

Tracking Payment Terms Compliance Using Reports

Oracle ERP provides comprehensive reporting tools that enable organizations to monitor payment terms compliance effectively. These reports typically include:

1. Aging Reports: These reports categorize outstanding invoices based on the number of days they have been outstanding. By comparing the age of invoices against the agreed payment terms, organizations can quickly identify overdue payments and assess compliance levels.

2. Payment Terms Reports: These specialized reports focus on the terms of payment, highlighting invoices that have met or missed their payment deadlines. They provide a clear overview of the organization's adherence to various payment terms and help pinpoint areas where compliance may be lacking.

Benefits of Monitoring Payment Terms Compliance

1. Improved Cash Flow Management: By adhering to payment terms, organizations can better manage their cash flow, ensuring that funds are available when needed and avoiding unnecessary interest or late payment fees.

2. Enhanced Vendor Relationships: Consistently meeting payment terms fosters trust and strengthens relationships with vendors. This can lead to more favorable terms, better service, and potential cost savings in the long run.

3. Opportunities for Early Payment Discounts: Monitoring payment terms compliance allows organizations to identify and take advantage of early payment discounts offered by vendors. These discounts can result in significant cost savings.

Strategies for Improving Payment Terms Compliance

1. Automated Payment Scheduling: Leveraging Oracle ERP's automation capabilities can help ensure that payments are scheduled and executed in accordance with agreed terms, reducing the risk of human error and delays.

2. Regular Monitoring and Reporting: Implementing regular reviews of payment terms compliance reports allows for timely identification of issues and corrective actions. This proactive approach helps maintain high compliance levels.

3. Vendor Communication and Negotiation: Open communication with vendors regarding payment terms and expectations can lead to mutually beneficial agreements. Periodic reviews and renegotiations can also help align terms with the organization's cash flow needs.

Invoice Processing Time

Importance of Invoice Processing Time

Invoice processing time is a critical metric that measures the duration from when an invoice is received to when it is approved for payment. Efficient invoice processing is essential for maintaining a smooth accounts payable operation, reducing bottlenecks, and ensuring timely payments.

Tracking Invoice Processing Time Using Reports

Oracle ERP's reporting tools offer detailed insights into invoice processing times through various report types:

1. Cycle Time Reports: These reports measure the total time taken to process invoices from receipt to payment. They provide a comprehensive view of the efficiency of the accounts payable process.

2. Exception Reports: These reports identify invoices that deviate from the standard processing time, highlighting bottlenecks and areas where delays occur.

Benefits of Monitoring Invoice Processing Time

1. Operational Efficiency: Tracking invoice processing time helps identify inefficiencies and streamline the accounts payable process, leading to faster turnaround times and reduced workload for AP staff.

2. Cost Savings: Faster invoice processing can help capture early payment discounts and avoid late payment penalties, directly impacting the organization's bottom line.

3. Vendor Satisfaction: Timely payments contribute to better vendor relationships, ensuring reliable supply chains and potentially more favorable terms.

Strategies for Reducing Invoice Processing Time

1. Implementing Automation: Utilizing Oracle ERP's automation features, such as automated invoice matching and approval workflows, can significantly reduce manual intervention and processing time.

2. Streamlining Approval Processes: Simplifying and standardizing approval processes can minimize delays. Clear guidelines and thresholds for approvals can expedite decision-making.

3. Continuous Monitoring and Improvement: Regularly reviewing invoice processing time reports and identifying recurring issues or bottlenecks allows for continuous process improvement and optimization.

Discounts Captured

Significance of Discounts Captured

Capturing discounts offered by vendors for early payments can result in substantial cost savings. These discounts are often a percentage of the invoice amount and can add up to significant savings over time.

Tracking Discounts Captured Using Reports

Oracle ERP provides detailed reports that help organizations monitor the discounts captured on accounts payable transactions:

1. Discount Reports: These reports list all discounts captured during a specified period, detailing the invoice amounts, payment dates, and discount values. They provide a clear picture of the savings achieved through early payments.

2. Variance Reports: These reports highlight instances where discounts were missed, helping identify patterns or reasons for missed opportunities and informing corrective actions.

Benefits of Monitoring Discounts Captured

1. Cost Savings: Regularly capturing early payment discounts directly reduces the overall cost of goods and services, positively impacting the organization's profitability.

2. Improved Cash Flow Forecasting: Knowing the potential discounts and their impact on cash flow helps in better financial planning and forecasting.

3. Enhanced Vendor Relationships: Taking advantage of early payment discounts demonstrates financial responsibility and can strengthen vendor relationships, potentially leading to better terms in the future.

Strategies for Maximizing Discounts Captured

1. Optimizing Payment Scheduling: Ensuring that payment schedules align with discount terms allows organizations to maximize savings. Automation tools in Oracle ERP can help schedule payments to capture discounts systematically.

2. Educating AP Staff: Training accounts payable staff on the importance of capturing discounts and providing clear guidelines can enhance awareness and encourage proactive efforts to secure discounts.

3. Regular Performance Reviews: Reviewing discount capture reports periodically helps identify missed opportunities and develop strategies to improve future performance.

Conclusion

Tracking key metrics such as payment terms compliance, invoice processing time, and discounts captured through Oracle ERP's reporting capabilities is essential for optimizing accounts payable processes. These metrics provide valuable insights that enable organizations to improve cash flow management, enhance vendor relationships, and achieve significant cost savings. By leveraging detailed reports and implementing targeted strategies, organizations can continuously refine their accounts payable operations and drive overall financial performance.

Through the effective use of Oracle ERP's reporting tools, businesses can ensure that their accounts payable processes are efficient, transparent, and aligned with strategic financial goals. The ongoing analysis and improvement of these metrics not only streamline day-to-day operations but also contribute to the long-term success and sustainability of the organization.

7.4.3 Emphasize the role of reports in continuous improvement of accounts payable operations

The role of reports in the continuous improvement of accounts payable operations cannot be overstated. Reports serve as the backbone of decision-making processes, providing essential insights that drive efficiency, accuracy, and strategic planning within the accounts payable function. Continuous improvement is a cornerstone of successful business operations, and leveraging reports effectively ensures that organizations remain agile, competitive, and fiscally responsible. This section delves into the multifaceted role that reports play in the ongoing enhancement of accounts payable processes, highlighting their impact on various aspects of financial management.

1. Identifying Process Inefficiencies:

Reports are instrumental in pinpointing inefficiencies within the accounts payable processes. By regularly reviewing detailed accounts payable reports, organizations can identify bottlenecks, such as delays in invoice processing or discrepancies in payment approvals. For instance, a report showing a high volume of overdue invoices might indicate a problem with the invoice approval workflow. Addressing these inefficiencies promptly can lead to significant improvements in the overall process, reducing delays and ensuring that vendors are paid on time.

2. Enhancing Accuracy and Compliance:

Accuracy and compliance are critical in accounts payable operations. Reports help in maintaining high standards by providing comprehensive data on transactions, enabling thorough audits, and ensuring adherence to company policies and regulatory requirements. For example, audit reports can highlight instances of non-compliance with tax regulations or internal policies, allowing the organization to take corrective actions. By continuously monitoring and analyzing these reports, companies can ensure that their accounts payable processes remain accurate and compliant, thereby avoiding potential legal issues and financial penalties.

3. Facilitating Strategic Planning:

Strategic planning in accounts payable involves making informed decisions that align with the organization's financial goals. Reports provide the necessary data to support these decisions. For instance, trend analysis reports can reveal patterns in spending and payment cycles, helping organizations plan their cash flow more effectively. Additionally, reports on vendor performance can inform strategic sourcing decisions, such as renegotiating contracts with high-performing vendors or identifying opportunities for cost savings. By using reports for strategic planning, organizations can optimize their accounts payable processes to support broader financial objectives.

4. Driving Data-Driven Decision Making:

Data-driven decision-making is essential for modern accounts payable operations. Reports provide the empirical evidence needed to make informed decisions. For example, a report showing a high incidence of late payments might prompt a review of payment schedules or approval processes. Similarly, reports on payment terms compliance can guide policy changes to ensure better adherence to agreed terms. By relying on accurate and up-to-date reports, decision-makers can implement changes that lead to continuous improvement in accounts payable operations.

5. Monitoring and Improving Vendor Relationships:

Vendor relationships are a crucial aspect of accounts payable management. Reports play a vital role in monitoring these relationships by providing detailed insights into vendor performance, payment histories, and overall reliability. For instance, a vendor analysis report can highlight vendors with frequent invoice disputes or delivery issues. Addressing these issues can improve the quality of vendor relationships, leading to better service and potentially more favorable terms. Continuous improvement in vendor management can result in cost savings and more efficient supply chain operations.

6. Measuring Performance Metrics:

Performance metrics are key indicators of the effectiveness of accounts payable processes. Reports provide the data needed to measure and analyze these metrics. Common performance metrics include invoice processing time, payment accuracy, discount capture rate, and payment cycle time. By regularly reviewing these metrics through reports, organizations can identify areas that need improvement and track the progress of implemented changes. For example, if the invoice processing time is consistently above the industry benchmark, the organization can investigate the cause and implement measures to streamline the process.

7. Supporting Financial Health and Risk Management:

Reports are essential for maintaining the financial health of an organization and managing risks associated with accounts payable. Cash flow reports, for instance, provide insights into the timing and magnitude of outgoing payments, helping organizations manage their liquidity effectively. Additionally, reports on outstanding liabilities can aid in risk assessment by identifying potential cash flow issues or exposure to financial risk. By using these reports to monitor financial health and manage risks, organizations can ensure the stability and resilience of their accounts payable operations.

8. Encouraging a Culture of Accountability:

A culture of accountability is crucial for continuous improvement in accounts payable operations. Reports promote accountability by providing transparent and objective data on individual and team performance. For instance, performance reports can highlight the productivity of accounts payable staff, such as the number of invoices processed or the accuracy of data entry. This transparency encourages employees to take ownership of their work and strive for continuous improvement. Additionally, reports can be used in performance reviews and goal-setting exercises, fostering a culture of accountability and excellence.

9. Enabling Proactive Issue Resolution:

Proactive issue resolution is a key component of continuous improvement. Reports enable organizations to identify and address issues before they escalate into significant problems. For example, a report showing a sudden increase in disputed invoices can prompt an immediate investigation into the root cause, whether it be issues with vendor communication or errors in invoice processing. By addressing these issues proactively, organizations can prevent disruptions and maintain smooth accounts payable operations.

10. Fostering Innovation and Adaptability:

Innovation and adaptability are essential for staying competitive in today's fast-paced business environment. Reports provide the insights needed to identify opportunities for innovation and adapt to changing circumstances. For example, reports on payment trends can reveal the potential benefits of adopting new payment technologies, such as electronic funds transfers or blockchain solutions. By continuously analyzing and acting on report data, organizations can innovate their accounts payable processes, leading to greater efficiency and effectiveness.

11. Enhancing Collaboration and Communication:

Effective collaboration and communication are vital for the success of accounts payable operations. Reports facilitate these by providing a common framework for discussing performance and identifying areas for improvement. For instance, regular review meetings can be structured around key reports, such as aging reports or payment accuracy reports. This structured approach ensures that all stakeholders are on the same page and can work together to implement improvements. Enhanced collaboration and communication lead to more cohesive and efficient accounts payable processes.

12. Leveraging Technology for Continuous Improvement:

Technology plays a significant role in the continuous improvement of accounts payable operations. Modern reporting tools, such as Oracle Business Intelligence (OBI), provide advanced capabilities for data analysis and visualization. By leveraging these tools, organizations can gain deeper insights into their accounts payable data and identify more sophisticated improvement opportunities. For example, predictive analytics can forecast future payment trends, enabling proactive adjustments to payment schedules or cash flow management. By integrating advanced technology with traditional reporting methods, organizations can achieve a higher level of continuous improvement.

13. Developing a Continuous Improvement Plan:

A structured continuous improvement plan is essential for systematically enhancing accounts payable operations. Reports are a critical component of this plan, providing the data needed to set goals, measure progress, and evaluate outcomes. For instance, a continuous improvement plan might include specific targets for reducing invoice processing time or increasing discount capture rates. Regularly reviewing progress through reports ensures that the plan stays on track and that any deviations are promptly addressed. A well-developed continuous improvement plan, supported by robust reporting, leads to sustained enhancements in accounts payable operations.

In conclusion, reports play a pivotal role in the continuous improvement of accounts payable operations. They provide the data and insights needed to identify inefficiencies, enhance accuracy and compliance, support strategic planning, and drive data-driven decision-making. By leveraging reports effectively, organizations can monitor and improve vendor relationships, measure performance metrics, support financial health, and foster a culture of accountability. Additionally, reports enable proactive issue resolution, foster innovation and adaptability, enhance collaboration and communication, and leverage technology for continuous improvement. Developing a structured continuous improvement plan, supported by comprehensive reporting, ensures that accounts payable operations remain efficient, effective, and aligned with the organization's broader financial goals.

CHAPTER VIII
Optimizing Accounts Payable Processes

8.1 Implementing Best Practices for Invoice Processing

8.1.1 Discuss best practices for streamlining invoice processing workflows and reducing errors

Efficient invoice processing is critical for any organization to maintain healthy cash flow, ensure timely payments, and foster positive relationships with suppliers. Implementing best practices in invoice processing can significantly streamline workflows and reduce errors. Here are some key strategies to consider:

1. Centralized Invoice Receipt and Management

One of the primary steps to streamline invoice processing is to centralize the receipt and management of invoices. By creating a single point of entry for all invoices, organizations can ensure that all documents are tracked and processed consistently. This can be achieved by using a dedicated email address for invoice submissions or an electronic invoicing system where suppliers can upload invoices directly.

Benefits:

- Reduces the risk of lost or misplaced invoices.

- Simplifies the tracking and status monitoring of invoices.

- Facilitates quicker identification and resolution of discrepancies.

2. Standardization of Invoice Formats

Standardizing invoice formats can help reduce errors and improve efficiency in processing. Organizations can provide suppliers with a standardized invoice template or specify the required fields and formats for invoice submission. This ensures that all necessary information is captured consistently and accurately.

Benefits:

- Minimizes the need for manual data entry and corrections.

- Enhances the accuracy of data captured.

- Simplifies the integration with accounting and ERP systems.

3. Automation of Data Capture

Manual data entry is time-consuming and prone to errors. Implementing automated data capture solutions, such as Optical Character Recognition (OCR) technology, can significantly reduce the time and effort required to process invoices. OCR can scan and extract data from paper or electronic invoices, reducing the need for manual input.

Benefits:

- Speeds up the invoice processing cycle.

- Reduces human errors in data entry.

- Frees up staff to focus on higher-value tasks.

4. Implementing a Robust Approval Workflow

A well-defined approval workflow is essential to ensure that invoices are reviewed and approved in a timely manner. Organizations should establish clear guidelines for who needs to approve invoices, the approval thresholds, and the steps involved in the approval process. Using workflow automation tools can help streamline this process by routing invoices to the appropriate approvers and sending reminders for pending approvals.

Benefits:

- Ensures compliance with internal policies and controls.

- Reduces bottlenecks and delays in the approval process.

- Provides a clear audit trail for all approvals.

5. Exception Management

Handling exceptions efficiently is crucial for maintaining smooth invoice processing workflows. Organizations should define clear procedures for managing exceptions, such as discrepancies between purchase orders and invoices or missing information. Automated workflows can help flag exceptions and route them to the appropriate personnel for resolution.

Benefits:

- Ensures timely resolution of discrepancies.

- Reduces the risk of payment delays or errors.

- Improves overall process efficiency and accuracy.

6. Supplier Communication and Collaboration

Maintaining open and effective communication with suppliers is key to resolving issues quickly and ensuring accurate invoice processing. Organizations should establish clear channels for suppliers to submit invoices, ask questions, and receive updates on the status of their payments. Supplier portals or collaboration platforms can facilitate this communication and provide suppliers with real-time access to information.

Benefits:

- Enhances supplier relationships and satisfaction.

- Reduces the volume of inquiries and follow-up emails.

- Improves the accuracy and timeliness of invoice submissions.

7. Regular Training and Education

Providing regular training and education for accounts payable staff is essential to keep them updated on best practices, new technologies, and changes in processes. Training should cover areas such as invoice verification, data entry, exception handling, and the use of automation tools.

Benefits:

- Ensures staff are knowledgeable and skilled in invoice processing.

- Reduces errors and improves efficiency.

- Encourages the adoption of best practices and new technologies.

8. Continuous Improvement and Performance Monitoring

Implementing a culture of continuous improvement is vital for optimizing invoice processing workflows. Organizations should regularly review their processes, identify areas for improvement, and implement changes to enhance efficiency and accuracy. Key performance indicators (KPIs) such as invoice processing time, error rates, and payment cycle times should be monitored to measure performance and identify trends.

Benefits:

- Drives ongoing improvements in process efficiency and accuracy.

- Provides insights into areas needing attention or enhancement.

- Supports data-driven decision-making and strategic planning.

9. Leveraging Technology and Automation

The use of technology and automation can transform invoice processing workflows, making them more efficient and less error-prone. Accounts payable automation solutions can handle various aspects of the process, from data capture and approval routing to exception management and payment processing.

Benefits:

- Streamlines and accelerates the entire invoice processing cycle.

- Reduces the risk of errors and manual interventions.

- Enhances compliance and control over the process.

Practical Tips for Implementing Best Practices

To successfully implement these best practices, organizations can follow these practical tips:

1. Conduct a Process Audit: Review the current invoice processing workflows to identify inefficiencies and areas for improvement. This can help pinpoint specific changes needed to optimize the process.

2. Engage Stakeholders: Involve key stakeholders, including finance, procurement, and IT departments, in the planning and implementation of process improvements. Their input and buy-in are crucial for successful adoption.

3. Pilot New Processes: Before rolling out new processes or technologies organization-wide, conduct a pilot program to test their effectiveness and identify any issues. Use feedback from the pilot to refine and improve the implementation plan.

4. Invest in Training: Provide comprehensive training for accounts payable staff on new processes, tools, and technologies. Ensure they understand the benefits and are comfortable using new systems.

5. Monitor and Adjust: Continuously monitor the performance of the new processes and make adjustments as needed. Use KPIs and feedback from staff and suppliers to identify areas for further improvement.

By adopting these best practices and continuously striving for improvement, organizations can achieve significant enhancements in their invoice processing workflows, leading to reduced errors, improved efficiency, and better overall financial management.

8.1.2 Emphasize the importance of automation, standardization, and exception management for efficient invoice processing

Efficient invoice processing is crucial for maintaining a smooth and effective accounts payable (AP) function. The role of automation, standardization, and exception management cannot be overstated in this context. Each of these components plays a vital part in reducing errors, speeding up processes, and ensuring compliance. Let's delve into why these elements are so important and how they can be effectively implemented in the accounts payable workflow.

The Role of Automation in Invoice Processing

Automation in invoice processing involves using technology to perform tasks that were traditionally done manually. This includes data entry, invoice matching, approval workflows, and payment processing. Automation brings several key benefits:

1. Reduced Errors: Manual data entry is prone to errors, which can lead to payment delays, duplicate payments, or even fraud. Automation ensures that data is accurately captured and processed, reducing the likelihood of mistakes.

2. Increased Speed: Automated systems can process invoices much faster than humans. This speed is critical for taking advantage of early payment discounts and avoiding late payment penalties.

3. Improved Compliance: Automated systems can be configured to ensure compliance with internal policies and external regulations. This includes enforcing approval hierarchies, checking for duplicate invoices, and ensuring that all necessary documentation is in place.

4. Enhanced Visibility: Automation provides real-time visibility into the status of invoices and payments. This transparency helps in better cash flow management and financial planning.

5. Cost Savings: By reducing the need for manual intervention, automation lowers labor costs and minimizes the risk of costly errors.

Best Practices for Implementing Automation

- Evaluate Current Processes: Before implementing automation, it's crucial to understand and map out the current invoice processing workflow. Identify pain points, bottlenecks, and areas that can benefit most from automation.

- Choose the Right Technology: Select an automation solution that fits the specific needs of your organization. Consider factors like integration with existing systems, scalability, user-friendliness, and support for different types of invoices.

- Standardize Data Entry: Ensure that data entry fields are standardized across the organization. This uniformity makes it easier for automated systems to process and interpret the data.

- Train Staff: Provide adequate training for staff to use the new automated system. This includes understanding how to handle exceptions and troubleshooting common issues.

- Monitor and Adjust: Continuously monitor the performance of the automated system and make adjustments as necessary. This includes updating rules and parameters to adapt to changing business needs and regulations.

The Importance of Standardization in Invoice Processing

Standardization involves creating uniform procedures and formats for invoice processing. This consistency is essential for efficient and error-free operations. Key benefits of standardization include:

1. Consistency: Standardized processes ensure that invoices are handled in the same way every time, reducing variability and errors.

2. Simplified Training: With standardized procedures, training new employees becomes simpler and more effective. Staff can quickly learn and adhere to established workflows.

3. Improved Efficiency: Standardization eliminates unnecessary steps and redundancies, streamlining the invoice processing workflow.

4. Better Compliance: Standardized processes are easier to audit and ensure that all invoices are processed in accordance with company policies and regulatory requirements.

5. Enhanced Collaboration: Standardized formats and procedures facilitate better communication and collaboration between departments and with external vendors.

Best Practices for Implementing Standardization

- Develop Standard Operating Procedures (SOPs): Create detailed SOPs for each step of the invoice processing workflow. Ensure these procedures are documented and easily accessible to all relevant staff.

- Use Standardized Templates: Implement standardized invoice templates for vendors to use. This ensures that all necessary information is included and formatted consistently.

- Set Clear Policies: Define clear policies for invoice submission, approval, and payment. Communicate these policies to all relevant parties, including vendors and internal staff.

- Conduct Regular Training: Regularly train staff on the standardized procedures and update them on any changes. Ensure that everyone understands the importance of following these procedures.

- Monitor Compliance: Regularly review and audit the invoice processing workflow to ensure compliance with the standardized procedures. Address any deviations promptly.

The Role of Exception Management in Invoice Processing

Exception management involves identifying, handling, and resolving discrepancies and issues that arise during invoice processing. Effective exception management is critical for maintaining smooth operations and minimizing disruptions. Key benefits of exception management include:

1. Reduced Delays: By quickly identifying and resolving exceptions, companies can prevent delays in invoice processing and payment.

2. Improved Accuracy: Exception management helps ensure that discrepancies are addressed and corrected, maintaining the accuracy of financial records.

3. Enhanced Control: Effective exception management provides better control over the invoice processing workflow, ensuring that issues are handled promptly and appropriately.

4. Increased Transparency: A robust exception management system provides visibility into the types and frequencies of exceptions, helping identify patterns and areas for improvement.

5. Compliance Assurance: By managing exceptions effectively, companies can ensure compliance with internal policies and external regulations, reducing the risk of fines and penalties.

Best Practices for Implementing Exception Management

- Define Exception Types: Clearly define the types of exceptions that can occur in the invoice processing workflow. This includes issues like missing information, duplicate invoices, and discrepancies in amounts.

- Establish Resolution Procedures: Develop procedures for resolving each type of exception. This includes identifying the responsible parties, steps for resolution, and timelines for addressing the issue.

- Automate Exception Handling: Use automation tools to identify and flag exceptions in real-time. Automated workflows can route exceptions to the appropriate personnel for resolution.

- Train Staff: Ensure that staff are trained on how to handle exceptions. This includes understanding the types of exceptions, resolution procedures, and the use of automated tools.

- Monitor and Report: Continuously monitor the occurrence and resolution of exceptions. Generate reports to identify patterns and trends, and use this data to improve the overall invoice processing workflow.

Conclusion

Automation, standardization, and exception management are essential components of an efficient invoice processing system. By implementing these best practices, companies can reduce errors, increase speed, improve compliance, and achieve significant cost savings. A well-designed and executed invoice processing workflow not only enhances operational efficiency but also contributes to better financial management and stronger vendor relationships.

In the next section, we will explore how leveraging automation can further streamline accounts payable processes and drive additional efficiencies and cost savings for your organization.

8.1.3 Provide practical tips and guidelines for implementing best practices

Optimizing invoice processing within the Accounts Payable (AP) module is crucial for ensuring efficiency, reducing errors, and maintaining a smooth financial workflow.

Implementing best practices involves a combination of automation, standardization, and effective exception management. Below are practical tips and guidelines to help you achieve these goals:

1. Standardize Invoice Submission Channels:

  - Digital Submission: Encourage suppliers to submit invoices electronically via email or an online portal. This reduces manual data entry and minimizes the risk of errors.

  - Centralized Processing: Establish a centralized location for receiving all invoices, whether physical or electronic, to streamline the intake process and ensure consistency.

2. Automate Invoice Data Entry:

  - Optical Character Recognition (OCR): Use OCR technology to scan and extract data from paper invoices automatically, reducing manual entry and errors.

  - Electronic Data Interchange (EDI): Implement EDI to facilitate the seamless exchange of invoices between your organization and suppliers, ensuring accurate and timely data transmission.

3. Implement Invoice Matching Processes:

  - Three-Way Matching: Verify that the details on the invoice, purchase order (PO), and receiving report match. This helps prevent discrepancies and ensures that payments are made only for goods and services received.

  - Automated Matching: Use software to automatically match invoices to POs and receiving reports. This speeds up the process and reduces manual intervention.

4. Establish Clear Approval Workflows:

  - Defined Roles and Responsibilities: Assign specific roles and responsibilities within the AP team for invoice approval to ensure accountability and prevent delays.

  - Automated Approval Routing: Implement automated workflows that route invoices to the appropriate approvers based on predefined criteria, such as invoice amount or department.

5. Utilize Invoice Management Software:

  - Integrated AP Solutions: Invest in comprehensive AP software that integrates with your ERP system, providing a unified platform for managing invoices, payments, and reporting.

- Real-Time Tracking: Ensure that the software provides real-time tracking and visibility into the status of each invoice, from submission to payment.

6. Streamline Exception Handling:

  - Clear Policies: Develop and document policies for handling invoice exceptions, such as discrepancies or missing information, to ensure consistent and efficient resolution.

  - Dedicated Team: Create a dedicated team or assign specific individuals to manage exceptions and resolve issues promptly.

7. Ensure Compliance and Accuracy:

  - Compliance Checks: Implement automated checks to ensure that invoices comply with company policies and regulatory requirements before processing.

  - Data Validation: Use validation rules to check for errors or missing information on invoices, such as incorrect vendor details or invalid tax codes.

8. Enhance Vendor Communication:

  - Vendor Portal: Provide a self-service portal for vendors to submit invoices, track payment status, and resolve discrepancies, reducing the burden on your AP team.

  - Regular Updates: Communicate regularly with vendors about any changes in invoice submission processes or requirements to maintain alignment and prevent issues.

9. Optimize Payment Schedules:

  - Early Payment Discounts: Negotiate early payment discounts with vendors and schedule payments to take advantage of these savings without compromising cash flow.

  - Batch Processing: Process payments in batches to streamline workflows and reduce the frequency of payment runs.

10. Continuously Monitor and Improve:

  - KPIs and Metrics: Establish key performance indicators (KPIs) to measure the efficiency and effectiveness of your invoice processing workflows. Common KPIs include invoice processing time, error rate, and cost per invoice.

  - Regular Reviews: Conduct regular reviews of your AP processes and performance metrics to identify areas for improvement and implement necessary changes.

Practical Implementation Steps:

1. Assess Current Processes:

   - Conduct a thorough review of your current invoice processing workflows to identify bottlenecks, inefficiencies, and areas prone to errors.

   - Gather input from AP team members, vendors, and other stakeholders to understand pain points and opportunities for improvement.

2. Develop a Roadmap:

   - Create a detailed roadmap for implementing best practices, including timelines, milestones, and resource allocation.

   - Prioritize initiatives based on their potential impact on efficiency, cost savings, and compliance.

3. Invest in Technology:

   - Evaluate and select the right automation tools and technologies that align with your organization's needs and budget.

   - Ensure that chosen solutions integrate seamlessly with your existing ERP system and other financial software.

4. Train and Educate:

   - Provide comprehensive training for AP staff on new tools, technologies, and workflows to ensure smooth adoption and effective use.

   - Offer ongoing education and resources to keep the team updated on best practices and industry trends.

5. Monitor and Adjust:

   - Implement regular monitoring and reporting mechanisms to track the performance of your invoice processing workflows.

   - Be prepared to adjust and refine processes based on feedback and performance data to achieve continuous improvement.

Case Study: Implementing Best Practices in a Mid-Sized Enterprise

A mid-sized manufacturing company faced challenges with their manual invoice processing, including high error rates, delayed payments, and strained vendor relationships. By implementing the following steps, they optimized their AP processes and achieved significant improvements:

- Automated Data Entry: The company adopted OCR technology to automate the data entry process for paper invoices. This reduced manual input errors by 80% and accelerated invoice processing times.

- Three-Way Matching: They implemented a three-way matching system that automatically verified invoice details against POs and receiving reports. This minimized discrepancies and ensured payments were made accurately.

- Approval Workflows: The company established automated approval workflows that routed invoices to the appropriate approvers based on predefined criteria. This streamlined the approval process and reduced delays.

- Vendor Portal: A self-service vendor portal was introduced, allowing suppliers to submit invoices electronically, track payment status, and resolve discrepancies. This improved vendor satisfaction and reduced the workload on the AP team.

- Regular Monitoring: The company set up KPIs to monitor invoice processing performance, including processing time, error rates, and cost per invoice. Regular reviews and adjustments based on performance data led to continuous process improvements.

Conclusion:

Implementing best practices for invoice processing within the Accounts Payable module of Oracle ERP is essential for achieving operational efficiency, reducing errors, and maintaining compliance. By standardizing workflows, leveraging automation, and continuously monitoring performance, organizations can streamline their AP processes and enhance overall financial management. Practical tips and guidelines, such as those outlined above, provide a roadmap for successfully optimizing invoice processing and reaping the benefits of a well-managed AP function.

8.2 Leveraging Automation to Streamline Workflows

8.2.1 Explain the benefits of using automation to streamline accounts payable processes

Automation in accounts payable (AP) processes offers a multitude of benefits that significantly enhance the efficiency, accuracy, and overall effectiveness of financial operations. By integrating automation technologies into AP workflows, organizations can transform what is often a cumbersome and error-prone process into a streamlined, precise, and highly efficient system. The key benefits of using automation in AP processes include:

1. Increased Efficiency and Productivity

Automation reduces the need for manual intervention in routine tasks such as data entry, invoice processing, and approval workflows. By automating these repetitive tasks, AP staff can focus on more strategic activities, such as analyzing spending patterns, negotiating with suppliers, and improving financial controls. This shift in focus not only boosts productivity but also enhances job satisfaction among employees by reducing monotonous work.

2. Enhanced Accuracy and Reduced Errors

Manual data entry is prone to human error, which can lead to discrepancies, missed payments, and issues with financial reporting. Automation ensures that data is captured accurately and consistently, minimizing the risk of errors. Automated systems can validate data against predefined rules, flagging any discrepancies for review. This level of precision helps maintain accurate financial records and reduces the likelihood of costly mistakes.

3. Faster Invoice Processing

Automated invoice processing systems can quickly capture, validate, and route invoices for approval, significantly reducing processing times. Optical character recognition (OCR) technology, for example, can extract data from scanned invoices and automatically populate the relevant fields in the AP system. This not only accelerates the invoice processing cycle but also ensures that invoices are paid on time, helping organizations take advantage of early payment discounts and avoid late payment penalties.

4. Improved Cash Flow Management

Automation provides real-time visibility into the status of invoices and payments, enabling better cash flow management. Organizations can more accurately predict their cash needs and optimize their cash reserves. Automated AP systems can also prioritize payments based on due dates, discount opportunities, and other criteria, ensuring that cash is used efficiently and strategically.

5. Enhanced Supplier Relationships

Timely and accurate payments are crucial for maintaining strong relationships with suppliers. Automation ensures that invoices are processed and paid promptly, reducing the likelihood of disputes and fostering trust with suppliers. Additionally, automated systems can provide suppliers with self-service portals where they can track the status of their invoices and payments, reducing the need for inquiries and improving communication.

6. Better Compliance and Audit Readiness

Automated AP systems can enforce compliance with internal policies and external regulations by ensuring that all transactions are properly documented and approved according to predefined rules. This level of control makes it easier to adhere to financial regulations and internal audit requirements. Automated systems also provide an audit trail of all activities, facilitating easier and more thorough audits.

7. Cost Savings

By reducing manual effort and errors, automation can lead to significant cost savings. The need for paper-based processes is minimized, reducing costs associated with printing, storage, and mailing. Furthermore, automation can decrease the amount of time spent on resolving errors and disputes, resulting in lower labor costs. The overall reduction in processing time and improved efficiency contribute to a lower cost per invoice processed.

8. Scalability

Automated AP systems can easily scale to handle increasing volumes of transactions without a corresponding increase in labor costs. This scalability is particularly beneficial for growing organizations that need to manage larger volumes of invoices and payments efficiently. As the organization expands, the automated system can adapt to accommodate new suppliers, additional invoice types, and more complex approval workflows.

9. Enhanced Data Analytics and Reporting

Automation allows for the capture and analysis of vast amounts of data, providing valuable insights into spending patterns, supplier performance, and process efficiencies. Advanced analytics tools can generate detailed reports and dashboards, helping organizations make informed decisions and identify areas for improvement. This data-driven approach enables continuous improvement and supports strategic financial planning.

10. Improved Security and Fraud Prevention

Automated AP systems incorporate security measures such as encryption, access controls, and audit trails to protect sensitive financial information. These systems can also detect and prevent fraudulent activities by flagging unusual patterns or transactions for further investigation. By reducing the reliance on manual processes, automation minimizes the risk of fraud and enhances the overall security of financial operations.

Conclusion

The benefits of automation in accounts payable processes are extensive and impactful. By leveraging automation technologies, organizations can achieve greater efficiency, accuracy, and control over their financial operations. The result is a more streamlined and effective AP process that supports the overall financial health and strategic goals of the organization. As technology continues to advance, the potential for further improvements in AP automation is vast, offering ongoing opportunities for organizations to optimize their financial workflows and achieve greater success.

8.2.2 Discuss the different types of automation tools and technologies available

Automation has revolutionized many business processes, including accounts payable (AP). By leveraging various automation tools and technologies, organizations can significantly improve the efficiency and accuracy of their AP workflows. This section will discuss the different types of automation tools and technologies available, their features, and how they can be integrated into the accounts payable processes.

1. Optical Character Recognition (OCR) Technology

Overview:

Optical Character Recognition (OCR) is a technology that converts different types of documents, such as scanned paper documents, PDF files, or images captured by a digital camera, into editable and searchable data.

Features:

- Data Extraction: OCR technology can accurately extract data from invoices, receipts, and other financial documents.

- Pattern Recognition: Advanced OCR systems use pattern recognition to identify different data fields, such as invoice numbers, dates, and amounts.

- Integration: OCR tools can be integrated with ERP systems to automatically populate data fields in AP workflows.

Benefits:

- Efficiency: Reduces the need for manual data entry, speeding up the invoice processing time.

- Accuracy: Minimizes human errors associated with manual data entry.

- Cost Savings: Reduces the labor costs associated with manual processing.

2. Robotic Process Automation (RPA)

Overview:

Robotic Process Automation (RPA) involves the use of software robots or "bots" to automate repetitive, rule-based tasks.

Features:

- Task Automation: RPA bots can handle various AP tasks, such as data entry, invoice validation, and payment processing.

- Integration: RPA can integrate with existing systems, including ERP and accounting software, without the need for major modifications.

- Scalability: RPA solutions can be scaled up or down based on the volume of transactions.

Benefits:

- Consistency: Ensures consistent execution of tasks, reducing variability and errors.

- Productivity: Frees up human employees to focus on more strategic tasks.

- Compliance: Enhances compliance by ensuring that all tasks are performed according to predefined rules and regulations.

3. Machine Learning (ML) and Artificial Intelligence (AI)

Overview:

Machine Learning (ML) and Artificial Intelligence (AI) technologies enable systems to learn from data and make intelligent decisions.

Features:

- Predictive Analytics: ML algorithms can analyze historical data to predict future trends, such as payment patterns and cash flow.

- Anomaly Detection: AI can detect anomalies in AP transactions, such as duplicate payments or fraudulent activities.

- Natural Language Processing (NLP): NLP can be used to interpret and process unstructured data from emails, invoices, and other documents.

Benefits:

- Enhanced Decision-Making: AI-driven insights help AP teams make informed decisions.

- Fraud Prevention: Detects and prevents fraudulent activities, reducing financial losses.

- Improved Accuracy: Continuously learns and improves from data, increasing the accuracy of AP processes.

4. Electronic Data Interchange (EDI)

Overview:

Electronic Data Interchange (EDI) is the electronic exchange of business information using a standardized format.

Features:

- Standardization: EDI uses standardized formats, such as ANSI X12 and EDIFACT, to ensure consistency and interoperability.

- Automation: Automates the exchange of invoices, purchase orders, and other financial documents between trading partners.

- Real-Time Processing: Facilitates real-time processing and reduces the time required for document exchange.

Benefits:

- Speed: Speeds up transaction processing and reduces the turnaround time.

- Cost-Effective: Reduces paper-based processing costs and improves operational efficiency.

- Accuracy: Minimizes errors associated with manual data entry and document handling.

5. Workflow Automation Software

Overview:

Workflow automation software is designed to automate and manage business processes, including AP workflows.

Features:

- Process Mapping: Allows organizations to map out their AP processes and identify areas for automation.

- Task Automation: Automates repetitive tasks, such as invoice approval, payment processing, and reconciliation.

- Collaboration Tools: Facilitates collaboration between AP teams and other departments, ensuring smooth workflows.

Benefits:

- Streamlined Processes: Streamlines AP processes, reducing bottlenecks and improving efficiency.

- Visibility: Provides visibility into the status of invoices and payments, enhancing transparency.

- Compliance: Ensures compliance with internal policies and external regulations.

6. Cloud-Based AP Solutions

Overview:

Cloud-based AP solutions are software-as-a-service (SaaS) platforms that provide AP automation functionalities over the internet.

Features:

- Accessibility: Accessible from any location with an internet connection, enabling remote work.

- Scalability: Scalable based on the organization's needs, allowing for flexibility in handling transaction volumes.

- Integration: Easily integrates with other cloud-based and on-premises systems.

Benefits:

- Lower Costs: Reduces the need for on-premises infrastructure and maintenance.

- Flexibility: Offers flexibility in terms of deployment and usage.

- Security: Provides robust security features, including data encryption and access controls.

7. E-Invoicing Solutions

Overview:

E-invoicing solutions enable the electronic exchange of invoices between suppliers and buyers.

Features:

- Standard Formats: Supports various e-invoicing standards, such as XML, UBL, and PEPPOL.

- Automation: Automates the generation, transmission, and processing of invoices.

- Validation: Includes validation features to ensure that invoices meet regulatory and business requirements.

Benefits:

- Efficiency: Speeds up invoice processing and reduces manual intervention.

- Compliance: Ensures compliance with local and international e-invoicing regulations.

- Cost Savings: Reduces the costs associated with paper-based invoicing and manual processing.

8. Payment Automation Tools

Overview:

Payment automation tools streamline the payment process by automating the creation, approval, and execution of payments.

Features:

- Automated Payments: Automates the generation of payment files and the execution of payments.

- Approval Workflows: Includes approval workflows to ensure that payments are reviewed and approved before execution.

- Reconciliation: Automates the reconciliation of payments with bank statements and accounting records.

Benefits:

- Accuracy: Reduces errors in payment processing and ensures accurate payments.

- Efficiency: Speeds up the payment process and reduces the time required for manual intervention.

- Control: Provides better control over the payment process, ensuring compliance with payment policies.

9. Supplier Portals

Overview:

Supplier portals are online platforms that facilitate communication and collaboration between organizations and their suppliers.

Features:

- Invoice Submission: Allows suppliers to submit invoices electronically through the portal.

- Status Tracking: Enables suppliers to track the status of their invoices and payments in real-time.

- Document Exchange: Facilitates the exchange of documents, such as purchase orders and delivery notes.

Benefits:

- Transparency: Provides transparency into the AP process, reducing inquiries and disputes.

- Efficiency: Streamlines the invoice submission and approval process, speeding up payments.

- Collaboration: Enhances collaboration between organizations and suppliers, improving relationships.

10. Mobile AP Solutions

Overview:

Mobile AP solutions provide AP functionalities through mobile applications, enabling on-the-go access and processing.

Features:

- Mobile Access: Allows AP teams to access and process invoices and payments from mobile devices.

- Notifications: Provides real-time notifications for approvals, payments, and other AP activities.

- Integration: Integrates with existing ERP and AP systems to ensure seamless workflows.

Benefits:

- Flexibility: Enables AP teams to work remotely and manage AP processes from anywhere.

- Speed: Speeds up approval and payment processes by enabling quick actions on mobile devices.

- Productivity: Increases productivity by allowing AP teams to manage tasks on the go.

Conclusion

Automation tools and technologies offer significant benefits for streamlining accounts payable processes. By leveraging OCR, RPA, AI, EDI, workflow automation software, cloud-based AP solutions, e-invoicing solutions, payment automation tools, supplier portals, and mobile AP solutions, organizations can enhance efficiency, accuracy, and compliance in their AP workflows. Each technology brings unique features and benefits, and organizations should carefully evaluate their specific needs and choose the right combination of tools to achieve optimal results. The integration of these technologies not only reduces manual effort but also enables AP teams to focus on more strategic activities, ultimately contributing to the overall success and growth of the organization.

8.2.3 Provide examples of how automation can be used to improve efficiency and reduce costs

Automation in accounts payable (AP) processes has become increasingly vital for organizations aiming to enhance efficiency and reduce costs. By integrating advanced technologies and automation tools, companies can streamline workflows, minimize manual tasks, and achieve greater accuracy and compliance. Below are detailed examples of how automation can be leveraged in accounts payable to improve efficiency and reduce costs.

Example 1: Automated Invoice Data Capture

One of the most labor-intensive tasks in accounts payable is the manual entry of invoice data. Automated invoice data capture solutions, such as Optical Character Recognition

(OCR) and Intelligent Document Processing (IDP), can significantly reduce the time and effort required to process invoices. These technologies extract data from invoices regardless of format, automatically populate AP systems, and validate the information against purchase orders and contracts.

- Efficiency Improvement: Automation reduces the need for manual data entry, leading to faster invoice processing times. By eliminating human errors associated with manual entry, organizations can ensure higher data accuracy.

- Cost Reduction: With fewer manual interventions, the need for extensive AP staff is diminished, resulting in lower labor costs. Additionally, faster processing times can help organizations take advantage of early payment discounts offered by suppliers.

Example 2: Automated Three-Way Matching

Three-way matching is a critical control process in AP, where the invoice, purchase order, and receiving report are compared to ensure consistency before payment approval. Automating this process can drastically cut down the time required for manual matching and reduce errors.

- Efficiency Improvement: Automated systems can instantly compare data from multiple documents and flag discrepancies for further review. This speeds up the validation process and reduces the backlog of pending invoices.

- Cost Reduction: By automating the three-way matching process, organizations can decrease the likelihood of overpayments and duplicate payments, thus saving costs associated with payment errors. The reduced need for manual intervention also lowers labor expenses.

Example 3: Automated Payment Processing

Automating the payment process involves using electronic payment methods such as Automated Clearing House (ACH) transfers, electronic funds transfers (EFT), and virtual credit cards. These methods streamline the payment process, enhance security, and provide better control over cash flows.

- Efficiency Improvement: Automated payment processing ensures timely and accurate payments, reducing delays and enhancing supplier relationships. Electronic payments are processed faster than traditional checks, which can take days to clear.

- Cost Reduction: Electronic payments eliminate the costs associated with printing and mailing checks. Additionally, virtual credit cards can generate rebates, creating a new revenue stream for the organization.

Example 4: Automated Approval Workflows

In many organizations, the approval of invoices and payments involves multiple layers of manual review and authorization. Automating these approval workflows can simplify and expedite the process by routing invoices to the appropriate approvers based on predefined rules and thresholds.

- Efficiency Improvement: Automated workflows ensure that invoices are promptly reviewed and approved, minimizing bottlenecks and delays. Notifications and reminders can be sent automatically to approvers, ensuring timely action.

- Cost Reduction: Reducing manual oversight and streamlining the approval process decreases the administrative burden on AP staff, leading to lower operational costs. Faster approvals also enhance cash flow management by ensuring timely payments.

Example 5: Automated Supplier Portal Integration

Supplier portals provide a centralized platform for suppliers to submit invoices, track payment statuses, and manage their information. Integrating supplier portals with AP automation tools can significantly streamline interactions between suppliers and the AP department.

- Efficiency Improvement: Suppliers can directly enter invoice data into the portal, reducing the need for manual data entry by AP staff. Real-time tracking of invoice status minimizes supplier inquiries, freeing up AP resources.

- Cost Reduction: By automating supplier interactions, organizations can reduce administrative costs associated with manual processing and handling of supplier inquiries.

Improved transparency and communication also strengthen supplier relationships, potentially leading to more favorable terms and conditions.

Example 6: Automated Expense Report Processing

For organizations that handle a large volume of employee expense reports, automating the expense management process can lead to substantial efficiency gains. Expense management software can automatically capture and categorize expenses, enforce policy compliance, and streamline reimbursement processes.

- Efficiency Improvement: Employees can use mobile apps to capture receipts and submit expense reports on the go. Automated policy checks ensure that expenses comply with company policies before submission, reducing the need for manual review.

- Cost Reduction: Automating expense report processing reduces the administrative burden on finance teams, allowing them to focus on more strategic tasks. Faster reimbursement processes also improve employee satisfaction and productivity.

Example 7: Automated Exception Handling

Despite best efforts, exceptions and discrepancies can occur in the AP process. Automating exception handling involves using advanced algorithms and machine learning to identify, categorize, and resolve exceptions without manual intervention.

- Efficiency Improvement: Automated systems can quickly identify discrepancies and route them to the appropriate personnel for resolution. Machine learning algorithms can also learn from past exceptions to predict and prevent future issues.

- Cost Reduction: By minimizing the time spent on resolving exceptions, organizations can reduce the operational costs associated with manual exception handling. Improved accuracy and faster resolution times also enhance overall AP efficiency.

Example 8: Automated Compliance and Audit Trails

Compliance with financial regulations and internal policies is crucial for any organization. Automating compliance checks and maintaining detailed audit trails can simplify the audit process and ensure adherence to regulatory requirements.

- Efficiency Improvement: Automated compliance tools can continuously monitor transactions and flag non-compliant activities in real-time. Detailed audit trails provide a clear record of all transactions and actions taken, simplifying the audit process.

- Cost Reduction: By reducing the manual effort required for compliance checks and audits, organizations can lower the associated labor costs. Automated systems also reduce the risk of non-compliance penalties, resulting in potential cost savings.

Example 9: Automated Analytics and Reporting

Automation tools can also enhance the capabilities of analytics and reporting within the AP department. By integrating with business intelligence (BI) tools, organizations can generate real-time reports and gain insights into AP performance.

- Efficiency Improvement: Automated reporting reduces the time spent on data gathering and report generation. Real-time dashboards provide instant visibility into key metrics, enabling proactive decision-making.

- Cost Reduction: By leveraging automated analytics, organizations can identify cost-saving opportunities, such as optimizing payment schedules and identifying process inefficiencies. The reduction in manual reporting efforts also lowers operational costs.

Conclusion

Leveraging automation in accounts payable processes offers substantial benefits in terms of efficiency and cost reduction. By adopting advanced technologies and integrating automation tools, organizations can streamline workflows, minimize errors, and enhance overall AP performance. From automated data capture and three-way matching to automated payment processing and compliance monitoring, the examples provided demonstrate the transformative potential of automation in optimizing accounts payable processes. By continuously exploring and implementing automation solutions, organizations can stay competitive and achieve long-term success in their financial operations.

8.3 Enhancing Controls for Internal Compliance

8.3.1 Describe the importance of internal controls for ensuring compliance with financial regulations and policies

Internal controls are critical mechanisms within an organization's accounts payable (AP) processes that ensure compliance with financial regulations and internal policies. These controls help prevent and detect errors, fraud, and inefficiencies, ensuring that financial information is accurate, reliable, and compliant with legal and regulatory requirements. In this section, we will explore the various dimensions of internal controls, their significance in maintaining compliance, and their broader impact on the organization's financial health and integrity.

1. Ensuring Accuracy and Reliability of Financial Reporting

One of the primary functions of internal controls is to ensure the accuracy and reliability of financial reporting. In the context of accounts payable, this involves verifying that all transactions are recorded correctly, all invoices are legitimate, and all payments are properly authorized and documented. Accurate financial reporting is essential for stakeholders, including management, investors, creditors, and regulatory agencies, who rely on financial statements to make informed decisions. Errors or inaccuracies in financial reporting can lead to significant consequences, including financial losses, reputational damage, and legal penalties.

2. Preventing Fraud and Mismanagement

Internal controls are vital in preventing fraud and mismanagement within the accounts payable process. Fraudulent activities, such as unauthorized payments, fictitious vendors, and kickbacks, can have devastating effects on an organization's finances and reputation. Implementing robust internal controls helps detect and deter fraudulent activities by establishing checks and balances, segregation of duties, and regular audits. For example, separating the responsibilities of invoice approval, payment processing, and reconciliation can reduce the risk of fraud by ensuring that no single individual has control over the entire process.

3. Ensuring Compliance with Legal and Regulatory Requirements

Organizations are subject to various legal and regulatory requirements related to their financial operations. These regulations can include tax laws, anti-corruption laws, financial reporting standards, and industry-specific regulations. Internal controls help ensure compliance with these requirements by establishing procedures and safeguards that align with legal and regulatory standards. For instance, maintaining accurate and complete records of all transactions, adhering to payment terms and conditions, and conducting regular audits are essential practices for compliance. Failure to comply with legal and regulatory requirements can result in severe penalties, legal actions, and loss of business licenses.

4. Enhancing Operational Efficiency

Effective internal controls contribute to enhanced operational efficiency within the accounts payable process. By standardizing procedures, automating routine tasks, and implementing best practices, organizations can streamline their AP operations and reduce the risk of errors and inefficiencies. For example, implementing automated invoice processing systems can significantly reduce the time and effort required for data entry, verification, and approval. This not only improves the accuracy and speed of invoice processing but also frees up valuable resources that can be redirected towards more strategic activities.

5. Building Trust and Confidence

Robust internal controls help build trust and confidence among stakeholders, including employees, management, investors, and customers. When stakeholders have confidence in the organization's financial integrity and compliance with regulations, it enhances the organization's credibility and reputation. This trust is particularly important for publicly traded companies, where investor confidence can significantly impact stock prices and market performance. Additionally, strong internal controls demonstrate the organization's commitment to ethical business practices, fostering a positive corporate culture and enhancing employee morale.

6. Facilitating Audit and Review Processes

Internal controls play a crucial role in facilitating audit and review processes. Auditors rely on the existence and effectiveness of internal controls to assess the accuracy and reliability of financial information. Well-documented internal controls and procedures make it easier for auditors to verify transactions, assess compliance, and identify potential risks. This, in turn, can lead to more efficient and cost-effective audits, reducing the time and resources required for external audits and reviews.

7. Supporting Risk Management

Internal controls are integral to an organization's risk management framework. By identifying potential risks and implementing controls to mitigate those risks, organizations can proactively manage their exposure to financial, operational, and compliance risks. In the context of accounts payable, risks can include duplicate payments, late payments, vendor disputes, and regulatory non-compliance. Effective internal controls help mitigate these risks by establishing procedures for verifying invoices, authorizing payments, and reconciling accounts. Regular monitoring and review of these controls ensure that they remain effective and aligned with the organization's risk management objectives.

8. Aligning with Corporate Governance

Corporate governance refers to the system of rules, practices, and processes by which an organization is directed and controlled. Internal controls are a fundamental component of corporate governance, ensuring that the organization's financial operations are conducted with integrity, transparency, and accountability. Strong internal controls support corporate governance by providing a framework for decision-making, risk management, and compliance. They help ensure that the organization's financial activities align with its strategic objectives and ethical standards, promoting long-term sustainability and success.

Conclusion

In conclusion, internal controls are essential for ensuring compliance with financial regulations and policies within the accounts payable process. They play a critical role in preventing fraud, ensuring the accuracy and reliability of financial reporting, enhancing operational efficiency, and building trust and confidence among stakeholders. Effective internal controls facilitate audit and review processes, support risk management, and align with corporate governance principles. By prioritizing and implementing robust internal controls, organizations can safeguard their financial integrity, comply with legal and regulatory requirements, and achieve long-term success in their accounts payable operations.

8.3.2 Discuss the different types of internal controls that can be implemented in the accounts payable process

Implementing robust internal controls within the accounts payable (AP) process is crucial for ensuring financial integrity, preventing fraud, and maintaining compliance with regulatory requirements. Internal controls in accounts payable can be categorized into several types, including preventive, detective, and corrective controls. Each type plays a distinct role in safeguarding the AP process, and collectively, they create a comprehensive control environment.

Preventive Controls

1. Segregation of Duties:

Segregation of duties is a fundamental preventive control that involves dividing responsibilities among different individuals to reduce the risk of errors or fraudulent activities. In the AP process, this means separating the roles of invoice approval, payment authorization, and record-keeping. For example, the person who approves invoices should not be the same person who processes payments. This control ensures that no single individual has excessive control over the entire AP process, thereby reducing the likelihood of fraudulent transactions.

2. Vendor Verification and Maintenance:

Regular verification and maintenance of vendor information help prevent fraudulent vendors from being added to the system. This includes verifying the legitimacy of new vendors, conducting periodic reviews of existing vendor data, and updating information as necessary. Establishing a process for verifying vendor credentials, such as tax identification numbers and business licenses, helps ensure that payments are made only to legitimate and approved vendors.

3. Invoice Matching:

Implementing a three-way matching process, where invoices are matched with purchase orders and receiving reports before payment is authorized, is an effective preventive control. This ensures that payments are made only for goods and services that were actually ordered and received. Discrepancies between the documents can be identified and resolved before payment, preventing overpayments and fraudulent invoices.

4. Authorization and Approval Hierarchies:

Establishing clear authorization and approval hierarchies ensures that only authorized personnel can approve invoices and payments. This control involves setting monetary limits for different levels of approval and requiring higher-level approvals for larger transactions. By enforcing strict authorization protocols, organizations can prevent unauthorized payments and ensure that all expenditures are properly vetted.

5. System Access Controls:

Restricting access to the AP system to authorized personnel only is a critical preventive measure. Implementing role-based access controls ensures that employees have access only to the functions and information necessary for their job responsibilities. Regularly reviewing and updating access permissions helps prevent unauthorized access and reduces the risk of internal fraud.

Detective Controls

1. Reconciliation Processes:

Regular reconciliation of AP records with general ledger accounts, bank statements, and vendor statements helps detect discrepancies and errors. By comparing AP transactions with financial records, organizations can identify and investigate any inconsistencies, such as duplicate payments, unauthorized transactions, or incorrect amounts. Timely reconciliation helps ensure the accuracy of financial records and facilitates early detection of potential issues.

2. Exception Reporting:

Exception reporting involves generating reports that highlight unusual or high-risk transactions, such as payments exceeding a certain threshold, payments to new or infrequently used vendors, and duplicate payments. Reviewing and investigating these exceptions allows organizations to identify potential errors or fraudulent activities and take corrective actions as needed. Exception reports should be reviewed regularly by management to ensure prompt resolution of issues.

3. Audit Trails:

Maintaining detailed audit trails that document every transaction and change made within the AP system is essential for detecting unauthorized activities and ensuring accountability. Audit trails should include information on who performed each action, what changes were made, and when they occurred. Regularly reviewing audit trails helps identify suspicious activities and supports investigations into potential fraud or non-compliance.

4. Periodic Audits:

Conducting periodic internal and external audits of the AP process helps ensure compliance with policies and regulations, identify control weaknesses, and assess the overall effectiveness of internal controls. Internal audits can be performed by the organization's internal audit department, while external audits are conducted by independent third-party auditors. Audit findings should be used to implement improvements and strengthen the control environment.

Corrective Controls

1. Error Correction Procedures:

Establishing clear procedures for correcting errors identified through reconciliation, exception reporting, or audits is a key corrective control. These procedures should outline the steps for investigating discrepancies, making necessary adjustments, and documenting the corrections. Ensuring that errors are promptly and accurately corrected helps maintain the integrity of financial records.

2. Root Cause Analysis:

Conducting root cause analysis of identified errors or control failures helps organizations understand the underlying issues and implement measures to prevent recurrence. This involves analyzing the reasons behind errors, such as process deficiencies, system limitations, or inadequate training, and taking corrective actions to address these root causes. Continuous improvement of processes based on root cause analysis enhances the overall effectiveness of internal controls.

3. Policy and Procedure Updates:

Regularly reviewing and updating AP policies and procedures based on audit findings, changes in regulations, and evolving business needs is essential for maintaining an effective control environment. Updating policies and procedures ensures that they remain relevant and aligned with best practices. Communicating changes to employees and providing training as needed helps ensure compliance with updated policies.

4. Disciplinary Actions:

Implementing disciplinary actions for employees who violate AP policies or engage in fraudulent activities serves as a deterrent and reinforces the importance of compliance. Disciplinary actions should be clearly defined in the organization's policies and communicated to all employees. Ensuring that violations are promptly and consistently addressed helps maintain a culture of accountability and integrity.

Conclusion

Implementing a comprehensive set of internal controls in the accounts payable process is essential for ensuring financial integrity, preventing fraud, and maintaining compliance with regulatory requirements. By combining preventive, detective, and corrective controls, organizations can create a robust control environment that safeguards their AP process and supports overall financial management. Regularly reviewing and enhancing these controls based on audit findings, technological advancements, and evolving business needs ensures that the AP process remains efficient, effective, and secure.

8.3.3 Provide guidance on implementing and maintaining effective internal controls

Implementing and maintaining effective internal controls within the Accounts Payable (AP) process is crucial for ensuring compliance with financial regulations, safeguarding assets, and enhancing the overall efficiency and accuracy of financial operations. This section will provide a comprehensive guide on how to establish, implement, and maintain robust internal controls in the AP module of Oracle ERP.

1. Establishing a Strong Control Environment

The foundation of effective internal controls is a strong control environment. This involves setting the tone at the top and ensuring that management demonstrates a commitment to integrity and ethical values. Key steps include:

- Leadership Commitment: Senior management should actively promote a culture of compliance and ethical behavior. This can be achieved through regular communications, training programs, and by setting a personal example.

- Clear Organizational Structure: Define roles and responsibilities clearly to ensure accountability. This includes establishing an appropriate segregation of duties to prevent conflicts of interest and reduce the risk of fraud.

- Policies and Procedures: Develop comprehensive policies and procedures that outline the AP processes and controls. Ensure these documents are easily accessible to all employees and are regularly updated to reflect changes in regulations or business practices.

2. Implementing Key Internal Controls

Once a strong control environment is established, the next step is to implement specific controls within the AP process. These controls can be categorized into preventive, detective, and corrective controls.

- Preventive Controls: These controls are designed to prevent errors or fraud from occurring. Examples include:

 - Segregation of Duties: Separate responsibilities for key tasks such as invoice approval, payment processing, and vendor management to prevent a single individual from having control over all aspects of a transaction.

 - Authorization Controls: Implement approval hierarchies for invoice processing and payments. Ensure that only authorized personnel can approve transactions and that approval limits are set based on the individual's role and responsibilities.

 - Vendor Verification: Conduct thorough due diligence on vendors before adding them to the system. This includes verifying their business credentials, reviewing their financial stability, and checking for any red flags such as a history of fraudulent activities.

- Detective Controls: These controls are designed to identify errors or irregularities after they have occurred. Examples include:

 - Reconciliation Procedures: Regularly reconcile AP sub-ledgers with the general ledger to identify discrepancies. This should include a detailed review of outstanding invoices, payment records, and vendor statements.

 - Exception Reports: Generate and review exception reports that highlight unusual transactions or patterns, such as duplicate invoices, invoices that exceed approved limits, or payments made to inactive vendors.

 - Audit Trails: Maintain comprehensive audit trails for all AP transactions. This includes logging details such as the date and time of transactions, the individuals involved, and any changes made to the transaction records.

- Corrective Controls: These controls are designed to correct errors or address issues identified through detective controls. Examples include:

 - Error Correction Procedures: Establish procedures for investigating and correcting errors identified during reconciliations or through exception reports. This should include documenting the nature of the error, the corrective actions taken, and any changes made to prevent similar errors in the future.

- Disciplinary Actions: Implement disciplinary measures for employees who violate AP policies or engage in fraudulent activities. This can range from additional training and warnings to termination of employment and legal action.

3. Leveraging Technology for Internal Controls

Technology plays a vital role in enhancing the effectiveness of internal controls within the AP process. Oracle ERP offers a range of tools and features that can be leveraged to implement and monitor controls.

- Automated Workflows: Use automated workflows to enforce approval hierarchies and ensure that all invoices and payments go through the appropriate levels of authorization. Automated workflows can also help reduce processing times and minimize the risk of errors.

- Access Controls: Implement strict access controls within the ERP system to restrict access to sensitive information and functions. This includes using role-based access controls (RBAC) to ensure that users only have access to the information and functions necessary for their job.

- Audit and Monitoring Tools: Utilize the audit and monitoring tools available in Oracle ERP to track user activities, monitor compliance with policies, and generate audit reports. These tools can help identify potential issues and provide valuable insights into the effectiveness of internal controls.

4. Continuous Monitoring and Improvement

Effective internal controls require continuous monitoring and improvement to adapt to changes in the business environment, regulations, and emerging risks. Key steps include:

- Regular Audits: Conduct regular internal and external audits to assess the effectiveness of internal controls. Use audit findings to identify areas for improvement and implement corrective actions.

- Performance Metrics: Establish key performance indicators (KPIs) to measure the effectiveness of internal controls. Examples of KPIs include the number of exceptions identified, the time taken to resolve issues, and the rate of compliance with AP policies.

- Feedback Mechanisms: Implement feedback mechanisms to gather input from employees and other stakeholders on the effectiveness of internal controls. Use this feedback to make necessary adjustments and improvements.

5. Training and Awareness Programs

Ensuring that employees are aware of and understand the importance of internal controls is crucial for their effective implementation. Key steps include:

- Training Programs: Develop and deliver regular training programs on AP policies, procedures, and internal controls. Ensure that all employees involved in the AP process receive appropriate training.

- Awareness Campaigns: Conduct awareness campaigns to promote a culture of compliance and highlight the importance of internal controls. Use various communication channels such as newsletters, intranet, and workshops to disseminate information.

- Ongoing Education: Encourage ongoing education and professional development for employees to stay updated on best practices, regulatory changes, and new technologies related to AP and internal controls.

6. Collaboration and Communication

Effective internal controls require collaboration and communication among different departments and stakeholders. Key steps include:

- Cross-Functional Teams: Establish cross-functional teams to oversee the implementation and monitoring of internal controls. These teams should include representatives from finance, IT, compliance, and other relevant departments.

- Regular Meetings: Hold regular meetings to review the effectiveness of internal controls, discuss any issues or challenges, and plan for improvements. Ensure that these meetings are documented and that action items are tracked.

- Clear Communication Channels: Establish clear communication channels for reporting issues, providing feedback, and sharing information related to internal controls. Ensure that employees know how to report concerns and that they feel comfortable doing so without fear of retaliation.

7. Adapting to Changes and Emerging Risks

The business environment and regulatory landscape are constantly evolving, and internal controls must be adaptable to these changes. Key steps include:

- Risk Assessments: Conduct regular risk assessments to identify new and emerging risks related to the AP process. Use the findings to update and enhance internal controls.

- Regulatory Updates: Stay informed about changes in financial regulations and standards that impact the AP process. Ensure that internal controls are updated to comply with new requirements.

- Scenario Planning: Engage in scenario planning to anticipate potential changes or disruptions that could impact the AP process. Develop contingency plans to address these scenarios and ensure business continuity.

8. Documenting and Reviewing Internal Controls

Proper documentation and regular review of internal controls are essential for maintaining their effectiveness. Key steps include:

- Documentation: Maintain detailed documentation of all internal controls, including policies, procedures, workflows, and control activities. Ensure that documentation is up-to-date and easily accessible.

- Regular Reviews: Conduct regular reviews of internal controls to assess their effectiveness and identify areas for improvement. This should include a review of control activities, performance metrics, and audit findings.

- Continuous Improvement: Use the findings from reviews and audits to continuously improve internal controls. Implement changes as needed to address any weaknesses or gaps and enhance the overall effectiveness of the control environment.

By following these guidelines, organizations can implement and maintain effective internal controls within the Accounts Payable module of Oracle ERP, ensuring compliance with financial regulations, safeguarding assets, and enhancing the efficiency and accuracy of financial operations.

8.4 Continuously Monitoring and Improving Performance

8.4.1 Explain the importance of continuous monitoring and improvement of accounts payable processes

Continuous monitoring and improvement of accounts payable (AP) processes are critical to maintaining an efficient, accurate, and compliant financial operation. The dynamic nature of business environments, regulatory changes, and technological advancements necessitates a proactive approach to managing AP processes. Here's why continuous monitoring and improvement are vital:

1. Ensuring Accuracy and Reducing Errors

The accounts payable process involves multiple steps, including invoice receipt, validation, approval, and payment. Each of these steps is susceptible to errors, such as duplicate payments, incorrect data entry, and missed invoices. Continuous monitoring helps identify these errors promptly, allowing for immediate corrective actions. By regularly auditing and reviewing the AP processes, organizations can reduce the occurrence of such errors, ensuring the accuracy of financial records.

2. Enhancing Efficiency

Efficiency in accounts payable is crucial for maintaining cash flow and ensuring timely payments to vendors. Continuous improvement initiatives often focus on streamlining processes, eliminating bottlenecks, and automating repetitive tasks. By regularly assessing the AP workflow, organizations can identify inefficiencies and implement process improvements, resulting in faster invoice processing times and reduced operational costs.

3. Maintaining Compliance

Regulatory compliance is a significant concern for all businesses. Continuous monitoring ensures that the AP processes adhere to financial regulations and company policies. This includes compliance with tax laws, anti-fraud measures, and internal financial controls. Regular audits and reviews help identify any deviations from compliance, allowing the organization to take corrective actions before they lead to legal or financial repercussions.

4. Improving Vendor Relationships

Timely and accurate payments are essential for maintaining good relationships with vendors. Continuous monitoring helps ensure that invoices are processed and paid on time, preventing disputes and fostering trust with suppliers. Improved vendor relationships can lead to better negotiation terms, discounts, and more favorable credit conditions, ultimately benefiting the organization's bottom line.

5. Optimizing Cash Flow Management

Effective cash flow management is a key aspect of financial health. Continuous monitoring of AP processes allows organizations to optimize their cash flow by managing payment schedules strategically. By analyzing payment patterns and cash outflows, companies can make informed decisions on when to pay invoices, thus maximizing available cash and avoiding unnecessary interest or late payment fees.

6. Adapting to Changes and Innovations

The business environment is constantly evolving, with new technologies and methodologies emerging regularly. Continuous improvement processes ensure that the AP department stays current with these changes, adopting new tools and practices that enhance efficiency and accuracy. This adaptability helps organizations remain competitive and responsive to market demands.

7. Data-Driven Decision Making

Continuous monitoring provides a wealth of data that can be analyzed to gain insights into the performance of the AP processes. By leveraging data analytics, organizations can identify trends, pinpoint areas for improvement, and make informed decisions. Data-driven decision-making enables a proactive approach to managing AP, rather than a reactive one.

8. Supporting Strategic Objectives

Efficient and effective AP processes support the broader strategic objectives of the organization. For example, by reducing the time and cost associated with invoice processing, the organization can allocate resources to other strategic initiatives. Continuous improvement in AP processes contributes to overall operational excellence and supports the company's growth and profitability goals.

Strategies for Continuous Monitoring and Improvement

To achieve continuous monitoring and improvement in accounts payable, organizations can adopt the following strategies:

1. Implementing Key Performance Indicators (KPIs)

KPIs are essential tools for monitoring the performance of AP processes. Common KPIs for accounts payable include:

- Invoice processing time

- Percentage of invoices paid on time

- Number of invoice exceptions

- Cost per invoice processed

- Vendor satisfaction scores

Regularly tracking these KPIs provides insights into the efficiency and effectiveness of the AP processes, highlighting areas that require improvement.

2. Regular Audits and Reviews

Conducting regular audits and reviews of the AP processes helps identify discrepancies, errors, and areas of non-compliance. These audits can be internal or external and should be performed at regular intervals. The findings from these audits should be used to implement corrective actions and improve the overall process.

3. Leveraging Technology and Automation

Technology plays a crucial role in continuous monitoring and improvement. Automated AP solutions can streamline workflows, reduce manual errors, and provide real-time data for monitoring. Tools such as electronic invoicing, workflow automation, and AI-powered analytics can significantly enhance the efficiency and accuracy of AP processes.

4. Employee Training and Development

Continuous improvement is not just about processes and technology; it also involves people. Regular training and development programs for AP staff ensure that they are up-to-date with the latest best practices, tools, and technologies. A well-trained team is better equipped to identify inefficiencies and contribute to process improvements.

5. Feedback and Collaboration

Encouraging feedback from employees, vendors, and other stakeholders can provide valuable insights into the AP processes. Collaborative efforts to address identified issues and implement improvements can lead to more effective and efficient operations. Creating a culture of continuous improvement within the AP department fosters innovation and proactive problem-solving.

6. Establishing a Continuous Improvement Framework

A structured continuous improvement framework, such as Lean or Six Sigma, provides a systematic approach to identifying and implementing process improvements. These methodologies focus on reducing waste, improving quality, and increasing efficiency. By adopting a continuous improvement framework, organizations can ensure a disciplined and consistent approach to enhancing AP processes.

Conclusion

Continuous monitoring and improvement of accounts payable processes are essential for maintaining accuracy, efficiency, compliance, and overall financial health. By adopting a proactive approach and leveraging technology, KPIs, audits, and employee development, organizations can create a culture of continuous improvement. This not only enhances the performance of the AP department but also supports the broader strategic objectives of the organization, ensuring long-term success and competitiveness in the market.

8.4.2 Discuss key performance indicators (KPIs) that can be used to measure accounts payable performance

Key Performance Indicators (KPIs) are crucial for monitoring and evaluating the efficiency and effectiveness of accounts payable (AP) processes. These metrics provide valuable insights into various aspects of AP operations, allowing organizations to identify areas of improvement, enhance efficiency, and ensure compliance with financial regulations. Here, we discuss several critical KPIs that can be used to measure accounts payable performance:

1. Days Payable Outstanding (DPO)

Definition: DPO measures the average number of days a company takes to pay its suppliers. It is calculated using the formula:

DPO = Accounts Payable/Cost of Goods Sold Number of Days

Importance: A higher DPO indicates that a company is taking longer to pay its suppliers, which could be beneficial for cash flow management. However, excessively high DPO may strain supplier relationships. Conversely, a low DPO suggests quicker payments, potentially resulting in better supplier terms but impacting cash reserves.

Best Practices: Organizations should aim for an optimal DPO that balances cash flow efficiency with strong supplier relationships. Regularly reviewing and adjusting payment terms based on cash flow forecasts and supplier agreements is recommended.

2. Invoice Processing Cycle Time

Definition: This KPI measures the time taken from receiving an invoice to its approval and payment. It tracks the efficiency of the AP process.

Importance: Shorter cycle times indicate a more efficient invoice processing system, reducing the risk of late payments and potential penalties. It also reflects positively on the company's ability to manage its liabilities effectively.

Best Practices: Implementing automation tools such as electronic invoicing and workflow automation can significantly reduce processing times. Additionally, standardizing invoice submission and approval processes helps streamline operations.

3. Invoice Exception Rate

Definition: The invoice exception rate is the percentage of invoices that require manual intervention due to errors or discrepancies.

Importance: A high exception rate can indicate issues with invoice accuracy, supplier data management, or the effectiveness of automated systems. Reducing the exception rate minimizes the need for manual intervention, thus improving overall efficiency.

Best Practices: Enhancing data accuracy through vendor education and automated data validation, and adopting robust exception management processes can help lower the exception rate. Regular training for AP staff on error detection and resolution techniques is also beneficial.

4. Cost per Invoice Processed

Definition: This KPI measures the total cost incurred to process a single invoice, including labor, technology, and overhead costs.

Importance: Understanding the cost per invoice helps organizations identify opportunities for cost reduction and efficiency improvements. Lower processing costs generally indicate a more efficient AP process.

Best Practices: Leveraging automation and reducing manual processing can significantly lower costs. Continuous review and optimization of AP processes, combined with investment in scalable technology solutions, can further enhance cost efficiency.

5. Payment Error Rate

Definition: The payment error rate tracks the percentage of payments that are processed incorrectly, resulting in overpayments, underpayments, or duplicate payments.

Importance: High error rates can lead to financial losses, strained supplier relationships, and compliance issues. Reducing payment errors is critical for maintaining financial accuracy and trust with suppliers.

Best Practices: Implementing stringent validation checks and automated payment systems can help reduce errors. Regular audits and reconciliations of AP transactions also play a crucial role in identifying and correcting errors promptly.

6. Supplier Satisfaction Score

Definition: This qualitative KPI measures the satisfaction levels of suppliers with the company's AP processes, often through surveys and feedback mechanisms.

Importance: High supplier satisfaction indicates strong supplier relationships, which can lead to better terms, discounts, and reliable supply chains. Conversely, low satisfaction scores may signal issues that need to be addressed.

Best Practices: Regular communication with suppliers, timely payments, and a transparent AP process can enhance supplier satisfaction. Gathering and acting on supplier feedback is essential for continuous improvement.

7. Early Payment Discounts Captured

Definition: This KPI tracks the percentage of available early payment discounts that the company successfully captures.

Importance: Capturing early payment discounts can lead to significant cost savings. It also reflects the efficiency of the AP process in terms of timely invoice processing and payment.

Best Practices: Ensuring invoices are processed and approved quickly allows companies to take advantage of early payment discounts. Implementing automated systems to prioritize invoices with available discounts can maximize savings.

8. Number of Invoices Processed per FTE (Full-Time Equivalent)

Definition: This KPI measures the number of invoices processed by each AP employee, indicating workforce productivity.

Importance: Higher numbers suggest a more efficient AP team, while lower numbers may indicate bottlenecks or inefficiencies that need addressing.

Best Practices: Providing AP staff with adequate training and the right tools can enhance productivity. Automation can also free up employees to focus on higher-value tasks, further improving efficiency.

9. Percentage of Electronic Invoices

Definition: This KPI measures the proportion of invoices received electronically versus paper-based invoices.

Importance: A higher percentage of electronic invoices typically indicates a more modern and efficient AP process, reducing manual data entry and errors associated with paper invoices.

Best Practices: Encouraging suppliers to submit invoices electronically and integrating electronic invoicing systems can improve efficiency and accuracy. Additionally, providing training and support to suppliers on electronic invoicing can facilitate the transition.

10. Cycle Time to Resolve Discrepancies

Definition: This KPI measures the average time taken to resolve discrepancies between purchase orders, invoices, and goods receipts.

Importance: Shorter resolution times enhance the overall efficiency of the AP process and reduce delays in payments. It also improves supplier relationships by ensuring timely resolution of issues.

Best Practices: Implementing robust discrepancy management processes and leveraging technology for automatic matching and discrepancy detection can speed up resolution times. Regular training for AP staff on effective discrepancy resolution techniques is also beneficial.

11. Supplier Inquiry Response Time

Definition: This KPI tracks the average time taken to respond to supplier inquiries regarding payments and invoices.

Importance: Quick response times indicate a well-organized AP process and contribute to higher supplier satisfaction. Delays in responding to inquiries can lead to frustration and strained relationships.

Best Practices: Establishing a dedicated supplier support team and using automated inquiry management systems can improve response times. Regularly monitoring and analyzing response time data helps identify areas for improvement.

12. On-time Payments

Definition: This KPI measures the percentage of payments made on or before the due date.

Importance: High on-time payment rates indicate an efficient AP process and contribute to maintaining good supplier relationships. Late payments can lead to penalties and damaged supplier trust.

Best Practices: Implementing automated payment scheduling and reminders can help ensure timely payments. Regularly reviewing payment schedules and aligning them with cash flow forecasts can further enhance on-time payment performance.

Conclusion

Effective monitoring and continuous improvement of accounts payable performance are critical for maintaining financial health and strong supplier relationships. By leveraging key performance indicators (KPIs), organizations can gain valuable insights into their AP processes, identify areas for improvement, and implement strategies to enhance efficiency and effectiveness. Regularly reviewing and analyzing these KPIs, coupled with a data-driven approach, ensures that the AP process remains optimized, compliant, and aligned with the organization's overall financial goals. As technology and automation continue to evolve, the role of KPIs in driving continuous improvement will only become more significant, enabling organizations to achieve greater levels of performance and competitiveness in their AP operations.

8.4.3 Provide a framework for establishing performance targets, measuring results, and implementing corrective actions

To achieve excellence in accounts payable (AP) processes, it is imperative to establish a robust framework for setting performance targets, measuring results, and implementing corrective actions. This approach ensures that the AP function operates efficiently, minimizes errors, and contributes positively to the organization's overall financial health. Below is a detailed guide on how to develop and execute this framework effectively.

1. Establishing Performance Targets

Setting clear, achievable performance targets is the first step towards enhancing AP processes. These targets should align with the organization's overall strategic goals and reflect the specific objectives of the AP department.

a. Identifying Key Performance Indicators (KPIs)

To set meaningful performance targets, it's essential to identify relevant KPIs that can provide insight into the efficiency and effectiveness of the AP process. Common KPIs include:

- Invoice Processing Time: The average time taken to process an invoice from receipt to payment.

- Invoice Accuracy Rate: The percentage of invoices processed without errors.

- Payment Cycle Time: The total time from invoice receipt to payment.

- Cost Per Invoice: The total cost incurred in processing a single invoice.

- Early Payment Discounts Captured: The percentage of available early payment discounts that are captured.

- Late Payment Penalties: The frequency and amount of penalties incurred due to late payments.

- Supplier Discrepancies: The number of disputes or discrepancies with suppliers regarding invoices or payments.

b. Setting SMART Targets

Performance targets should adhere to the SMART criteria:

- Specific: Clearly define what is to be achieved.

- Measurable: Quantify the target to track progress.

- Achievable: Ensure the target is realistic and attainable.

- Relevant: Align the target with the department's and organization's goals.

- Time-bound: Set a clear timeframe for achieving the target.

For instance, a SMART target could be "Reduce invoice processing time from an average of 10 days to 7 days within the next six months."

c. Benchmarking

Benchmarking against industry standards or best-in-class performers can help set realistic and competitive targets. This involves comparing your current performance metrics with those of similar organizations to identify areas for improvement.

2. Measuring Results

Once targets are set, it is crucial to measure actual performance against these targets. This involves collecting data, analyzing it, and reporting the findings.

a. Data Collection

Implementing robust data collection methods is essential. This can be achieved through:

- Automation Tools: Utilize AP automation software to track and record relevant data in real time.

- Manual Logs: Maintain detailed records of AP activities if automation tools are not available.

- Supplier Feedback: Gather feedback from suppliers to gauge the accuracy and timeliness of payments.

b. Data Analysis

Analyzing the collected data involves:

- Trend Analysis: Examine data over time to identify trends, patterns, and anomalies.

- Variance Analysis: Compare actual performance with targets to identify deviations and understand the reasons behind them.

- Root Cause Analysis: Investigate the underlying causes of any performance gaps to develop effective solutions.

c. Reporting

Regular reporting is essential for monitoring progress and communicating results to stakeholders. Effective reporting should:

- Be Timely: Provide regular updates (e.g., weekly, monthly) to ensure issues are addressed promptly.

- Be Clear and Concise: Present data in an easy-to-understand format, using visuals like charts and graphs where appropriate.

- Highlight Key Findings: Focus on significant insights, such as performance gaps, trends, and areas needing improvement.

3. Implementing Corrective Actions

When performance does not meet targets, corrective actions must be taken to address the issues and improve processes.

a. Identifying Corrective Actions

Develop a range of corrective actions based on the root cause analysis. Common corrective actions include:

- Process Redesign: Streamline or re-engineer processes to eliminate inefficiencies.

- Training and Development: Provide additional training to staff to improve their skills and knowledge.

- Technology Upgrades: Invest in new or upgraded technology to automate and enhance AP processes.

- Supplier Collaboration: Work closely with suppliers to resolve discrepancies and improve payment terms.

b. Action Planning

Create detailed action plans to implement the identified corrective actions. These plans should include:

- Specific Steps: Outline the precise steps required to implement each corrective action.

- Responsible Parties: Assign responsibility for each action to specific individuals or teams.

- Timelines: Set clear deadlines for completing each action.

- Resources: Identify any resources (e.g., budget, technology, personnel) needed to implement the actions.

c. Monitoring Implementation

Ensure that the implementation of corrective actions is closely monitored:

- Progress Tracking: Regularly track the progress of action plans to ensure they are on schedule.

- Performance Reviews: Conduct periodic performance reviews to assess the effectiveness of the corrective actions.

- Feedback Loops: Establish feedback loops to gather input from staff and suppliers on the impact of the changes.

d. Continuous Improvement

Adopt a culture of continuous improvement to ensure ongoing enhancement of AP processes:

- Regular Assessments: Conduct regular assessments of AP processes to identify new opportunities for improvement.

- Employee Involvement: Encourage employees to suggest improvements and participate in process optimization efforts.

- Performance Rewards: Implement performance-based rewards to incentivize employees to contribute to continuous improvement.

4. Utilizing Technology for Performance Monitoring and Improvement

Modern technology plays a critical role in monitoring and improving AP performance. Leveraging the right tools can significantly enhance the efficiency and effectiveness of AP processes.

a. Automation Tools

AP automation tools can streamline processes, reduce errors, and provide real-time data for performance monitoring. Features of AP automation tools include:

- Invoice Capture and Processing: Automatically capture and process invoices, reducing manual data entry.

- Workflow Automation: Automate approval workflows to speed up invoice processing and ensure compliance.

- Payment Processing: Automate payment processing to ensure timely and accurate payments.

b. Data Analytics

Advanced data analytics tools can provide deeper insights into AP performance. These tools can:

- Visualize Data: Use dashboards and visualizations to present performance data in an easily understandable format.

- Predictive Analytics: Employ predictive analytics to forecast future performance and identify potential issues before they occur.

- Benchmarking: Use benchmarking tools to compare performance against industry standards and best practices.

c. Continuous Monitoring Solutions

Continuous monitoring solutions can track AP processes in real-time and alert managers to any deviations from established performance targets. These solutions can:

- Detect Anomalies: Identify anomalies and potential issues in real time, allowing for prompt corrective actions.

- Monitor Compliance: Ensure compliance with internal policies and external regulations by monitoring transactions and workflows.

- Generate Reports: Automatically generate reports on AP performance, providing insights for continuous improvement.

Conclusion

Establishing a framework for setting performance targets, measuring results, and implementing corrective actions is essential for optimizing accounts payable processes. By leveraging KPIs, SMART targets, data analysis, and modern technology, organizations can ensure their AP function operates efficiently and contributes to overall financial success. Continuous monitoring and improvement efforts, supported by robust internal controls and automation tools, will further enhance AP performance, reduce costs, and improve compliance.

Appendix

Glossary of Accounts Payable Terms

Understanding the various terms and concepts used within the Accounts Payable (AP) module is essential for efficient navigation and utilization. This glossary provides definitions and explanations of key terms and phrases associated with Accounts Payable in Oracle ERP.

Accounts Payable (AP)

A module within Oracle ERP that manages the payment of invoices and the handling of the company's short-term debt obligations. AP ensures timely payments to vendors and accurate financial reporting.

Accrual

A method of accounting that records expenses and revenues when they are incurred, regardless of when the cash transactions actually occur. In AP, accruals might include recording expenses for services received but not yet invoiced.

Aging Report

A report that categorizes a company's payables based on the length of time an invoice has been outstanding. It helps in managing overdue invoices and assessing the effectiveness of credit control.

Approval Workflow

A predefined sequence of steps or processes that an invoice or payment request must go through to obtain necessary approvals before payment is made. This ensures compliance with organizational policies.

Automated Clearing House (ACH)

A network for processing electronic financial transactions, such as direct deposit, payroll, and vendor payments. ACH payments in AP are used to facilitate secure, efficient transfer of funds.

Batch Processing

A method of processing transactions where multiple invoices or payments are processed as a single group or batch, improving efficiency and accuracy in the AP module.

Cash Management

A module that works closely with AP to ensure that an organization has adequate cash flow to meet its obligations. It includes forecasting, monitoring cash balances, and managing liquidity.

Chart of Accounts (COA)

A structured list of an organization's general ledger accounts, used to classify transactions. In AP, COA ensures that expenses are recorded in the correct accounts.

Credit Memo

A document issued by a vendor to acknowledge that a customer has returned goods or services, leading to a reduction in the amount owed. It can be applied against future invoices.

Debit Memo

A document issued by a buyer to indicate a reduction in the amount owed to a vendor due to discrepancies such as returned goods or overbilling.

Discount Terms

Conditions under which a buyer can reduce the amount payable to a vendor by paying the invoice early. These terms are often denoted as "2/10, net 30," indicating a 2% discount if paid within 10 days, with the full amount due in 30 days.

Due Date

The date by which an invoice must be paid. Effective AP management ensures payments are made on or before the due date to avoid late fees and maintain good vendor relationships.

Electronic Data Interchange (EDI)

A system that allows the electronic exchange of business documents, such as invoices and purchase orders, between companies. EDI improves the speed and accuracy of transactions in AP.

Expense Report

A detailed list of expenditures incurred by an employee that needs reimbursement. AP processes these reports to ensure timely and accurate repayment.

General Ledger (GL)

A complete record of all financial transactions over the life of an organization. AP transactions flow into the GL, impacting the company's financial statements.

Goods Receipt

A document confirming that goods ordered have been received. It is used in the three-way match process in AP to verify that the goods received match the purchase order and invoice.

Invoice

A document issued by a vendor requesting payment for goods or services provided. Invoices must be matched with purchase orders and goods receipts for accuracy before payment is processed.

Invoice Matching

The process of comparing an invoice with the corresponding purchase order and goods receipt to ensure that the details match before approving the invoice for payment.

Net Payment Terms

The total time allowed for payment of an invoice, often specified in terms such as "net 30," indicating that the full amount is due within 30 days.

Payables Aging

A technique used to categorize unpaid invoices by the length of time they have been outstanding. It helps in managing cash flow and prioritizing payments.

Payment Hold

A temporary suspension of a payment due to various reasons such as disputes or incomplete documentation. AP places invoices on hold until issues are resolved.

Payment Run

A scheduled process in which multiple invoices are selected and paid in a single operation. It streamlines the payment process in the AP module.

Payment Terms

The conditions under which a vendor will complete a sale. These terms include the due date, discount offered for early payment, and any penalties for late payment.

Purchase Order (PO)

A document issued by a buyer committing to purchase goods or services from a vendor. POs are matched with invoices and goods receipts in AP to ensure accuracy.

Reconciliation

The process of ensuring that two sets of records (such as the accounts payable records and bank statements) are in agreement. It helps in identifying discrepancies and ensuring accuracy in financial reporting.

Remittance Advice

A document sent to a vendor detailing which invoices have been paid, the amount paid, and any deductions. It helps vendors reconcile their accounts.

Three-Way Match

A process in AP that involves matching the purchase order, goods receipt, and invoice before approving a payment. This ensures that only valid and accurate invoices are paid.

Vendor

An individual or company that supplies goods or services to another company. Maintaining accurate vendor records in AP is essential for effective invoice processing and payment management.

Vendor Master File

A database containing all relevant information about the company's vendors, including contact details, payment terms, and transaction history. Accurate vendor master data is crucial for efficient AP operations.

Voucher

A document that supports the payment of an invoice and is used to authorize disbursements. It includes details such as the invoice number, payment amount, and date.

Workflow Automation

The use of technology to streamline and automate the approval processes in AP. It enhances efficiency, reduces manual errors, and ensures compliance with organizational policies.

Understanding and effectively managing these terms and processes within the Accounts Payable module will enhance efficiency, ensure compliance, and improve overall financial management within an organization.

Conclusion

As we reach the end of "Oracle ERP Essentials: Navigating the Accounts Payable Module," it's clear that Oracle ERP is a powerful tool that can transform the way organizations operate. This book has guided you through the various modules and functionalities, offering a comprehensive understanding of how to leverage Oracle ERP to enhance efficiency, accuracy, and overall business performance.

Implementing an ERP system is no small feat. It requires careful planning, robust execution, and continuous improvement. By following the best practices, strategies, and detailed processes outlined in this book, you are well-equipped to successfully implement and utilize Oracle ERP in your organization.

Remember, the journey doesn't end here. As technology evolves, so too will Oracle ERP. Staying informed about updates, new features, and industry trends is crucial for maintaining the competitive edge that Oracle ERP offers. Continue to explore, learn, and adapt, ensuring that your ERP system remains a cornerstone of your business strategy.

We hope this book has provided valuable insights and practical guidance, empowering you to unlock the full potential of Oracle ERP. The road to mastering ERP systems is ongoing, but with the knowledge gained from this book, you are well on your way to achieving operational excellence.

Acknowledgments

First and foremost, we would like to extend our heartfelt gratitude to you, our readers, for choosing this book. Your decision to invest in "Oracle ERP Essentials: Navigating the Accounts Payable Module" is greatly appreciated. We hope that the knowledge and insights shared within these pages will prove invaluable in your ERP journey.

A special thank you to the team of experts and contributors who provided their insights, experiences, and knowledge. Their dedication and hard work have made this book a comprehensive resource for Oracle ERP users.

We also wish to acknowledge the countless professionals who have shared their real-world experiences and challenges. Their stories and feedback have been instrumental in shaping the content of this book, ensuring it is both practical and relevant.

To our families and friends, your unwavering support and encouragement have been a source of strength throughout this writing process. Thank you for believing in us and for your patience during the countless hours spent bringing this book to life.

Lastly, we would like to thank the broader Oracle ERP community. Your commitment to innovation, collaboration, and excellence is truly inspiring. It is our hope that this book will contribute to the ongoing success and growth of this dynamic community.

Thank you once again for your support. We wish you every success in your ERP endeavors and hope that "Oracle ERP Essentials: Navigating the Accounts Payable Module " becomes a valuable companion on your journey to operational excellence.